Integrative Performance

Integrative Performance serves a crucial need of twenty-first-century performers by providing a transdisciplinary approach to training. Its radical new take on performance practice is designed for a climate that increasingly requires fully rounded artists. The book critiques and interrogates key current practices and offers a proven alternative to the idea that rigorous and effective training must separate the disciplines into discrete categories of acting, singing, and dance.

Experience Bryon's Integrative Performance Practice is a way of working that will profoundly shift how performers engage with their training, conditioning, and performance disciplines. It synthesizes the various elements of performance work in order to empower the performer as they practise across disciplines within any genre, style, or aesthetic.

Theory and practice are balanced throughout, using:

- Regular boxes, introducing the work's theoretical underpinnings through quotes, case studies, and critical interjections.
- A full programme of exercises ranging from training of specific muscle groups, through working with text, to more subtle structures for integrative awareness and presence.

This book is the result of over twenty years of practice and research working with interdisciplinary artists across the world to produce a training that fully prepares performers for the demands of contemporary performance and all its somatic, emotive, and vocal possibilities.

Experience Bryon is Senior Lecturer in Performance Practices and Research at the Royal Central School of Speech and Drama, London.

Integrative Performance

Practice and Theory for the Interdisciplinary Performer

Experience Bryon

Illustrations by Paul Zacharek

Routledge
Taylor & Francis Group
LONDON AND NEW YORK

First published 2014
by Routledge
2 Park Square, Milton Park, Abingdon, Oxon OX14 4RN

and by Routledge
711 Third Avenue, New York, NY 10017

Routledge is an imprint of the Taylor & Francis Group, an informa business

British Library Cataloguing in Publication Data
A catalogue record for this book is available from the British Library

Library of Congress Cataloguing in Publication Data
A catalog record for this book has been requested

ISBN: 978-0-415-69446-9 (hbk)
ISBN: 978-0-415-69448-3 (pbk)
ISBN: 978-0-203-14778-8 (ebk)

Typeset in Joanna and Bell Gothic
by HWA Text and Data Management, London

To Alec Rubin
(my grandfather and first teacher of performance)

Contents

Exercises

Acknowledgements

THIS BOOK WOULD NOT HAVE BEEN POSSIBLE if not for the many committed and talented artists I have worked with over the years in classrooms, workshops, and as part of productions, especially members of the Front Room, The Mercurious Ensemble, and Experience Vocal Dance Company. With gratitude to my colleagues at the Royal Central School of Speech and Drama for their support and for the stimulating intellectual environment created as part of the ongoing debates around all things research and practice. A special thank you to my editor Ben Piggott and his team at Routledge, for their patience and unwavering support.

I would like to also thank those that helped in the making of this book by reading and commenting on chapters, and/or joining me in the studio to test out the articulation of the exercises as written. Thank you to Alix Atwell, Antonia Batzoglou, Kevin Corbett, Caroline Colomei, Katerina Damvoglou, Tony Fisher, Jessica Hartley, Helen Heaslip, Sarah Goddard, Karen Jolicoeur, Linda King, Lola Maury, Julia Munrow, Robin Nelson, Ita O'Brien, Douglas Paulson, Rosalind Philips, Aurea Romero-Alvarez, Joanne Scott, Emma Savell, Simon Spencer, Lisa Turner, Konstantinos Thomaidis, Lynn Wichern, and Angela Zacharek.

So much gratitude goes to my dear friend and collaborator for many years now, David Wolfson, who contributed the musical examples, read and re-read every word many times, made pivotal suggestions, and acted as comma police. To the love of my life, and illustrator of this book, my husband Paul Zacharek, thank you for being here.

Introduction

IF YOU ASK VERY YOUNG CHILDREN TO SING, they invariably dance and act; if you ask them to dance, they sing and act; if you ask them to recite a poem or play a character, they sound and move with their entire breathing body and voice. It's glorious. Why, then, when we learn to become performers, do we disintegrate ourselves and suppress our intuitive impulses by separating aspects of expression into categories of singing, dancing, and acting?

This book is for performers first. It speaks from the performer's perspective and to performers as they live and work within their practice(s). This book is also for practitioners who are teaching, writing, directing, devising, or choreographing with performers. It is for all who are interested in what happens when we merge or cross the disciplines of dance and movement, singing and voice, and acting, in no particular order or necessary privileging of any of them.

You will find in this book a new perspective on the ways we think about how we (performers) do things and how we approach our discipline(s). The practice and research within these pages are not there to advocate an abandonment of past trainings or techniques, but rather to offer a reconfiguration of how we approach our work as performers as we integrate our disciplines. As a result, you will not find a new "technique", but rather an Integrative Performance *Practice*.

As an artist who can sing, dance, or act, or any combination thereof, your training and practice sessions are most likely multiple. With the Integrative Performance Practice (IPP) you learn a way of working that may radically shift how you engage with your current training, conditioning, and performance disciplines, while offering a more streamlined and synthesized approach, helping you to develop a unified practice that compromises no one discipline.

You will find that you actually can do it all! It is, for instance, possible to do extended movement, including ballet and acrobatics, while at the same time singing a high C, while acting a role, without compromising any aspect of movement, sound, or emotive expression. You will learn that this is possible not by a clever negotiation of many techniques but rather through one practice that allows for the emergence of any combination of disciplinary expression.

The need for a practice that supports the artist working within today's climate of increasingly interdisciplinary performance is overdue. It has become essential that we as performers re-evaluate our systems of training, conditioning, and performance practice. When many of the training models that we still use today were developed, separate expressions of dance, theatre, musical theatre, and opera were the norm. Up until the middle of the last century the disciplines rarely crossed; the life of the artist was quite different and training was highly specialized.

For instance, less than a century ago, it was not unusual for classical singers to apprentice under a master while they were sponsored for up to five years. An actor might have entered into a conservatoire and trained there and lived there, day in and out, for at least four years before even making a debut (in some places, for instance in Russia, this still happens). Dancers were sometimes recruited into "schools" that monitored everything from diet to shoes to training and rehearsal regime for many years before allowing a principal role.

Today, the systems, methods and languages around what it means to practice, condition, and train remain in many ways unchanged, even as the models and culture for which they are situated have altered drastically. Where we might once have trained in concentrated conservatoire environments, the liberal arts education and double major is a norm for many talented artists-to-be. Economy, time, and the changing landscape of where performance sits within Western culture are also large factors. Postmodernism has left the arts and media altered forever. All of this (explored in greater detail in Part I of this book) has inspired new types of work, the adoption and adaptation of new technologies, and has given birth to the invention of new hybrid performance forms. It is time to reconsider how we look at the way we work, and examine what it means to practise as a performer in today's climate.

One could argue that an integrated, interdisciplinary, and unified theatre has been sought for many years, from the time of Ancient Greece up through to the philosophies and works of Wagner and, more recently, since the 1960s. Since the 1960s we've seen an exponential growth in creation and the production of interdisciplinary performance that has seriously altered the landscape. This growth was catalyzed by a series of confrontations around what were perceived as artificial or unhelpful separations between and within the fine arts, philosophy, politics, social sciences, and performance. Interdisciplinarity within and across scholarship and creative work has taken hold. Since the 1960s there has been an explosion in aesthetics and in the ways we categorize and value performance as an entity and a practice. Part I of this book goes into detail about the implications of this dynamic and discusses key creative visionaries and influential scholars who have affected how we think about what it means to be a performer doing this thing we now call performance.

Well into the 21st century, we are at a juncture where the industry has evolved. However, while the demands on the performer have become increasingly interdisciplinary, the training of the performer still tends to take place within an outdated set of categories. Many of us still train in the arts of acting, singing, and dancing within discrete models, techniques, and vocabularies of learning. Within this book you will see mention of key experiments and developments of practices that have embraced a crossing of disciplines. In general, however, these have often been in the service of a company's aesthetic, a director's vision, a devisor's mission, and/or in the service of a particular work or genre. The IPP aims to serve no one genre, philosophy, or aesthetic, but rather to offer a practice that can be used within any creative context. In the IPP the integrated artist does not adhere to any type, shape, tone, or look, but rather to a "way" of doing that balances the dynamic web of all that our expressive possibilities allow, within an exacting practice, allowing optimum possibilities across the performing disciplines.

It is increasingly apparent that there is more being expected of us as actors, singers, and dancers, or any combination thereof. The parking-and-barking days of opera are gone. Actors are required to have skills in extended movement, as the creation of more physical expressions of theatre is becoming the norm. In dance, the language of *Tanztheater* is increasingly adopted, and we can no longer rely on beautiful gestures or spectacular physical feats to hold attention. Moreover, dancers are also being asked to voice and move at the same time. Innovative work by Pina Bausch, Cirque Du Soleil, Meredith Monk, DV8 Physical Theatre, Faulty Optik, Forced Entertainment, Frantic Assembly, The Robert Pacitti Company, Robert LePage, The Lust Collective, Primitive Science, Station House Opera, Theatre De Complicite, Theatre Pur, Volcano, Robert Wilson, The Wooster Group (to name just a few) has contributed to the changing landscape (and sincere apologies to all those who may have been left out).

What was in the last century often considered an experimental or radical exercise in hybrid, cross-over, or interdisciplinary performance is now often the expectation. Interdisciplinarity has entered the mainstream of pop, opera, music(al) theatre, and "straight" theatre. A few current examples: the pop singer Pink sang her top hit "Glitter in the Air" at the 2010 Grammy Awards while doing a physical routine suspended in mid-air. In opera, artists placed in a giant fish tank expressing key dramatic moments in Sasha Waltz's *Dido and Aeneas* at Sadler's Wells provide another example. At the San Francisco Opera, diva Nadja Michael had great critical success, raising expectations for all future Salomes, when she expertly performed the Dance of the Seven Veils herself. The recent Broadway revival of *Pippin*, directed by Diane Paulus, is circus-based, with principal performers as well as chorus members singing and acting while doing aerial work, sliding on poles, jumping through hoops, and hanging upside down. Are we as performers being trained and prepared for this type of work?

The Integrative Performance Practice offers a transdisciplinary approach (a concept explained in detail in Chapter Three). The IPP offers a performance practice: conditioning and training for the actor-singer-dancer that does not require a negotiation, juggling, or even coordination of different techniques or disciplines. It is one practice, which allows the rigorous expression of acting, singing/sounding, and dancing/moving, without the compromise of technical excellence that might normally be associated with practices that depart from rigid specialization. The practice outlined within this book stems from over twenty years of practical research working with actors, vocalists (including those of musical theatre and opera), and dancers from both modern and ballet schools. Although it is true that the IPP makes it possible to do any combination of these as one, without compromise to technical excellence, it also has proven time and time again to strengthen and streamline an approach to traditional methods, when this is what is desired. Within this practice, the integrated instrument is one that is available to itself, in all its somatic, emotive, and vocal possibilities.

As you read further you will see that this book proposes something quite simple in action; it is not complicated, but perhaps initially complex to think about, as it challenges much current thinking and practice around performance. To do this, the IPP proposes a radical shift, not so much in *what* we do but more in the *way* we do our practices as performers, and in doing so it flips the entire way we look at ourselves and the function we serve within current critical thinking and culture(s) around *how* we do. In order to fully make possible and to discern the subtleties of this distinction, a new term, *active aesthetic*, is introduced in the context of current critical discourse around performance, and then employed as a foundation of the practice in exercises integrating voice, movement, acting, and text analysis. The active aesthetic is offered as a new way of looking at practice, creating a working construct that puts the performer and the act of performance in a place of privilege: within the act of doing, as an integrated agent of making meaning. In doing so, it confronts some of the conventional wisdom and practices around breath, centre, and presence, and turns on its head the very notion of what it means to perform within performance.

Participating in an active aesthetic, the integrative performer is able to respond in the creation of performance and maintain a position of responsibility in the areas of conditioning, training, practice, and performance. With this, we can begin to ask questions such as: In what way does a performer create meaning? Where does the art of performance reside? How do we initiate a multi-disciplinary technique that integrates discipline(s) in action? The introduction of an active aesthetic offers a deeper look at these questions through the way of doing, rather than what is/was done.

Research in the neurosciences, physiology, and psychology, along with ancient knowledge of the relationships among the breath, mind, and body, shows that we are wired as integrated artists and are set up for models of learning, training, and performance that do not require a disintegration of our talents or a false categorizing of our artistic selves. But disintegration is inherent in the languages whereby we identify ourselves as artists, reinforced by current models within our academies, studios, and conservatoires. At present, the actor/singer/dancer learns disciplines separately, in seemingly uncomplementary conditionings of the body and breath, approaching gesture, text (including both music and word), and expression of emotion in very different ways.

It is likely that many will find within this book a radical but sensible alteration to what they have learned as a method of breathing. Some might also find a profound difference in the place or initiation of centre. The idea of what it means to be present within the act of doing might also seem a little different. This practice is quite unapologetically specific about these terms and concepts. Centre, presence, and breath are currently surprisingly different and mercurial across the various techniques of dancing, singing, and acting. This is a fundamental disintegrating dilemma when working across the performance disciplines. With the IPP there is no such conflict. As it stands now, the interdisciplinary artist spends years mastering their disciplines, only to struggle later to put them together, creating a working negotiation of different approaches in an attempt to re-integrate themselves as a fully capable performance artist.

With a re-evaluation of the thinking around the act of performance and the concept of interdisciplinarity, along with serious examination of the techniques and practice of the performer who sings, dances, and acts, we can begin to create an integrative model from which to practise. It is time to seriously examine what we do in the rehearsal room, the classroom, the studio, at the barre, and in front of the piano. What we do now is problematic and in many ways out of touch with current interdisciplinary needs within both the commercial and non-profit world of performing arts.

HOW TO USE THIS BOOK

If you have a quick flip through the book you will see that it is in four parts. Part I: *Performers — Performing — Performance* has three chapters on theory that explore philosophy, neuroscience, consciousness studies, performance theory, and conceptual ideas drawn from quantum physics to help us better understand ourselves as integrative artists, our role in the making of performance, and the ways we might draw from other areas to better understand the dynamics of integration. Theory of this kind is often written by scholars for scholars; in this book every attempt is made to frame the theory for the performer, working to better understand what it means to be an artist/"self" who does this thing called performance. Chapter One is dedicated to the artist as self, exploring the dilemmas inherent in the dissonances between various techniques, and offers new ways to think about who we are as practitioners as we work across the disciplines. This is important because what is expected of the dancer, singer, and actor as a self can often be unnecessarily contradictory. In Chapter Two we look at how performance, as an evolving term and entity, has changed and been influenced by new thinking, new emerging technologies, and aesthetic trends. While these have radically changed what it means to be a performer, many of our trainings and techniques have remained strangely unchanged. Chapter Three offers a new way of viewing what it might mean to integrate the disciplines within a cohesive, personal practice, a practice that allows for the integration of all the performance disciplines without compromising any one. Here we will introduce the concept of *active aesthetic*, which will serve as the methodological framework through which the practice will then be experienced in the following chapters.

If you flip forward to Parts II and III, you will observe that we leave the tone and language of critical discourse and enter into the vocabulary and tone of the studio. Here you will find many detailed practical exercises. These have been developed over the last twenty-two years with professional actors; singers of opera and musical theatre; dancers, including those of ballet and modern dance; and also physical theatre practitioners, working in America, New Zealand, Australia, and England, all aiming to integrate the disciplines without compromising any one disciplinary value or aesthetic.

Part II: *Working in the Field of Performing* is in many ways the defining section of this book. It reconciles the theory and the practice with the concept of an active aesthetic. There is no one way to read this book. You may wish to go directly to the exercises, or you may wish to only read the theory. You will find it helpful, however, to read and work through Part II to fully understand the basis of the theory and to set you up for the practice. This is where much of the theory and the practice integrate to establish the fundamentals of the working process.

Throughout the entire book, you will find cross-references between the theory section and the practice; so in an exercise you may be directed to return to a section on theory to remember why we are approaching a particular exercise in a particular way. Likewise, a reader more conversant with theory might work through the exercises, especially in Part II (as these are possible for most) to fully understand what much of contemporary performance theory actually means as we take these concepts off the page and into the studio.

The thirty-five exercises in this book are all essentially equally acting, movement, and vocal exercises. You will find in the introduction of an exercise that a familiarity with certain other exercises is recommended before progressing. Once you become more familiar with the practice, you will be able to pick and choose from the catalogue of exercises to suit a rehearsal process, disciplinary challenge, training session, or lesson plan. The *Conscious Practice Journal* at the end of Part II offers a process for making these choices.

Part III: *Integrative Performance Practice* begins with Chapter Five, titled *Working from the Integrative Centre*. Here you will find exercises in isolating the iliopsoas muscle system and then relating it to interdisciplinary challenges. Here you will find a critical account and a detailed survey of the way centre is employed across other techniques. You will learn that integration depends on a most exacting use of centre in order to integrate the emotive breath-body in a way that allows full emotional expression with unimpeded movement while sounding and keeping the integrity of sonic line and harmonics. You will see how the iliopsoas is connected not only to the physicality of the performer but also the entire mind/body, along with the relationship of the iliopsoas to the parasympathetic and sympathetic nervous systems. We will explore the work's profound implications for the performer in terms of emotional availability and the ability to sound without compromise in any physical position. We then move to the next stage in understanding centre with the IPP, which is in the use of the perineum as a place of initiation for all tasks of the breath-body. The practical implication of this very precise centre as an initiator of breath servicing vocal/physical and emotive challenges is made clear.

The second chapter in Part III, *Voicing as a Breath Dance*, is dedicated to how we sound, and moves forward after establishing a precise three-part breathing practice, in line with exacting iliopsoas work, which works equally for dance, singing, and acting. Here you will find exercises to condition and establish the discipline of integrative breath in application to various requirements of sounding within interdisciplinary performance challenges. You will find somatic exercises to aid the practitioner to discern between habitual patterning and disintegrating aspects of other techniques. By the end of the chapter, it will be clear that these exacting uses of centre within the IPP literally integrate the vocal, physical, and emotive instrument.

The last chapter in Part III, *Acting is Doing*, offers a critical review of the many articulations around acting as a discipline, speaking specifically to the act of doing, the expectation of presence, and the ways in which we may employ the various techniques of acting within interdisciplinary work.

In Part IV you will find a new way to approach text analysis that includes plays, scores, blocking, choreography, and improvisational structures across the disciplines. In the IPP, text is considered just another active partner in the process of making and doing. Here you learn how you, as a performer in the flow of your practice, can *generate* meaning, rather than show or depict the meaning in a work. This will become key as you formulate and integrate your discipline(s) in the act of your own personal integrative practice.

PART I

Performers – Performing – Performance

Chapter 1

Who is an integrative performer?

BY THE TIME YOU FINISH THIS CHAPTER, hopefully you will agree that the answer is: you. You are an integrative performer!

As you progress through the book, you will begin to understand that integrative performance is largely a matter of what you integrate and what you understand you are performing.

By the time you finish this book, you will have gained a new perspective on what it means to practise, along with a set of tools that will help you integrate the performance disciplines in any combination you wish.

In the twenty years that this work has been in development, Integrative Performance Practitioners have learned a crucial lesson. The lesson is that in order to work in a way that integrates performance disciplines effectively, we must come from an integrated self: body, breath, and mind all working from an integrated instrument toward an integrated outcome. As we move forward, you will learn that this integrated self does not mean a "cleansed" self, "clear" of histories and "defects", but in some cases the exact opposite. We will also learn that this integrative instrument does not adhere to any type, shape, tone, or look, but rather to a "way" of doing that balances the dynamic web of all that our expressive possibilities allow, within an exacting practice, creating excellence across the performing disciplines.

This book does not offer a "technique", but rather a *practice*, and perhaps a new way of thinking about practice. As you progress you will be able to incorporate this work into your own "tool kit", creating a personal practice and expanded awareness of yourself as an interdisciplinary performing artist. You may consider yourself as any combination of singer, dancer, and/or actor. You may also be a practitioner working with performing artists, exploring philosophies and new ways of making work through direction or choreography. You may be critiquing, devising, or writing for interdisciplinary work, or perhaps you are helping to advance performance through developing technologies, philosophies, and techniques. This particular work offers an Integrative Performance *Practice*, through which many combinations of performance discipline(s) can be activated.

New vocabularies and skill sets are presented in the spirit of putting YOU at the heart of YOUR life's work, YOUR practice as an integrated mind/body with a history and given talents. Some of your talents may be more developed than others. How you identify as a practitioner may also differ. For instance, you might say, "I am an actor first, singer second, and dancer third". It is recommended that you come to this work with what you have at this time and from this, in each action, we will move forward.

For the purposes of finding a starting point, knowing there can never be only one in the experience of the performer and their practice, we will begin at a biological beginning, through the lens of developmental psychology, starting with early childhood.

As mentioned in the introduction, if you ask most young children to sing, they invariably also dance and act; if you ask them to dance, they also sing and act; if you ask them to recite a poem or play a character, they sound and move with their entire breathing body and voice. As very young children, we rarely compartmentalized artistic expression into categories of movement, voice, or gesture. We hadn't started to edit ourselves as agents of expression or categorize our choices of expressive activity into disciplinary signs and signifiers. We didn't identify ourselves as belonging to a discipline that would inhibit, through delineation, aspects of our physical, vocal, and emotive patterning. Rather, we were little people doing something (that might fall into disciplinary categories). More simply put, we didn't come from the idea that we were either dancers, singers, or actors, and further, we didn't decide that the way to express an idea was through set gestures expressed through select skill sets. (We will discuss later how this has implications for *self* in terms of categories of race and gender, but for now let's stay with performance disciplines.)

Of course, as little children we couldn't do a perfect pirouette or sing a Bellini cadenza, and a Shakespearian monologue might have eluded our abilities for a few years yet. The point for now is that we may start with less sophistication and skill, but we do start as integrative performers... But wait, were we really less sophisticated practitioners? After all, we learned greater amounts, and faster; we adapted better, and were open and present. We were centred in our bodies, our breath was free, we had incredible vocal resonance in any physical position, we were emotionally available and unapologetically spontaneously creative. These are things that are asked of the best dancers, singers, and actors. Aren't these also some of the very aspects that define great performers and, further, separate them from the mere technicians?

Could it be that in learning a specialism we also start to categorize, and in doing so we sometimes block out not only creative but also physical, emotive, and vocal technical possibilities? How can we retain an integrative philosophy and skill sets while attaining excellence? This book is all about that question, and offers a practice and philosophy toward this goal.

In Part I we will look at some of the current thinking that sits at the very core of how we consider practice, discipline, and performance. We will look at key concepts that have been adopted and adapted from science, philosophy, anthropology, and literary theory by the diverse field of critical theory of performance. We will explore certain ways these ideas have influenced a disintegration of our practice(s) and even marginalized performers in our own realm of performing. In this chapter we will look at how we identify as *self* when in practice. In a few pages we will return to the latest knowledge about how our brains worked as children to better understand how we might be able to harness some of the immediacy, integration, and lack of inhibition of childhood in balance with the level of excellence required in our specialism(s). But first, let's look at our craft(s) of performance and establish a working vocabulary from which we will explore further.

THE ALCHEMY OF THE PERFORMER

Whether we are singers, dancers, actors, or any combination of these, we can agree that we are all artists in the vocation of performance. In essence, we are people called *performers*, who do something called *performing*, towards an outcome called *performance*.

A	B	C
Performer	**Performing**	**Performance**
Who is doing.	Way of doing.	What is done.

> **NOTE:** *From here on when we use the terms performer, performing, or performance within the context of this working distinction, the words will be italicized, and may also have the corresponding letter in brackets next to them if a particular distinction in their relationship is being emphasized.*

Performance (C) may be a work of choreography, a play, or a score. It can also be an exercise, executed in the classroom or practice studio, such as barre work, scales, or sensory work. A performance can even be a doing or a verb, when that doing becomes the object. (We have all made the act of singing, dancing, and acting a *thing* to tackle. This often happens in practice or in a lesson.) *Performance* is an outcome of you, the artist, doing something in a certain way. We will learn that when you try to *do* an outcome directly you leave the *way* of *Performing* and change that desired outcome. In short, we work under the understanding that we are *performers* (self), *performing* (way of doing) *performance* (what's done).

From here on we will work with this distinction made between *performer* (A), *performing* (B), and *performance* (C). Within Part I, Chapter One will examine (A), Chapter Two will examine (C), and in Chapter Three we will define a distinct, active field of *performing* (B), from which the practice in Parts II, III, and IV of this book will unfold.

How the *performer* (A) is perceived by our culture, science, and philosophy affects the ways we work in and across our disciplines. The ways in which *performance* (C) is considered and is given prime value in analysis and the making of work also has very serious ramifications for our craft. We will look at these two categories in detail, offering a reconfiguration of the ways we consider ourselves in performance that puts the performer, our craft(s) and most importantly the *act of performing* front row and centre.

What will be brought to light is that *performing* (B) as a discrete category is exciting but also problematic, in that it does not fit easily into fundamental Western concepts such as reason, objectivity, reductive measurement, and paradigms of cause and effect. However, it is the stuff of *performing* (B), our *way of doing*, where our alchemy happens, and where our real work, our discipline of doing, resides. It is only in the field of *performing* (B) that our singing, dancing, and acting selves can integrate. Bracketing *performing* as its own distinct field provides a conceptual framework that highlights the kernel of our work, separating it from the "what I do" or the "who am I doing it", forefronting and giving prominence to a "way of doing". This *way of doing* will be made distinct from the "aesthetic values" of performance and will shift us out of the limitations of *performer* (A) doing *performance* (C) into a new concept, the *active aesthetic*, operating in a field of *performing* (B). An active aesthetic is distinguished from the term aesthetic, as commonly applied to performance and the performer, in that it is concerned with the steps before the product or outcome is usually evaluated. It is the *way of doing*. As we move through the book we will learn how, by engaging with the active aesthetic, you can witness or evaluate the *way of doing* in process, the qualities within the *activation* of *generating a process*. Through an embedded process of witnessing in the act of doing, active aesthetic differs from the general application of aesthetic in performance in that it is self-critical.

By the end of Part I you will have been taken through select philosophies, key scientific concepts and a few mind tasks to help reveal some *dis-integrative* influences embedded within aspects of our discipline(s). The ideas presented are designed to help us collapse the distinctions between (A), (B), and (C) as you begin to see how *performer* (A) and *performance* (C) can be viewed as emergent properties of *performing* (B) and that in this central field we can begin to conceive of a practice whereby the disciplines of acting, voice, and dance integrate.

For those of us not used to reading theory, some of the writing in Part I (Chapters 1, 2, and 3) can be complex and challenging. It can be like entering a foreign land that shifts not only your thinking if you allow it, but also your way of thinking. Do, however, feel free, as stated in the introduction, to skim and skip to the writing on practice starting in Part II to help facilitate your own personal understanding of the relationship between the practice and theory. To aid this, throughout the book corresponding sections will be signposted for practical exploration.

For now, let's return to the idea that we are people called *performers* (A), who do something in a certain way called *performing* (B), towards an outcome called *performance* (C).

In the distinction between (A), (B), and (C), the *performer* (A) is who we are, the self that we bring to the task. It includes the condition and intricacies of yourself as an instrument and as a physical, emotional, and spiritual being. It includes how you live in and of the world. It includes your attitudes and beliefs. We will leave the English language for a second to somewhat ironically use one German word to define another. We will learn in this chapter that much influential thinking around what it means to *experience* as *self* in the act of *doing* is found in the works of German philosophers, within the field of Phenomenology.

The German word *Haltung*, for which there is no equivalent in English, is most appropriate here. *Haltung* translates as *attitude*, but also includes posture, position, stance, manner, keeping, and composure. *Haltung* might come from cultural indoctrination or teachings; it might influence your level of commitment and affect what you consider discipline in service to your craft. It will include behavioural, emotional, and physical patternings, family history… It's the *gestalt* that you bring to the table as you work.

Gestalt

Gestalt, as a concept, suggests that something is greater than the sum of its parts and, further, that the whole cannot be predicted from the parts. It suggests that in order to understand something (an event or aspect of a person, for instance), you must consider the entire situation and the components that create it. The term has been adopted by disciplines interested in higher-order cognitive processes such as psychology, philosophy, and learning, especially in relation to perception and problem solving.

"Gestalt" is a German word for which we have no equivalent in English. It translates as a noun to figure, image, form, human shape, shape, mould, and symbol, and as a verb to configure, arrange parts to form a particular configuration, fashion, shape, form, adjust, create, make, frame, model, display, mould, and pattern.

Of course all this is dynamic: we change as we interact with the world. We are changed by the act of *performing* (B) in the engagement of *performance* (C). Further, we are not always aware of our self/*performer* (A) first and *performance* (C) last; sometimes (C) starts and we find (A). Later we will discuss theories that propose, for instance, that *self* is the result of being culturally "performed on" or that performance in itself is always performing. We will consider how key postmodernist ideas, adopted by the field of performance theory, have blurred the boundaries of the three categories of A, B, and C.

Try this:

Let's do a little exercise. As you are reading this page there is you, the *performer* (A) doing the performance of *reading* (C). You are *reading*, (A to C) — but wait, what's happening in (B)? Are you skimming the pages to get the basic idea? Are you searching for things that apply to you? Are you connecting the ideas on this page to your own knowledge base? Are you trying to make sense of the ideas? Are you criticizing the text as it unfolds? Are you thinking about what you might have for dinner tonight? What do you bring to the act of reading as far as attitude? Are you suspicious, eager, dispassionate, interested?

In that exercise, what was the "doing" of your reading? What was your way of reading? This is the stuff of *performing* (B). You (A) are not simply reading (C), but rather you are performing (B) reading.

If we take this further, perhaps a *performer* (A) does not simply do dance, song, or acting (C). Asking what we are actually doing, what is the "doing of our doing", opens this field to further scrutiny, letting us explore where we may be disintegrating or integrating our vocal, physical, and emotive instruments in the act of doing. It is through this field that we will learn how Integrative Performance Practice works.

When reading, it is not so important to understand or even work intimately with all the *ways* we might read; however, for the performer, the singer, dancer, and actor, it is precisely in ways of doing, in the field of *performing* (B), that our skills are honed, quality of doing is determined, and where the acts of vocalizing, moving, and expressing are joined or disjoined. It is where the discipline of our discipline resides. It is this field that makes us more than mere puppets or agents of representation and, very possibly, where our stage presence is determined. It is through this active field of doing that the artistry of the performer and also the performance emerges.

In the Integrative Performance Practice we practise *a way of doing* (B) that allows the performer (A) not to negotiate all the doings of acting, singing, and dancing, but to do one practice that allows the emergence of acting, singing, and dancing (C). There is one breathing practice, one physical centre to initiate from, and one notion of action. Repeatability and reliability is possible only by doing a doing again. What emerges through the way of doing does not adhere to linear laws of causation, or subject/object paradigms. It is whole and complex, but it is not disjointed or complicated.

The sweetness of emergence

Emergence is a term used in philosophy and in the human and physical sciences. It is a term that is widely applied in discussions on interdisciplinarity, complexity, and systems theory (discussed in Chapter Three). Emergence describes what parts of a system do together that they would not do alone, or how collective properties arise from the properties of parts. It can also speak to a system's function in that it can describe what something might do in relation to its environment that it would not do by itself. In this way it is very much about the dynamic relationships between things and is an essential aspect in the study of integration.

A common example from chemistry is that of the structure and properties of sugar. Carbon, oxygen, and hydrogen atoms form the structure of sugar, but none of these elements have a sweet taste. It is through the interaction (or possibly performing) of these molecules that a new property, sweetness, emerges.

The field of performing (B) in many ways is a field of the unknown, as it does not settle. It lives in motion, as process. For this reason, it is easier to grasp onto some stable idea of (A) or (C) instead. Field (B) can be uncomfortable to work in, as it offers no easy answers or quick fixes. It is a practice, not a "thing" to attain, an identity to make, or a goal to achieve. There is no *getting* it — it is a practice that is returned to anew each time. It is a way of doing; however, through this way of doing, the self may alter and the goal may be achieved — something will emerge.

This is not new. Many acting teachers, for instance, have a finely tuned lie detector that knows when the student leaves the field of the way of doing and instead jumps to indication, faking, or watching self: exhibiting a doing rather than doing the doing. Many movement or dance teachers have an acute sense of the way a body moves in space and recognize when the artist leaves the way of motion, when the head gets in the way: the instrument gets disconnected and the body becomes cumbersome, losing its simplicity in motion, gaining heaviness, compromising coordination, and making combinations mechanical. Many singing teachers can hear the loss of upper harmonics and agility when the breath is manufactured, causing superfluous tensions and making sound production and quality burdensome. Finding the ways in which the crafts of acting, singing, and dance cross, collide, and interact as ways of doing (when working optimally) has been key to the integration of these disciplines and the emergence of an Integrative Performance Practice.

So let's return to that child, the one who when asked to sing or dance or act does something from a sense of self whereby a more integrated outcome emerges. When did we begin to separate things into linear categories? What has this done to the *performer* (A) as self? How does this act of categorizing of skill and self happen?

THE PERFORMER'S BRAIN

Children have that wonderful gift of being so in the moment of doing, absorbed in the act of the act. It can be really enchanting to watch. This lack of self-consciousness and inability to contextualize what one is doing within a larger context can also be seen as childish, unsophisticated, and primitive. Much of this has to do with the fact that in children the part of the brain that categorizes knowledge has yet to develop.

The development of our prefrontal cortex has much to teach us about integration and categorization. The prefrontal cortex sits at the front of our brains. It is, in psychological terms, considered the seat of *executive function* in that it is associated with planning, decision-making, and the way we moderate our behaviour. It is also the very last part of our brain to develop, usually in early adulthood. Through repetition, learning, environment and all the other things that make our world what it is, the brain starts to make connections that get established, the way a river etches out channels in the land. As we etch in the patterns, our mind is made up — literally — and with it the more random, often expansive, and also less effectual neural pathways get weaker and disappear. In many ways, the sophistication of adulthood is also a necessary form of disintegration.

> **The integrated mind of a baby**
> If you look at a map of a baby's brain it would look like old Paris, with a lot of winding, interconnected little streets. In the adult brain those little streets are replaced by fewer but more efficient neural boulevards, capable of much more traffic. Young brains are also much more plastic and flexible — they change more easily.
> Alison Gopnik in *The Philosophical Baby: What Children's Minds Tell Us About Truth, Love & the Meaning of Life* (Gopnik 2009: 12)

Child psychologist Alison Gopnik writes against the old prevailing notion that babies are somehow "defective adults" and argues that children are, in fact, the Research and Development department of the human species. She posits that in the way a baby's brain works, with its heightened learning capacity and knack for experimentation, "any child will put the most productive scientist to shame". Here we could substitute performer for scientist, since it is the breadth of effective, productive exploration, and creativity that is being discussed. She says that "when it comes to imagination and learning, prefrontal immaturity allows children to be super adults" (Gopnik 2009: 9–15).

As babies, our brain map shifts radically multiple times as we live in the field of performing, playing, exploring, imagining, and investigating without the filters, judgements, and inhibitions that we develop in adulthood. We may not have the type of focus that comes with maturity but we are very conscious, purposeful, and highly innovative with our activities. In fact, there is evidence to suggest that "High IQ is correlated with later maturing and more plastic frontal lobes. Keeping your mind open longer may be a part of what makes you smarter" (Gopnik 2009: 14). How do we stay free and disciplined, flexible but not flaccid, and focused but not dismissive of all possibilities? This is a fundamental question underlying the practice and philosophy of integrative performance. As you will see in the following chapters, it may entail a slight reconfiguring of what we often consider "discipline" and perhaps a shift in how we approach our practice. We may even need to rethink how we position the "self" as artist within what we consider the "discipline".

The brain maps that Gopnik speaks of are born of the mind-dance that makes us who we are, and as this dance changes, so do we. The good news for us is that although neuroplasticity slows down in adulthood, it does not stop. There is much accumulating evidence that proves you can literally change your mind. Through improvements in imaging technology, scientists can now collect data on and create mind maps of living people at different ages, in various degrees of recovery after major brain injuries, in stages of learning, moving, sounding, making music, playing sports... and in a diverse array of conditions. It is a developing field, with new information being discovered daily. Emerging evidence is being adopted by scientists, philosophers, and artists as they formulate their experiments and frame the findings to suit various agendas. Neuropsychology, neurophysiology, neurophenomenology, psychoneuroimmunology, and neuroplasticity are just a few avenues of inquiry. Interdisciplinary relationships between neuroscience and the performing arts are taking various forms and new emerging fields of study are being established. It is all relatively new and there is a lot yet to be discovered.

What we do know is that we are not fixed, and further that specific types of intention, attention, and perception will actually change our brains. We also know that even our perception and what we imagine can change our brain. This all happens through nerve cell connections. Thoughts can turn certain genes on and off; this will alter the insides of the nerve cells, which will then make proteins, which will then change the structure of our brains.

The plastic paradox

The plastic paradox is that the same neuroplastic properties that allow us to change our brains and produce more flexible behaviours can also allow us to produce more rigid ones. All people start out with plastic potential. Some of us develop into increasingly flexible children and stay that way throughout our adult lives. For others of us, the spontaneity, creativity, and unpredictability of childhood gives way to a routinized existence that repeats the same behaviour and turns us into rigid caricatures of ourselves. Anything that involves unvaried repetition — our careers, cultural activities, skills, and neuroses — can lead to rigidity.

Norman Doidge in *The Brain that Changes Itself*
(Doidge 2007: 242)

Working in a conscious way is an important part of Integrative Performance Practice. When I teach I often distil this basic point down to "There is no such thing as not doing" (Part II explores how this works in practice). Importantly, the next stage of understanding the integrative performer is to see that to change and pattern our minds is to change and pattern our body (and vice versa). To change and pattern our mind/body is to alter our perceptions and very consciousness. As a student I was often told that talent is "the greater capacity to experience". If this is true, then as we act in and of the world, mindfully or not, we are altering our very talent. This will become a key factor in our relationship with our exercises and practice as an integrative performer.

THE PERFORMER'S MIND/BODY

It is only recently that we have begun to think of the brain and body as joined in the dynamic web that makes us who we are. As we leave behind a mechanistic notion that a brain is a thing that thinks and merely tells the body what to do or feel, we have begun to embrace the idea that consciousness and mind are processes that engage the entire organism.

> **The mind is in the body**
> We know that the immune system, like the central nervous system, has memory and the capacity to learn. Thus it could be said that intelligence is located not only in the brain but in the cells that are distributed throughout the body, and that the traditional separation of mental processes, including emotions, from the body is no longer valid... we may conclude that the *mind* is in the body, in the same sense that the mind is in the brain, with all that that implies.
> Candace Pert in *Molecules of Emotion: Why You Feel the Way You Feel*
> (Pert 1997: 187–188)

In speaking about the relationship between the mind and body it is impossible to avoid the legacy of René Descartes (1596—1650), the father of modern philosophy. His profound influence on Western thinking revolves around a received understanding about the relationship between the mind and the body. Many read his treatise as advocating a separation between the mind and body in the understanding of knowledge and self. This separation is in a slow dissolve, and was arguably misunderstood in the first place. However, it affects how we as artists approach performance challenges and how we perceive ourselves in our work, even today. Descartes' influence on Western thought is exemplified by his famous statement "Cogito ergo sum" (I think therefore I am). This statement "signaled the centrality of the self and the rejection of authority from without, the authority of both texts and teacher" (Garber 2005: 189).

In order to better understand how we got into the mind/body divide in the first place, we need to return to the seventeenth century. At that time, Descartes proposed the idea that there was a distinction between the rational mind, based in the brain, capable of discerning objective reality, and a less trustworthy sensory reality, perceived through emotion, based in the body. Part of his objective was to create a measurable model and rigorous mode of inquiry that was free from the influence of the Church. He was working toward something rigorous and objective, a reliable method he could count on. What happened was that in the adoption and adaptation of his ideas over the years, intuition, felt senses, emotional experience, memory, and arguably feminine-anything and embodied knowledge got thrown in the same suspicious bucket as the irrational and non-rigorous, because not being of the "objective" mind made it slippery, immeasurable, non-reducible, and therefore unscientific and, even worse, subjective.

We will discuss shortly, in the section on the performer's self, how the very field of *performing* (B) is unapologetically subjective, and look at how consciousness is now being embraced as a subjective emergence of dynamic processes among the mind, body, and environment. It may be more likely that "to think" is one emergent property of self, not the one defining factor of self. This shift does two things: it takes us out of the mechanical dualism of mind/body and also out of the idea that self is born of linear and reductive models. It might also affect what performers value as correct, proper, and good discipline in the act of training, learning, and performing. The often primary status of "getting the values of performance right", or "being a better performer" might now be understood as emergent properties of the field of *performing* (B).

Subjectivity, culture, creativity, and self

Had subjectivity not begun, even if very modestly at first, in living creatures far simpler than we are, memory and reasoning are not likely to have expanded in the prodigious way they did, and the evolutionary road for language and the elaborate human version of consciousness we now possess would not have been paved. Creativity would not have flourished. There would have been no song, no painting, and no literature. Love would never have been love, just sex. Friendship would have been mere cooperative convenience. Pain would never have become suffering — not a bad thing, come to think of it — but an equivocal advantage given that pleasure would not have become bliss either. Had subjectivity not made its radical appearance, there would have been no knowing and no one to take notice, and consequently there would have been no history of what creatures did through the ages, no culture at all.

Antonio Damasio in *Descartes' Error* (Damasio 2010: 4)

Descartes' influence on scientific reason and physics "represented the rejection of the scholastic physics of matter and form, and its replacement by a mechanistic physics of matter and motion" (Garber 2005: 189). However, with the latest work in quantum theory, the Cartesian model of scientific reason is in question; many philosophers and scientists are now coming to the view that there can be no objective description or account of nature. If it is a human being doing the observing, and if our mind/body are not divided, but rather integral systems by which consciousness emerges, through a process of being in and of the world, then the observer and the observed are both changeable and also changed by the very act of observation. When a performer checks to see if they are doing that movement, that sound, that dramatic moment correctly, they cease to be in the act of doing those and shift to the doing of "checking". Both the task — the movement/sound/moment — and the artist are changed. In the field of *performing* (B), watching technique objectively is impossible, and also a guaranteed way to lose presence in the act of performing. It also separates the self from the doing of the doing of the task. The entirety of Part II offers practical exercises for the performer, addressing this split between practice and self.

Looking more specifically into the mind/body issue, this is far more than a philosophical shift. Philosophy did come to the same conclusions in many ways before science, most notably in the work of Merleau-Ponty in the 1940s, discussed in the following section on Phenomenology. The mind/body as an integrated paradigm has been gaining empirical evidence that may affect how we approach some of our practices, many of which were developed before they were supported by science.

Candace Pert, working in the field of receptor pharmacology and chemical neuroanatomy, has been one of the leading advocates for approaching the mind/body as a network, stressing the interconnectedness of all the systems that make up our organism. Her research shows us that through the wide distribution of peptides and other informational substances acting as biochemicals of emotion, feelings can start in many areas of the body, including the small intestine (talk about a gut feeling!). "Mind doesn't dominate body, it *becomes* body — body and mind are one" (Pert 1997: 187).

In addition, new technology in brain imaging is allowing us to both confirm what we have instinctively known about the mind/body connection and also provide some surprises. One example of something performance teachers have known instinctively for years is found in a study from the University of Wisconsin. Psychology professor Martha Alibali proved that "Being able to use your body in problem solving alters the way you solve the problems" (Association for Psychological Science 2011, June 3). The study employed a group of people solving problems with their hands bound and another with hands free. Those with their hands free were more accurate. This helped to prove that the mind/body relationship is not unidirectional. The study reinforced the idea that we use visual-spatial metaphors all the time to solve problems and conceptualize things — even in domains that don't, on the face of it, seem physical.

In another study from UC Santa Barbara, it was established that when a dancer reaches into the visual realm, as in grasping their partner's hand during a performance, and when they reach initiating the movement from an internal experience of the body, as in scratching their leg in the dark, they actually employ different mind maps. As stated by Scott T. Grafton, professor of psychology, it was observed that when "the brain is trying to make a map of the world…one map is what you see, which is provided by the visual system. The other map is where the body is in space. This map is based on proprioception — the sense of limb position — which is derived from receptors in the skin, muscles, and joints" (University of California 2010, December 5).

This led them to observe that these maps are very different and question how we may connect them. They concluded that "Either the visual map or the body map may be fixed, or neither may be fixed" (University of California 2010, December 5).

One study that might be surprising came out of UC Berkeley. It measured differences in the mind/body connection between trained dancers and long-time practitioners of Vipassana meditation. The two groups, plus a control group, were wired with electrodes to measure their physical responses while watching emotionally charged films. They each rated the degree of various feelings while their bodily responses were monitored. The rating of the depth of feelings was similar, but the relationship between the feelings and bodily responses were quite different. The dancers and the control group were very similar, while meditators showed a stronger sense of "attunement". It was concluded that dancers are not as emotionally in sync with their bodies as are people who regularly practise meditation. An explanation posited by Robert Levenson, a UC Berkeley psychology professor and senior author of the study, was that while dancers hone their craft, and in doing so habitually shift focus between time, music, space, and muscles, achieving heightened awareness of muscle tone, body alignment, and posture, "These are all very helpful for becoming a better dancer, but they do not tighten the links between mind and body in emotion" (Anwar, 2011, February 23). The implication of this study is connected to the plastic paradox found on page 16.

Some very useful studies for the performing artist come from the area of sports. Sports psychologist Antonis Hatzigeorgiadis looked into the role of "self-talk" and its relationship to performance. In addition to finding, as expected, that positive self-talk does help in the execution of a task, he found that there is a difference in the effectiveness in types of talk for different types of challenges. For more exacting tasks, and those requiring fine skills, a more specific, instructional self-talk was effective. For a singer, this might translate to "release tongue, connect to breath", rather than positive reinforcement or motivational self-talk such as "you can do it — you can hit that note, go for it baby!" Hatzigeorgiadis believes that self-talk, like visualization and meditation, works twofold: "to enhance your potential; and to perform during competition in terms of your ability and not less." And further, "The mind guides action. If we succeed in regulating our thoughts, then this will help our behavior" (Association for Psychological Science 2011, May 25). In Part II, as part of a "conscious practice", we will learn how to support a task in the act of *performing* through a type of self-talk. We will also learn that in this practice the mind will guide the action as much as the body will guide the action and, further, that the action will also guide the mind/body.

As mentioned previously, I believe performers have been ahead of the game in acknowledging a mind/body connection — at a mechanistic level at least. Earlier, I described the weakening of Descartes' influence as a "slow dissolve". Slow because, even in the performing arts, where we have been quite revolutionary against received Cartesian thought, largely due to the fact that much of our *knowledge* is effective only when it is consciously "embodied",[1] there are some surviving legacies. We still, for instance, speak of the practice of the performer in terms of the psychophysical, as if there were any possible way that an action could be either just psychological or just physical. Other discussions around the mind/body tend to be to do with how we position *self* (performer) in relation to task (practice), whether that task is within the discipline of singing, acting, or dancing.

THE PERFORMING SELF

If the mind and body are connected, where do *we* reside; who and what is *self*; *who* is doing the action in the scene, the movement of the dance, the breath of singing — who learns to do these? Who are we as the do-er? Does this matter? Are we best when we come from a place of no-self and non-ego, simply giving ourselves to the task? Are we best on the flip side of this, as self-possessed artists doing the action? Do our back-stories define us as artists? Does technique condition and alter the self, making one an artist? Where does intention come in? What relationship does intention have to movement, emotional expression, and sound in the aesthetics and practice(s) of our disciplines? How can we best prepare an integrated self towards an integrated doing?

Self is a huge topic, and at times it would be tempting to just go through life and discover it or ignore it as it comes. However, for the dancer, singer, and actor, having some sort of knowledge, mindfulness, or access to self is a generally accepted crucial aspect of being a performer. In performance trainings, *self* is often situated in relation to technique. Recall the self as a *performer* (A) who *does performing* (B) towards *performance* (C).

For now, let's explore the way that different performance disciplines and different techniques situate *self* in radically different places in relation to the doing of the practice(s). This is not to say that there is one hard and fast way that self is seen in the discipline of dance and another in singing and/or acting; however, some approaches are worth exploring even in general terms in order to highlight that there clearly are differences and, more importantly, serious implications for the performing *self* when practising multiple disciplines as they are often configured.

In speaking about self and discipline, the following examples may seem somewhat reductive. It is precisely this account and its effects on practice that I aim to reveal. Obviously, what happens in the studio and with different teachers and teachings of discipline can vary. More subtle accounts of techniques of acting, dance and movement, and voice and singing will be discussed in Parts III and IV as we integrate these disciplines and apply the practice. For now, we look at some prevailing conversation around the issue.

Martha Graham, the mother of modern dance, said, "The acquiring of technique in dance has been for one purpose — so to train the body as to make possible any demand made upon it by that inner self which has the vision of what needs to be said". Mark Franko, Scholar of Dance and Performance Studies, observed this as a "statement of the body's instrumentality in the service of a self" (Franko, 1996: 50). This statement can also be seen to reveal another position, which asserts that self is given voice through an external conditioning acquired through technique. It can be said that in dance one gives oneself over to technique in the promise that technique, developed over many years, will eventually deliver a conduit for self — at a later time.

An important consideration here is that those of us who have taken the practice of dance to a professional level often started at a very young age, sometimes before adolescence and before a full development of our frontal lobe (see first section), which arguably allows the practice to categorize and define the boundaries that help to mould the adult self.

As vocalists, we generally start the serious training later. It is inadvisable to train the voice until our breath-body is fully developed; for most, this is between the ages of eighteen and twenty-seven. By then we have been around for a while; our bodies have experienced joys and traumas. We have lived, and therefore have been patterned by our culture, our personal lives, and our educations in complex ways. Might not one think that this patterning is the very definition of self? Interestingly, many voice trainings start with a focus on "freeing" us of the many effects of this patterning, so as to let a "true" voice come forth. What is "true", "free", "natural" and even "correct" is not always completely agreed upon or defined. In much voice training there is a concentration on "getting out of bad habits", finding a "neutral" condition for the optimum breath-body and then "building" a new technique in line with the particular vocal tradition that one is conditioning toward. It is often an implicitly psychological approach and can be fairly subjective. It is also worth noting that many singing lessons happen one on one, giving the teacher's opinion a certain status and amplifying the personal importance of this one-on-one relationship to the student's sense of self.

In Richard Knowles's analysis of the writings of three of the seminal voice pedagogues of our time, those of Cicely Berry, Kristen Linklater, and Patsy Rodenburg, he focuses on the implications of particular language within voice training as evidenced and repeated in their texts. He mentions that "It is worth noting the incongruity between the rhetoric of 'freeing' something 'natural,' 'allowing' the true self to speak (and again, 'free,' 'let,' and 'allow' are most often used in the imperative mood), and the frequent adjuration to 'recondition your whole way of communicating' … resulting in 'reprogramming' … 'reconditioning your use of yourself'" (Knowles 1996: 112).

Acting in many ways situates the self at the core of how it defines itself as a discipline. Although to varying degrees the same can be said of voice and dance, acting as a discipline puts a more intense focus on the mind/body self as instrument, with constant discussion around dualistic themes such as internal/external, psychological/physical, personal/societal, higher/lower selves, and sacred/secular. In fact, different acting trainings are often defined by their different and often passionate rhetoric redefining the balance between these dialectical themes to do with self in action and representation.

In Chapter Seven we learn about acting practices in greater detail, but for now we continue with the question of how the performer (A) or *self* is considered within current discourses. In Auslander's essay *Just be your self*, he explores acting practice in relation to Derrida's reading of logocentrism and *différance* (a particular term, distinct from "difference", that we will learn more about in Chapter Two). Auslander first draws attention to a Joseph Chaikin quote: "Acting is a demonstration of self with or without a disguise" (Chaikin 1980: 2). Disguise in this instance can be construed as that thing between self and the practice of performing acting. Auslander states that, "For Stanislavsky, the disguise must be based on the actor's own emotional experience; Brecht wants the disguise to be separable from the actor's own persona. Grotowski believes that the actor must use the disguise by her role to cut away the disguise imposed on her by socialization and expose the most basic levels of self" (Auslander 1995: 60). Taking this further, we could say that for Strasberg the disguise and self become one in the service of truth, for Meisner the disguise and self converge in a place called the present, and for Chekhov the disguise is a transcended other, through the departure of the everyday self towards a heightened self in service to a higher art.

Everything is both manufactured and natural in man

It is impossible to superimpose on man a lower layer of behavior which one chooses to call "natural", followed by a manufactured cultural or spiritual world. Everything is both manufactured and natural in man, as it were, in the sense that there is not a word, not a form of behavior which does not owe something to purely biological being — and which at the same time does not elude the simplicity of animal life, and cause forms of vital behavior to deviate from their pre-ordained direction, through a sort of leakage and through a genius for ambiguity which might serve to define man.

Maurice Merleau-Ponty in *Phenomenology of Perception*
(Merleau-Ponty 2002: 220)

As mentioned, we will draw out some of the differences between Integrative Performance Practice and other trainings in dance, acting, and voice throughout the book, while offering a practical approach towards an integrated self that engages with practice(s). For now, the simple point is that the disciplines of acting, voice, and dance (and subsets of these disciplines) position *self* in various ways. Where is self when we work in more than one of these disciplines or their techniques at once? Do we lose self? How can I be both my singing self and my acting self at the same time, if I am being asked to come from different places in my self by each? Many of us have come to our own personal understandings of this as we negotiate separate techniques across performing disciplines. We may even have this down to a fine art form. However, the IPP aims to free us from the need to negotiate different selves or different practices. This work comes from one self, doing one practice, whereby the singer, dancer, and actor and any combination of performance discipline(s) can emerge.

Whether self is positioned as a potential instrument that technique conditions to render it an artist; or self comes to technique as a flawed object there to be cleansed, neutralized, and reconditioned for an optimum aesthetic expression; or self is considered a mind/body, struggling to reconcile inherent psychophysical questions of the human condition in order to access, become, or portray a heightened or more "natural" and "authentic" being ready for expression in performance: *self* is still positioned *against* or *next to* the action or task and therefore *outside* of its practice, with one the subject and the other the object.

With the IPP we will come to be wary of the idea that the self is equivalent to a "thing" that exists in the same way that an object exists. This will be important as we move into the Practice in Parts II and III. With the IPP, the performer is not there to be passively conditioned by a technique. We *engage* with practice.

But first, in the following sections, Phenomenology, Performativity and Cognitive Science, we will learn a few modes of thinking where self is considered as a dynamic practice.

Phenomenology: experiencing of, as, and in self

As our first stage in beginning to consider self as a kind of practice, let's turn to the field of phenomenology. Proponents of phenomenology such as Husserl, Heidegger, Sartre, and Merleau-Ponty *et al* interpret the field differently, but share a thought inquiry that reveals "a method of philosophical investigation which results in a radical ontological revision of Cartesian Dualism". In phenomenology, "subjects and objects are essentially interrelated, a fact which any adequate account of subjects and objects must preserve". Further, "Phenomenological accounts of subjects emphasize action and the body; accounts of objects emphasize the significance they have for us" (Howarth 2005: 791).

If we follow the line of thought that within the disciplines of acting, singing, and dancing there is a tradition of self being positioned as either subject or object and technique/task as the other, it follows that as this book is for performers in the act of practice, looking at our *experience* as *self* in practice may be helpful. Phenomenology instigates a dissolution of subject and object through just that, *experience*.

David R. Cerbone, in *Understanding Phenomenology*, offers a wonderful account of some of the most complex and varied articulations of phenomenology. To help illuminate what is meant by *experience* in phenomenology, he offers this simple exercise, which could be seen as a further development from our reading exercise on page 24.

He writes:

> I happen to wear glasses. If I were to take them off while looking at the page of the book held at the usual half-arm's length away, the letters, words and page would, as I might put it, become blurry, while restoring my glasses would render them sharpened once again. Of course, I do not for a moment think that the blurriness characterizes the things I am looking at in and of themselves, as though my removing my glasses had the magical power to soften the actual ink, paper and so on. (Think here of the difference between removing your glasses and taking your wet hand and rubbing it across the printed page. Doing the latter, wetting the paper and smearing the print, really does affect the object.) That there are descriptions that apply to visual experience without necessarily applying to the objects of that experience helps to make vivid the distinction we are trying to *delineate between what we see and are seeing of it. To concentrate on the latter, to focus one's attention not so much on what one experiences out there in the world but on one's experience of the world*, is to take the first step in the practice of phenomenology. The word "phenomenology" means "the study of phenomena", where the notion of phenomenon coincides roughly with the notion of experience. Thus, *to attend to experience rather than what is experienced is to attend to the phenomena*. (emphasis added)
>
> David R. Cerbone in *Understanding Phenomenology* (Cerbone 2006: 2)

Here let's consider phenomenology in relation to our practice(s). One can substitute for Cerbone's seeing the words on the page here the bending in a plié as a dancer, breathing in a voiced scale as a singer, or the executing of a character's actions as an actor. In order to attend to the experience of any of these as phenomena you might shift your attention away from "the things that you are doing" (bending, breathing, executing) toward "your experience of doing them". So in a phenomenological inquiry, instead of being asked to describe the exercise or task, "the object of your experience", you would be asked to consider *your experience of the doing of them*. This would move focus from *you* doing *tasks* — recalling the distinction in: *performer (A)* doing *performance (C)* — and rather move towards your "attending to your experience" in the act of doing the task(s). This will open up the middle field of *Performing (B)* towards an *active aesthetic*.

This attending to *experience* in this way might begin to move us away from the discipline(s) as abstract schematizations and toward practice as a lived experience. But here it is most important to clarify that this "attending to experience" as "experience itself" is not about telling stories, creating narratives, recalling action and/or working it out through judging and diagnosing. It is also not about investigating a biological account (often understood as mechanism) or a psychological explanation (often understood as behaviorism). These would take us away from the domain of phenomenology. "Phenomenology emphatically rejects the idea that attending to experience be construed as a kind of 'introspection'" (Cerbone 2006: 4).

One thing to note here is that reliance on personal narrative is often a public relations device in the performing arts. "Backstory" is a somewhat over-fetishized construction in our industry. The most extreme instances of this trend are seen on "reality" talent shows and TV depictions of our industry that tend to misrepresent the integrity of practice and the reality of life as a performer and rather focus on self as a narrative/subject in search of fame/object. When the king of pop talent shows Simon Cowell was interviewed in London's *The Guardian*, he said it all: "Contestants as young as 12 now understand the concept of a strong 'backstory' and talk about their lives in those terms. I once had a guy who came rushing out on stage and literally shouted, 'I've got cancer!' Like it was great news. He was so happy that he had a sad story" (Brockes 2011). This account is extreme, granted; however, as discussed earlier, a focus on personal history is currently found in certain systematic approaches to our discipline(s). This is not to say that such an approach is not valuable, especially if framed as an exercise in witnessing the things we have brought to the work, but if constantly delving into a narrative sense of self becomes the primary tool of a discipline, then the work can become a glorified therapy and/or the work can be in danger of serving only the personal narrative. Fine, if that is the choice, but few of us are *that* interesting or exclusively interested in ourselves.[2]

Returning to the idea of "attending to our experience" within the performing disciplines, we might begin to ask not what we do, but what our *way* of doing might be, the doing of our doing, the practice of our practice.

This brings us to the term "intentionality". Let's not confuse this with the use of the word "intention" as understood in acting techniques. We will return to the better-known definition as used in various acting practices in Chapters Seven and Eight. However, for the rest of this section we will speak of "intentionality" within the context of phenomenology.

How does intentionality affect experience? *Experience* in phenomenology includes thought, emotion, imagination, desire, perception, memory, bodily awareness, physical and psychological action, social and linguistic activities. "The structure of these forms of experience typically involves what Husserl called 'intentionality', that is, the directedness of experience *toward* things in the world, the property of consciousness that it is a consciousness *of* or *about* something. According to classical Husserlian phenomenology, our experience is directed toward — represents or 'intends' — things only through particular concepts, thoughts, ideas, images, etc. These make up the meaning or content of a given experience, and are distinct from the things they present or mean" (Smith: Fall 2011).

In phenomenology, intentionality has to do with directionality, and differs from purely scientific, objective, or sequential understandings of process often referred to in cause-and-effect paradigms attributed to naturalism. "One of the dangers of scientific naturalism, according to the phenomenological tradition, is that such a preoccupation makes one lose sight of (and sometimes deny) the idea that things are manifest at all" (Cerbone 2006: 8). A more scientific, naturalist, and objective explanation of the singing of a tone might go like this: "I am standing by the piano and mentally place a pitch in my mind. I exhale and my vocal folds are hit by the air. They slam together, they vibrate at 392 times a second and I sound a G above middle C". It is rational, clear, and makes a linear sort of sense. It is also most unlikely that an artist would consider their experience of singing a G in this way. But we can learn a few things from this extreme account: the above singer is goal-oriented. This singer does not witness the effects on her body, the feeling of subtle resistance on her upper palate as the breath releases, the experience of the largeness or smallness of the room. By contrast, the artist witnessing herself in the act of sounding might say "I am standing, conscious of my body close to the piano, with my teacher looking at me. I am sensing her eyes on my lower belly. I can feel my lungs are full and at the ready. As my palate releases up, I sense apprehension in my jaw. I know that I will sound, I know what pitch I will sound, I sound, I sense my diaphragm release upwards and I feel the vibrations dance around my head..." ...it could go on. It will be reflective, inherently subjective, in recognition not just of the "I" doing something called singing but inclusive of what the singing is doing with me. This will not be a reductive account spoken through the lens of justification and explanation but an active opening-out of possibilities and, through that, a dissolve of the dualistic relationship whereby the singer (with everything she might be) is one and singing (with everything that might hold) is another; for that moment, we are in "singing-ness".

This mode of reflecting on experience, as "me" being of or about something — in this example, something being the sounding of the note G — is the domain of "intentionality". In this example the singer is in "practice-ness", and there is a possibility of emergence. The note G is but one of the things that emerge. This environment is one of becoming. Through this type of account of experience, *performance* (C) of the note of G and the *performer*/self (A) both emerge through the field of *performing* (B).

This idea that a body is not just a material thing that does stuff, but is also receptive and perceptive in its living, is what Husserl illustrated and Merleau-Ponty took further. This idea, called the *double constitution*, is best described in a little game of a *double touch*.

Try this:

Stroke the top of your right hand with your left three middle fingers. Continue slowly and attend to your experience for a few moments... What is happening? Are your left fingers stroking your right hand? Is this the action? Are you sure? Or is your right hand sensing being stroked? Of course as the body is a "lived-body", one and both are happening! Lived-body is a term that dissolves the Cartesian dualism in that we are not here speaking of the body as just material or a container. "A lived-body is a 'localized field of sensations', not merely a causal conduit of sensations, but the place in and on which those sensations occur" (Cerbone 2006: 104).

The subject that I am is inseparable from this body and this world
In so far as, when I reflect on the essence of subjectivity, I find it bound up with that of the body and that of the world, this is because my existence as subjectivity is merely one with my existence as a body and with the existence of the world, and because the subject that I am, when taken concretely, is inseparable from this body and this world. The ontological world and body which we find at the core of the subject are not the world or body as idea, but on the one hand the world itself contracted into a comprehensive grasp, and on the other the body itself as a knowing-body.

Maurice Merleau-Ponty in *Phenomenology of Perception*
(Merleau-Ponty 2002: 475)

With the examples offered we see how the field of phenomenology can offer the performer guidance on self-ness in the act of doing, through attending to *experience*, within a field of *intentionality*, engaging and being engaged by the *lived-body*.

In the chapters outlining the practice these concepts will help us to engage as an integrative self within an integrative practice.

For instance, in the Integrative Performance Practice, it is crucial that the act of doing a task, be it a scale, a plié, or the learning of lines, does not happen in a zone-out, trance-like state or with a by-rote quality, but rather with an awareness of and attending to experience between you the performer in-and-of-and-with the task. The exercises do not exercise you, and you do not master the exercise; rather, the practice, when engaged with, allows the emergence of mastery, one that is not discipline-based or aesthetic-based but active, in process, and lived. Its quality is that of the active aesthetic within the field of performing.

Performativity — making of self — self as making

Where phenomenology is largely concerned with experience, performativity is a term largely concerned with doings: things we do, things that are done around us, about us and to us and, importantly for the purposes of this section, how these doings help to make what we understand as self, a self that performs and is performed on.

When Schechner states that the term *performativity* is "A hard term to pin down" (Schechner 2002: 110), he is not only being accurate but embracing a certain irony. This is because much of what *performativity* is about, as a concept, is opposed to any situating, pinning down, centralizing, or authorizing a source from which inherent meaning is spoken or even radiates. As we will see, this extends to the idea that *self* does not come from any essential place but is an ever-developing dynamic, created through production and reproduction.

But let's back up. The term has roots in the philosophy of language and, largely through poststructuralist critique initiated by Jacques Derrida, it has become a vibrant tool and at times an annoyance for sociologists, anthropologists, architects, literary theorists, film theorists, cultural theorists, and those in performance studies. It can be an annoyance partly because it is a hard term to pin down, but more importantly because it sets things that we thought were nicely pinned down out, up, and spinning. For our purpose, in this section we will focus on the term's implication for the performer when considering the *self*. (In Part IV we will return to this concept when applying the practice to choreography, the script, and the score as text. In Chapter Two we will look at the term in relation to performance.)

We can trace current understanding of the term to J.L. Austin and John Searle's developments of a speech act theory, where the concept of a "performative utterance" was first defined. Austin aimed to show that we understand utterances only because of socially shared conventions. Performatives, as described by Austin, are instances of one type of use of language that *do* something. Examples may include when a judge says, "I sentence you to ten years" and bangs down his gavel, or when a dignitary crashes a bottle of champagne against a boat and says "I name you the SS Integrative Performance Practice". Bracketing these types of utterances shifts the emphasis from language as being the mere vehicle of some intent or meaning to the way in which language functions as a social force and how it performs.

But what happens when such utterances are not spoken by a real judge and not in front of a boat at all? Regardless of what may be "intended" or "who" utters them, do they hold weight? What happens if they are a scene in an opera, play or musical? In the case of performatives in their strictest sense, statements uttered by the clergy, judges, and law enforcers, and statements such as promises and commitments, only work successfully in legitimate contexts. When taken out of legitimate contexts (which Austin spends some time distinguishing), they become, as he states, infelicitous (inappropriate).

Although Austin does come around to say that all utterances are performative, even if only to inform, both he and Searle assert to varying degrees that words (Auslander 1995) spoken in a play, fiction, or a poem, i.e. not in the "normal real world", are in some way "parasitic". Schechner takes umbrage with this use of the term with his assertion that "Searle and Austin take this position because they don't recognize that art can be a model for rather than a mirror of life" (Schechner 2002: 111). Oscar Wilde might have had it right when he stated, "Life imitates art more than art imitates life".

It is at this point in the ongoing debate about meaning and doing, through the understanding of the term "performativity", that things get really interesting. In Derrida's essay *Signature Event Context*, he insists that this dismissal of fictive or parasitic utterances is illegitimate. This turns things on their head. Derrida asks, how can Austin decide what constitutes a genuine or parasitic performative? Austin makes this decision with regard to contexts. A performative uttered on stage is infelicitous or parasitic, Austin argues, in relation to genuine cases. But what Derrida aims to show is that all language acts have this infelicitous or parasitic character that exceeds the limit of context, and he makes this argument by way of the notion of an event.

How is it that shared contexts of meaning are generated? Austin treats language as something that takes place within context. Because of this, he can distinguish between legitimate and illegitimate interpretations. But if we take Austin's theory seriously, we see that this is not possible. Firstly, it is the very repeatability or conventionality of words that renders all contexts essentially open. A word only works if it is repeatable, or if it can be used in more than one context. And so this means that a context cannot limit or ground a word.

A performative can be uttered on stage and a promise can be used in fiction precisely because there is nothing limiting the use of these utterances. And this is why such utterances are essentially unstable. We can extend this to the interpretations of texts for performance. It's possible that we could argue for legitimate interpretations of *Hamlet* by appealing to the context of Renaissance drama and the conventions of tragedy, and we could even appeal to what we know about the life of Shakespeare as a way of providing a limit and legitimacy to possible interpretations. But, according to Derrida's theory, the fact that we have to appeal to a context shows that no text harbours a meaning in itself, and that texts are therefore essentially open to re-interpretation and re-contextualization.

For us as performers, this is particularly interesting, especially since we are so often asked to express, interpret or honour some supposed inherent meaning in a text. If the meaning of the performance is not *in* or *held* by the text, then where does meaning reside? What meaning are we interpreting? How do we as the performer generate meaning? These questions are at the heart of the discussions around performativity. We will continue to discuss this aspect in Chapter Two when speaking of postmodernism, meaning and *performance* (C) within the context of *event*. In Part IV, a practical solution for working across the disciplines with text is offered. For now, however, let's return to the question of self, and therefore to identity, in order to further explore what happens to the *performer* (A) through the lens of this concept of performativity.

Let's now follow this train of thought to the idea that it is not only text but also *self/performer* (A) and *identity* that can be determined in context and in repetition from, about, and within social, linguistic, and cultural contexts. Culture here might also include the specific culture(s) of our discipline(s), such as the culture of dancers, actors, or singers. Here we begin to enter a fascinating territory that goes to the heart of how we may begin to re-consider our artistic identities.

You'll remember that Austin aimed to show that we understand utterances only because of socially shared conventions through repetition. Butler takes this into the idea of gender: gender as *performative*. If we can say that a word on its own before repetition and situation within the context of various socio-cultural paradigms holds no essential meaning, might we not say the same for self as inherently holding gender, for instance?

Butler argues that gender is *made* through sustained social performances. If Derrida can say that there is no inherent meaning, grounded in context, or repetition, or utterance, perhaps we are not born man or woman. Perhaps gender is not something one *is*, but something one does (and is done to one). Butler asserts that gender is a particular type of process. "Gender is the repeated stylization of the body, a set of repeated acts within a highly rigid regulatory frame that congeal over time to produce the appearance of substance, of a natural sort of being" (Butler 1988: 36).

> **I know it's controversial, but that's my claim.**
> We act as if that being of a man or that being of a woman is actually an internal reality or something that is simply true about us, a fact about us, but actually it's a phenomenon that is being produced all the time and reproduced all the time, so to say gender is performative is to say that nobody really is a gender from the start. I know it's controversial, but that's my claim.
> Judith Butler in an interview with Max Miller
> (Butler 2011, January 13)

And as this discussion develops, if gender can be seen to be performative, what about race, sexuality, political affiliations, illness identification such as "I'm a cancer survivor" (in the aforementioned backstory as identifying narrative), or self as identifying with disciplinary affiliation: I am a dancer?, I am an actor?, or I am a singer?... Destabilizing some of these can be highly contentious and quite challenging to consider. To consider self as somewhat mercurially constructed, as opposed to embodying an inherent essence of "I am", can be strange. But there is value in considering self as performative. It highlights that what we do produces self; we think, move, talk, approach, position, glance, speak, act, breathe in ways that produce a series of effects that create the impression of you being you.

For actors, singers, and dancers, this is important. Everything you do in the studio makes an imprint on your practice and yourself. It does not matter if it was on purpose, clumsy, ill-considered, conscious, by rote, taught well or badly. What you practise, what you actually *do* in practice, is what you get good at. Also, what is done to you and about you, which may live in the culture of your practice and rehearsal space, is performative too. In short, *all doings do something*. There is no such thing as not doing! Part II takes us through exercises that help to make this point about practice clear, and further to help us to harness this dynamic towards an integration of the discipline(s) of performance.

In many performance practices one is asked to simply *be*. In such thinking just to *be* is considered an essential aspect of presence and authenticity; however, performativity questions this: to live and practise is to do. To do is *active being*. Performativity as a concept questions "being" as an inherent self. In this way, performativity may not offer a set practice, but it will help us to deconstruct some of our conventions, habits, and even lived-body patternings in and out of the studio.

Through this lens we begin to see that the relationship between the *performer* (A) and the *performance* (C) is not linear and goes many ways. It further opens out "performance" as a term raising new questions to do with intentionality in the phenomenological sense and cause and effect in the scientific sense (more on this in the next chapter). For now, however, in the context of this discussion on self, performativity has helped to open the way for the possibility of a middle field, *performing* (B), through which both the *performer* (A) and the *performance* (C) are *activated*. But what is this? How would this work? How do we as integrative practitioners harness this knowledge? What do we do? And how do we know what we are doing?

Cognitive science — self in knowing — knowing of self

Where performativity can be seen to speak to action and phenomenology to experience, cognitive science can be seen to deal with the nature of knowing. What might it mean to *know* what we are doing, to know what/or where is *self*? What is it to know one's experience? Cognitive science is at its core interdisciplinary, drawing from philosophy, psychology, neuroscience, linguistics, anthropology, sociology, and even artificial intelligence. It is a huge field that is having a bit of a revolution due in part to the aforementioned advances in neural technology and the mass of data emerging daily. We will explore in this section not only that you are an integrated artist, but moreover that you and your practice are an integrated system.

> **Mind with a twist**
> What is consciousness made of? Mind with a twist, it seems to me, since we cannot be conscious without having a mind to be conscious of. But what is mind made of? Does mind come from the air or from the body? Smart people say it comes from the brain, that it is in the brain, but that is not a satisfactory reply. *How does the brain do mind?* (Emphasis added)
>
> Antonio Damasio in *Self Comes to Mind,Constructing the Conscious Brain* (Damasio 2010: 5)

Within this constantly developing and changing field there are presently a few camps of thought. There are those who describe a brain as analogous to a computer; some discuss the mind in largely physical terms, others in mystical terms, others as a dualism where the brain and body intersect in patterns creating consciousness, and some are working on the premise that consciousness is a biological phenomenon. (There are a myriad of combinations.) As I am not arguing for any one camp and suspect that they may all be onto something, at least in providing analogies leading towards greater conceptual understanding of mind and consciousness, we will sit with the latter camp that is exploring consciousness as a biological phenomenon, partly because this perspective seems most in line with the performer's environment, especially when in relation to practice, process, and experience. This is particularly true when practice requires a mastery of an integrative lived-body. Some cognitive scientists in this area of inquiry are Varela, Damasio, Searle, and Gallagher, who to varying degrees posit that "consciousness is a natural, biological phenomenon ... as much a part of our biological life as digestion, growth, or photosynthesis" (Searle 1997: xiii).[3]

Within this group, it is mostly agreed that while the brain plays a part in producing mind, it does so as a whole and not as discrete sections dedicated to solely separate functions. Damasio puts it beautifully: "Surprisingly as it may sound, the mind exists in and for an integrated organism; our minds would not be the way they are if it were not for the interplay of body and brain during evolution, during individual development, and at the current moment. The mind had to be first about the body, or it could not have been" (Damasio 2006: 12).

Seeing consciousness as a biological phenomenon leads us out of the idea that consciousness is a thing and rather directs the conversation to consciousness and cognition as processes.

The Santiago Theory of Cognition

Together, Humberto Maturana and Francisco Varela came up with a theory of cognition that stemmed from an examination of living systems in terms of processes and interrelationships. Maturana was a biologist who departed from the habitual traditions of his discipline in the 1960s and Varela was a celebrated cognitive scientist and pioneer of neurophenomenology. Their work became known as *The Santiago Theory of Cognition*.[4] It is concerned primarily with the knowing of knowing. For them, human cognition is viewed as effective action, which pertains to a biological domain. For them, knowing was not a *thing*, but rather a continuous *process* of the mind/body.

They posited a radical change in the traditional scientific perspective. They effectively argued, through an examination of history and heredity, cellular construction, social phenomena and behavioural and linguistic domains, that "cognition does not concern objects" but rather "cognition is effective action; and as we know how we know, we bring forth ourselves. Knowing how we know does not consist of a linear explanation that begins with a solid starting point and develops to completion as everything becomes explained" (Maturana 1992: 244). In fact, the concept of certainty in their approach was most problematic, since certainty can stymie change and growth. We will explore in the exercises in Part II that, in order to let one's *self* enter the field of performing where integration is possible, a relaxing of certainty is an important aspect of progress.

The knowledge of knowledge

The *knowledge of knowledge compels*. It compels us to adopt the temptation of certainty. It compels us to recognize that certainty is not a proof of truth. It compels us to realize that the world everyone sees is not *the* world but *a* world which we bring forth with others.

Humberto R. Maturana and Francisco J. Varela in *The Tree of Knowledge, The Biological Roots of Human Understanding* (Maturana 1992: 245)

The Santiago Theory is directly connected to a concept called *autopoiesis* (Greek *autos* = self & *poiein* = to do), meaning a living system or network that produces self from within self. We are such a living system, from the most basic cellular level to the more complex behavioural, cultural, and linguistic levels. If I were to adjust the position of a wooden artist mannequin, being a non-autopoietic system, it would alter in movement, but generally would remain the same mannequin, both in structure and organization. However, if I adjust a performer's body, a performer who has a living body, behaviour, knowledge, experience, opinions, words, memory, and cognition (all considered non-discrete parts of the biological system within The Santiago Theory of Cognition), this artist will be altered, by the nature of the touch, the emotional experience of who is touching, the sense of intention within the touch and any personal history of being touched. The fact that the artist is human will not change (termed the *organization*), but the encounter may alter the *structure*, which in this sense denotes "the components and relations that actually constitute a particular unity and make its organization real" (Maturana 1992: 47).

As we understand our environment, we change and grow partly in response to encounters with it. At a biological level, these changes occur as adjustments allowing us to respond to interactions or disturbances, which Maturana and Varela refer to as *perturbations* to our systems.

Maturana and Varela called this dynamic of reciprocal interaction "structural coupling". Capra summarizes, "According to the theory of autopoiesis, a living system couples to its environment structurally, i.e. through recurrent interactions, each of which triggers structural changes in the system. For example, a cell membrane continually incorporates substances from its environment into the cell's metabolic processes. An organism's nervous system changes its connectivity with every sense perception. These living systems are autonomous, however. The environment only triggers the structural changes; it does not specify or direct them" (Capra 2003: 30).

It is interesting to consider this in relation to how we might "structurally couple" to the practices or exercises in our disciplines. Do they change us? Where are we in the conditioning? Two people may learn from the same teacher and the same method; why do they come out as completely different artists? What determines our knowing of the knowing and how does this determine us as self, as *performer* (A)?

To help answer this sort of question, they argue that we are encountering and changing in relation to environment, but we are also autonomous. It may seem contradictory, but that is exactly the point of their revelation. "The most striking feature of an autopoietic system is that it pulls itself up by its bootstraps and becomes distinct from its environment through its own dynamics, in such a way that both things are inseparable" (Maturana 1992: 46). The effects of this structural coupling within an autopoietic system transcend that of a linear progression of cause and effect and that of mind and matter. Within this understanding, cognition is an emerging process within our living network.

We as systems are changed by how we structurally couple with the systems of discipline. However, we stay the system that is us and the practice stays the system that is practice. Most performers will be aware of a moment in which practice has altered them. We might also be aware of the ways in which we stayed us even as we were altered.

Practice is changed by how it encounters us too. As a long-term example, singers of the 1720s learning the practice of *bel canto* technique may have sung with a slightly different sound or tonality due to the sonic environment they lived and worked in. We as singers have changed — in the 1720s there were no recordings to copy, no cars, planes, ring tones, hums of household media; the loudest noises would have been the church bells or an orchestra. Throughout the centuries of singing, emerging technologies have changed students of voice. They remained singers, however. *Bel canto* as a practice is likely to have been altered in little yet profound ways by the singer as it coupled for centuries with its changing environment. *Bel canto* is still its own system, however. The singer is still the singer.

Our dynamic structure is a part of the couplings that came before (our history) and in flow with what is happening in the now. Here, behaviour is considered determined by our organism's own structure. Capra concludes that this sheds light on the debate about freedom and determinism: "behaviour of the living organism is both determined and free" (Capra 2003: 31). Capra states that "According to Maturana and Varela, you can never direct a living system; you can only disturb it" and summarizes that "a living system maintains the freedom to decide what to notice and what will disturb it... Cognition, then is not a representation of an independently existing world, but rather a continual bringing forth of a world through the process of living" (Capra 2003: 32).

Effective action leads to effective action

We are continuously immersed in this network of interactions, the results of which depend on history. Effective action leads to effective action: it is the cognitive circle that characterizes our becoming, as an expression of manner of being autonomous living systems... The business of living keeps no records concerning origins. All we can do is generate explanations, through language, that reveal the mechanism of bringing forth a world. By existing, we generate cognitive "blind spots" that can be cleared only through generating new blind spots in another domain. We do not see what we do not see, and what we do not see does not exist. Only when some interaction dislodges us — such as being suddenly relocated to a different cultural environment — and we reflect upon it, do we bring forth new constellations of relation that we explain by saying that we were not aware of them, or that we took them for granted.

Humberto R. Maturana and Francisco J. Varela in *The Tree of Knowledge, The Biological Roots of Human Understanding* (Maturana 1992: 242)

In this first chapter we looked at self, the *performer* (A), and that self's *performing* (B). It was about how we as performers live the performing of experience, doings, and knowledge. Phenomenology helped us to collapse the boundaries between the subject and object, showing us a way to consider the performer and performing as a mutually interdependent dynamic, which includes the condition of experience. In looking at performativity we considered how the performer doesn't necessarily do performing, but is in fact an emergent property of the myriad ways performing acts upon our society and culture and the ways we institute repeated acts of performing. We are performed on and perform ourselves into self/performer. Performing makes performer, not the other way around. Within cognitive studies, especially within the notion of structural coupling, we considered that the performer never stabilizes, but is a constant system of *performing* (B) that is disturbed and changed, yet also patterned with its interaction in and of the world. In neuroscience and in early childhood development we learned that self and performer happens as a result of the constant firings and patternings between the mind and the body. We do not decide self in the mind and tell the body what to do, or have the body constitute self, which the mind later labels. Further, we learned that this mind-body connection is plastic, meaning constantly performing and shifting and changing what it means to be a performer. The reading in this chapter is there to support a collapse in the distinction between *performer* (A) and *performing* (B) and to bring forth the importance of a discrete field of *performing* (B). It is within the field of *performing* (B) that all the integrative exercises in Parts II, III, and IV will be realized.

If you would like to practise some of the concepts that have been shared in this section on the *Performer* (A), skip to Chapter Four before returning to Chapter Two. In the next chapter we continue with select theory that interrogates the ways in which the concept of *Performance* (C), as it has developed in the last century, has directly affected how we consider what practice is and how we practise.

NOTES

1 Embodiment is a much-debated term in cognitive studies and, more recently, within performance theory; here it is used in the sense that the body/mind is a mutually interdependent dynamic that produces a sense of knowledge in and of practice.

2 This is not meant to diminish the power of doing one's own personal story on the stage when there is something interesting to be shared; however, in these cases, a little distance from it is often necessary in order to allow our practices to do their work.

3 For those wishing to further investigate the other "camps" of thought, John R. Searle's *The Mystery of Consciousness* along with William Seager's *Theories of Consciousness* are good places to start.

4 Fritjof Capra called the work of Maturana and Varela the Santiago Theory of Cognition because they developed it together at the University of Santiago in Chile. Capra's popularizing of the theory, with his particular brand of adaptation to his own agenda, has drawn some criticisms along the lines that it may have simplified and thus undermined the rigour of the original thesis. A good account of the concerns surrounding appropriations of the theory can be found in R.D. Whitaker's 1997 paper *Exploring and employing autopoietic theory: Issues and tips*, which was presented at Biology, Language, Cognition and Society: International Symposium on Autopoiesis, Belo Horizonte, Brazil. Although I choose to quote Capra (in addition to the original authors of the theory), I do so aware of the implications and with discernment and an appreciation that all the takes have a certain merit.

Chapter 2

What is integrative performance?

LET'S REVIEW OUR WORKING TERMS: we are people called *performers*, who do something called *performing*, towards an outcome called *performance*.

A	B	C
Performer	**Performing**	**Performance**
Who is doing.	Way of doing.	What is done.

In much the same way that we examined the *Performer* (A)–*Performing* (B) dynamic through the lens of self in Chapter One, in this next section we look at the *Performing* (B)–*Performance* (C) dynamic through an examination of the term "performance". We will start with a look at what performance has come to mean, and challenge some of the received thinking around what it means to perform in the thing called "performance". You will see that this has ramifications for where the practice of our discipline(s) is thought to reside, and also for what holds or activates meaning within performance. We will also look at how these issues directly affect our perceptions of ourselves, our work, and our practice as we integrate the disciplines.

Performance has come to mean different things. This is important for us as performers because the different ways in which the term "performance" has come to be used has greatly influenced what it means to be a performer and what is asked of us as performers. In the first chapter, we looked at some of the ways the performer/self might be reconfigured through the forefronting of an active aesthetic (*a way of doing*) that is a part of a separate field: the field of performing (B). But to fully understand how the *performer* (A) can no longer be understood to simply do *performance* (C) and, further, why a discrete field of *performing* (B) is so crucial, we need to look at why performance as a term no longer serves us as the thing we *do* within the performing arts. Later in this chapter, we will also see how *performance* (C), when perceived as the end goal for the *performer* (A), carries within it a prejudice against the performer in the act of performing.

As a quick review, in the last chapter we explored the idea that performers do not *do* performance; rather, performers engage in a field of *performing* (B) through which the performance and performer emerge. What we will explore in this chapter is how the *act* of performing has been somewhat compromised within the practice(s) of theatre, dance, and music, especially when viewed through select understandings to do with the function and operations of what is currently understood as *performance* (C).

An expansion of the use of the term "performance", along with its perceived functions, is central to and in perfect alignment with the evolution of the field called Performance Studies. In Chapter One, we heard from scholars and practitioners such as Butler, Schechner, Turner, Phelan, and Conquergood, all considered scholars and in some instances founders of this interdisciplinary field of study. In tracing the implications of the term "performance" and its influence on the contemporary performance practitioner, we also trace the origins of Performance Studies as a field. The journeys are synonymous, and offer some insights into the gifts and also the complications of the term "performance", especially around notions of interdisciplinarity as applied to performance practice.

PERFORMANCE, AN EXPANDING CONCEPT

On the basic level, performance can be understood in terms of a theatrical form, practice, or event, such as a play, an opera, a piece of musical theatre, or a dance. The term has taken on different nuances as it has encountered other disciplines, and then brought those nuances back to the performing arts upon its return. This has not always been a good thing for us as practitioners who work in the field of performing.

In reclaiming the practice of our practice, or the doing of our doing as an active aesthetic, we need to understand the implications of what has come to be meant by the term currently understood as performance.

> **Performance "is"?**
> One cannot determine what "is" a performance without referring to specific cultural circumstances. There is nothing inherent in an action in itself that makes it a performance or disqualifies it from being a performance... every action is a performance... What "is" or "is not" performance does not depend on an event in itself but on how that event is received and placed.
>
> Richard Schechner in *Performance Studies, An Introduction* (Schechner 2002: 30–31)

Schechner's comment in the box extends to his well-known *as/is* distinction. He identifies *is performance* as a self-evident aesthetic performance, such as a piece of theatre, and *as performance* as indicating "...any behavior, event, action or thing that can be analyzed in terms of doing, behaving, and showing" (Schechner 2002: 32). We have already encountered examples of *as performance* earlier in Part I, in the section on self; we looked at gender, race, and personal narrative as *as performance* within the dynamic of performativity (see pages 27–30). This *is/as* distinction speaks to a received understanding about distinct *functions* of the term performance.

Amanda Kemps, in speaking about her piece *This Black Body*, a "one woman show that might be performed by an ensemble", written about in detail in

Phelan's *The End of Performance*, offers a more complex model. Kemps' piece, which is theatrical in format, is born of her experience and research. She speaks of it as being "a critical record of fieldwork" and "a performative analysis of the field" through various contradictions that are played out. For Kemp, performance functions "*both as a way of knowing and a way of showing*" (Phelan 1998: 116). This statement encapsulates how performance has moved beyond simply a theatrical or artistic practice to now constitute a means by which we understand social and cultural processes. Here we see how theatrical performance can be both *as* and *is* at the same time. Part I of this book aims to show that it *has* to be both, further defining a new term, *active aesthetic*, which lives in full recognition of a middle field that serves as a dynamic fulcrum between performer (A) and performance (C): the field of performing (B).

Conquergood offers a three-prong breakdown of the term "performance" and with it leans more in the direction of process, for him articulated as a process of knowing. "We can think through performance along three crisscrossing lines of activity and analysis. We can think of performance (1) as a work of *imagination*, as an object of study; (2) as a pragmatics of *inquiry* (both as a model and method), as an optic and operator of research; (3) as a tactics of *intervention*, an alternative space of struggle". This way of thinking through performance helps in the challenge of "braiding together disparate and stratified ways of knowing" (Conquergood 2002: 152).

TRACING THE EVOLUTION OF PERFORMANCE

These wider definitions of "performance" followed an important shift in global thinking that is worth reviewing. It not only explains trends in current performance practice(s) but strikes at the very heart of the problems of interdisciplinarity and integration, particularly within our own discipline(s).

We can trace the most major shifts in thinking to various events and movements that took place across many disciplines during the 1960s. A key moment was the student uprisings in France in 1968. They set off a turn against modernist ideology, confronting political doctrine, historic materialism, and social reality. In America, a counterculture emerged marked by a rejection of the status quo that energized race riots, anti-war marches, and civil rights demonstrations, in addition to antiestablishment violence. The events brought forth recognition of complex social networks and helped to dissolve established hierarchies.

It was the end of modernism, which had been typified by a faith in "grand narratives, rational logic, nation-states, naturalism, patriarchal authority, mandatory coherence and beginning-middle and end stories" (Schechner 2002: 116). New ways of thinking and constructing performance emerged, typified by an embracing of fragmentations, difference, juxtapositions, pastiche, and contradictions, manifested in hybrid, cross-disciplinary, and contemporized work in the arts. The ground was set for postmodernism and poststructuralism to take hold in the 1970s.

During this vibrant time in the arts there was a blurring of boundaries along with a questioning of status and agency within the arts. Warhol's pop art blurred the lines between the commercial and the avant-garde, while also subverting the romantic mystique of the artist's own hand through the use of silk screening and mass production at The Factory. Warhol's rebellion against style confronted how an artist categorizes themselves not only into one discipline but into categories within their own discipline. In 1963 he famously said, "How can you say one style is better than another? You ought to be able to be an Abstract Expressionist next week, or a Pop artist, or a realist, without feeling you've given up something... I think that would be so great, to be able to change styles. And I think that's what's going to happen, that's going to be the whole new scene" (Andy Warhol in *Interview with Gene Swenson* (Goldsmith 2004)).

There were parallel movements in dance and music. For instance, the important collaborations between Merce Cunningham and John Cage blurred boundaries and stretched the very identities of what we consider dance and music. Intermedial and interdisciplinary *events* sprang up in the form of *performance art* and in the works of cross-disciplinary communities, with *Fluxus* being a major proponent.

Within theatre, rebellion was expressed in various ways. Theatre shifted away from quasi-realistic depictions based on text to more physical approaches to acting. With this there came the need for rigorously trained performers, committed physically, politically, spiritually, and creatively to often dogmatic and fiercely protected practices, within what was often a closed community of ensemble players. For directors such as Grotowski, Brook, Chaikin, Beck, and Malina, there was an adoption of communal authoring/creating and a marked shift of emphasis from rhetoric to action.

Pavis, a noted scholar of Performance Studies, summarizes the shift into the crossing of disciplines by stating that the years between 1958 and 1968 contained a "rather logocentric conception of theatre in spite of the influence of Brechtian dramaturgy", while 1968 to 1978 marked "the beginnings of theatre semiology; theory of theatre discourse and intertextuality" (Pavis 2001: 155).

It was in this climate, an environment of blurring boundaries and dissolution of categories, that a shift occurred — or what performance theorist Fisher-Lichte refers to as a "performative turn" (Fisher-Lichte 2008: 22). It was here that the field of Performance Studies established itself, a field stemming largely from literary theory and anthropology, with discursive criss-crossings in areas such as meaning, language, ritual, identity, society, behaviour, and culture. During the 1970s and 80s New York University and Northwestern University led the way.[1] Jon McKenzie characterizes the two variations of the field as they spread to other institutions as "Eastern" and "Midwestern", respectively (McKenzie 2001: 47). Similar developments were also happening in Europe. However, there were slight differences in approaches across the pond: "German programs in *Theaterwissenschaft*... never suffered from the tensions and divisions between theatre and performance that were frequently felt in the states" (Carlson in Fischer-Lichte 2008: 4).

Pavis characterizes this era as "signifying practices, deconstruction and performance under the influence of American poststructuralist theory; hence the promotion of the interartistic" and, further, from 1988 to 1998 as the rise of "theatre anthropology (influenced by Schechner and Barba); performance and interculturalism; the sociology of the theatre (Shevtosa)" (Pavis 2001: 155).

The fact that Performance Studies has roots in social sciences and literary theory is significant to the way in which performance has come to be defined. As we will see in the next pages, it has also presented some problems with respect to how performance practitioners are characterized. It is particularly of interest when looking at how our *way* of practice is often pulled away from subtle understandings of process, and instead categorized as a performative object that is embedded or positioned in the construction of a performance.

Not for the first time, presence and performance

A central fetish around the term *performance* comes jointly from social sciences and literary theory and has to do with issues of repeatability and citation. When we go to the theatre, we see work that is often rehearsed and is being repeated through pre-established sequences of words, actions, and movements. Erving Goffman expanded this idea to performance in everyday life. Using the theatrical analogy, he sought to better understand "parts", "roles", "routines", "play", "audience", and "observer" within everyday rituals and sociocultural paradigms (Goffman 1959).

Following from Goffman's use of performance as an analogy for socio-behavioural and cultural constructs, as a *rehearsed theatre* of sorts, Schechner coined the term "restored behaviour", meaning "Physical or verbal *actions that are not-for-the-first time*, prepared, or rehearsed". Further, "A person may not be aware that she is performing a strip of restored behavior" (emphasis added) (Schechner 2002: 22). This *not-for-the-first-time* is where the difficulty exists.

Presence, as in being in the here and now, fully available in the act of learning, practice, conditioning, and performance, is a widely accepted notion embedded in the vocabularies and in the skill sets of many performance practices within movement, acting, and voicing.

When we think of presence, especially as practitioners, we might ask, is not every moment for the first time? The here and now? Are you not reading this for the first time, taking it in as a new? Or are we living life repeating, citing socially learned behaviour within cultural rituals, constantly "re-doing performance"? The latter is certainly what Schechner suggests when he states that "The long infancy and childhood specific to the human species is an extended training and rehearsal period for the successful performance of adult life" (Schechner 2002: 23). How much of your act of reading is now a citation or a repetition of how you learned to read such stuff? (Recall the Exercise on page 13 where we looked at reading as part of a dynamic of performance.)

> **No one steps into the same river twice**
>
> Ever-newer waters flow on those who step into the same rivers. No man ever steps in the same river twice, for it's not the same river and he's not the same man.
>
> Attributed to Heraclitus

When Stanislavsky spoke of "the illusion of the first time", explaining how an actor needs to do the actions of the character in the given circumstances of the play anew each time, he was not just speaking of the practice of the actor in himself but also of the nature of presence within the *skill* of acting. Repeating what a character would do would be the action of "repeating", and if that is not the action of the character (which it rarely is), it would take the character out of the role and of the given circumstances of the drama — out of the presence of the character and the actor in the act of the character's act.

This is where current theoretical discourse in performance leaves the performer: in the act of practice. Carlson explains, "Schechner's useful concept of 'restored behavior' points to a quality of performance *not* involved with the display of skills but rather with a certain distance between 'self' and behavior, analogous to that between an actor and the role this actor plays on stage" (Carlson 2004: 3). If this is so, then how do we as performers reconcile the self and the character, self and technique, self and practice and self and discipline, self and *skill*? Chapter One sought to do exactly this by positing a way of seeing both self/performer and aspects of performance as emergent properties of a field: performing. In Chapter Four you will find a series of practical exercises that reconcile the self and practice, making it clear what is meant by *presence* in *action* within Integrative Performance Practice.

We will see next how neither notions of *inherent presence* nor *inherent repeatability* will work in this new recognition of an active aesthetic within a model of emergence from the field of *performing* (B). Perhaps as/is, present/restored, and first time/repeat are not useful dualisms or even the central paradoxes for the performer in the act of doing. Perhaps these are false dualisms, especially when discussing an embodied practice that integrates disciplines. I aim to go some way to both resolve and dissolve these issues of repeat, presence, and the doing of the doing for the performer in the act of performance in the following pages through a transdisciplinary methodology; but first, let's look at what literary theorists have to say about repetition, presence, and meaning, since so much of what is said, thought, and now even constructed as performance is influenced by the ways in which they set in motion a reversal in the modernistic order of aesthetic interpretation.

Repeatability, text, event

In literary theory, particularly the writings of Roland Barthes and Jacques Derrida, the idea of repeatability took hold, confronting ideas about meaning within text(s), authorship, and reading and writing within the notion of *event*. These confrontations are important for the performer because *text*, be it the script, score, blocking, choreography, or director's concept, is often the "thing" that we are trained to serve, represent, repeat, and/or bring to life. In a nutshell, literary theory brought into question modernistic and structuralist ideas about what/who/which "thing" or even linguistic or semiotic "dynamic" held meaning. Who/what is the custodian of meaning? Where does meaning reside? These are questions central to literary theory within postmodernism. The nature of these questions still affects the ways we make and consider performance and, as a result, have shifted, irrevocably, what it even *means* to *practise*. Many of the central fetishes of the postmodern era are losing their appeal; however, key concepts still affect performers' practice, our position in the act of making meaning, and our perceived place in a work.

You may remember Austin (from pages 27–9, introducing the term *performativity*), who spoke of performative utterances and posited that meaning was nothing other than the shared and recognized forms of social and linguistic exchange. Statements uttered by the clergy, judges, and law enforcers, and statements such as promises and commitments, were said to only work successfully in legitimate contexts. For him, that meant that meaning was not something that is harboured by words themselves but rather is produced through social exchange, conventions, and recognized contexts. You may also recall that such utterances spoken out of "context" were considered parasitical or infelicitous. This included all such utterances said in a play, musical or opera, as they are taken out of the original context (see pages 28–9).

A take on postmodernism

Postmodernism is, almost by definition, a transitional cusp of social, cultural, economic and ideological history when modernism's high-minded principles and preoccupations have ceased to function, but before they have been replaced with a totally new system of values. It represents a moment of suspension before the batteries are recharged for the new millennium, an acknowledgment that preceding the future is a strange and hybrid interregnum that might be called the last gasp of the past.

Gilbert Adair, quoted in an article in the *Sunday Times* (Adair 1991)

You may also recall from the last chapter that Jacques Derrida for the most part accepted the first premises of this theory, but balked against the last stage. In "Signature, Event, Context" (Derrida, 1972: 1–23), the first in a series of essays directed against the theory of performatives, Derrida aimed to show that *all* language acts have this infelicitous or parasitic character that exceeds the limit of context. This is pretty much where we left the argument in Chapter One as we were speaking of the performer (A). In this section we are exploring the term performance (C), and so will follow the discussion into the new territory of *event*.

Event as a working term will prove a most crucial tool in reconciling the three aspects of performer-performing-performance. In Part IV, you will see it become a shifting template within Integrative Performance Text Analysis, allowing you to make creative choices and aid the integration of the performing disciplines in practice. In the IPP the term *text* refers not only to the written word, but also to music and choreography. In fact, with the IPP, text is anything *pre-scribed*, which will include blocking, exercises when set out ahead of time, and anything pre-worked out. All texts, as part of the *event*, will provide practical strategies for making creative choices while integrating the disciplines of dance, singing, and acting. The following section helps to unpack some of the theory behind this working method. It can be challenging, so feel free to skip between Chapter Eight and Chapter Two if you are getting bogged down with either mode of delivery in the exploration of *event*.

You may recall from Chapter Two that Derrida takes us further from Austin in the exploration of the term performativity. He does this by plotting the path to a new, dynamic understanding of the term *event* by way of a journey through context. In order to undertake this critique, Derrida begins with the notion of "iterability".[2] A word will only work or have force if it is repeatable or iterable. If there is merely a singular use of a term — a one-off sound — then it cannot be meaningful. Meaning is generated only through repeatability or through its re-iteration. For instance, if we get jabbed by the costume designer's pin, most of us don't say "yum", we say "ouch"! We all know what "ouch" means because it has been repeated in many instances. It is because a word can be used in more than one instance that it functions as a word, and not just a sound. When a word or sound is recognized, or works, as a word, it is because two speakers recognize the same function. There can be no singular sense, for meaning and sense are only possible through shared and repeatable conventions. At this juncture Derrida is in agreement with Austin. But the difference begins to emerge when he examines the consequences of repeatability or iterability.

We can extend this to the interpretation of texts for performance. You will recall from Chapter One, in the section on performativity, that it's possible to argue for legitimate interpretations of *Hamlet* by appealing to the context of Renaissance drama and the conventions of tragedy, and we could even appeal to what we know about the life of Shakespeare as a way of providing a limit and legitimacy to possible interpretations. But, according to Derrida's theory, the fact that we have to appeal to a context shows that no text harbours a meaning in itself, and that texts are therefore essentially open to re-interpretation and re-contextualization.

Now, if it is the case that a context is a shared background of meaning and conventions, how is it that such contexts arise and are subsequently recognized? According to Derrida, while a word only works through repetition and iterability, it is also the case that each repetition is never a full and faithful repetition but is also always a singular event. It is in this way that we will work in the chapters on practice in this book; each movement, each sound, and each action will be recognized as an event in itself, even when it is repeated. It is through the *way of doing*, and from an agreed practice of *awareness*, that we will honor these "iterations" as part of a singular event.

Derrida's follow-through on Austin's premise has a number of consequences. First, a context is never a stable ground, *for each use of the word, gesture, or meaning is also an event in itself*, and therefore changes the shared context. For us, each repeat of an exercise, an arpeggio, a plié, or preparation of a *moment before* for a scene will adhere to the same premise and will be considered an event in itself.

Second, a context cannot operate as some ground or horizon within which meanings can be limited, for a context itself is a textual event. For example, to say that the meaning of a work (as in the example of *Hamlet*) is determined by its context, one has to appeal to other works that are themselves also interpretable, repeatable, and essentially unstable. This means that while performance of *Hamlet* is, on the one hand, the repetition of a recognized and conventional meaning, it is at the same time also singular. There are also those essentially singular events that make this general meaning possible: the materials of production; accidental features of each repetition that exceed the text's sense, such as the actor's timbre of voice, the coughing of an audience member, the blowout of a light; and other enabling conditions that are neither subject to interpretation nor decision. Because of this, Derrida concludes that a context is never a pre-given and stable unity but itself a textual event, open to repetition, decision, interpretation, and re-inscription. Third, while texts and meanings only work and have force through repeatability, there must also be the event of their particular inscription on each and every occasion, and this renders a certain singularity and non-semantic dimension to language. Taking this back to IPP, Derrida helps to establish that each performance (A) emerges from its singular performing (B) event.

We now turn to Roland Barthes to further look at what we mean by *text*. In his essay "From Work to Text" (Barthes 1977: 155–164), Barthes helps to redefine "text", distinguishing it from "work". For Barthes the term "work" is like a book, operatic score, a novel, or a play. He describes work as a "fragment of substance, occupying a part of space" that can also be "held in the hand" and "caught up in the process of filiation". (Barthes 1977: 156–157).

"Text", however, is a more active term. For Barthes it differs from *work* in the way it occupies space. "Text" is a "methodological field", "not to be thought of as an object that can be computed". Further, it is a process, more specifically "a process of demonstration", and "exists in the movement of a discourse" and is "experienced only in an activity of production" (Barthes 1977: 156–157). In keeping with Barthes' definition of text, in Chapter Eight you will learn a method of analysis whereby text is not an object that *holds* some inherent meaning that you, the performer, are obliged to depict or allow to passively come through you. In the IPP we recognize that text(s) set themselves free in the act of performing and as a result they hold no essential meaning. We will work with text as just another active partner in the process of making and doing in the field of performing (B). Text in this work is viewed as a collaborator in the doing of performing; it is seen as just one of the components woven into the performance event. In Chapter Eight you will start to use text(s) as a partner in integrating the disciplines.

With Derrida and Barthes we begin to see text *not* as the custodian of meaning or agent of the author or authority, but rather as a *process*. For the performer this can be liberating, because this means that the operatic score, the play or the prescribed choreography no longer holds a meaning that we are then supposed to bring to life. We are not merely puppets that *indicate* the texts' supposed inherent meaning, but our process in the act of performing generates the meaning as it crosses, collides, and intersects with these texts. It is the qualities within this *process of doing* that we will come to use as our *active aesthetic*.

When Jacques Derrida described the history of Western philosophy as "logocentrism", the assumption that truth, meaning, or sense exist prior to their specific textual incarnations, he confronted key ideas that adhered to the notion that there is inherent meaning within text. As we progress, the working definition of "text" within the Integrative Performance Practice will be informed by both Derrida and Barthes. In Derrida's arguments "text" refers to all those pre-semantic features that make meaning possible, including inscription, tone, rhythm, or syntax. His evoking of "the event" helped to confront this aspect of Western thought. Within the Integrative Performance Practice text is all things vocal, including things spoken, sung, or uttered. Text includes movement, such as choreography, blocking, or gesture; and also things emotive, such as action, feeling, and/or intention. It can also be the structure, instruction, and realization of exercises such as those shared throughout the following chapters.

As Barthes insists, "text" is "not a co-existence of meanings but a passage, an overcrossing; thus it answers not to an interpretation, even a liberal one, but to an explosion, a dissemination" (Barthes 1977: 159). Text thus becomes a network extending itself "as a result of a combinatory systematic (an image, moreover, close to current biological conception of the living being)" (Barthes 1977: 161).

For us this will boil down to the idea that text is a live creative partner in the process of making and performing work.

Responsibility and text

After exploring an expanded understanding of what we mean by *text*, we as performers might find a newfound freedom. Within this freedom there is also *responsibility*. Derrida argues in *Signature Event Context* that a text's essential undecidability leads to an intensified interpretive responsibility. No interpretation or reading can appeal to some context as a pre-given ground, for a context itself is an issue of interpretation. As performers we both interpret and re-interpret our directors', choreographers', conductors', and teachers' readings of everything from the play, the song, or the combination to the instruction of an exercise in the studio. Each interpretation or reading is, therefore, a decision. If texts are essentially undecidable, and if each reading is an event — and not just the replication of a pre-given meaning — then this raises the stakes of interpretation.

Derrida rejects the notion of autonomy — the idea that interpretation can be grounded in some self-present intention that can control aspects of the text. A plié, for instance, does not hold any essential meaning, or even an essential intended action. There are lots of reasons and ways to do a plié. But he also insists on the idea of responsibility: a text is an event that has a certain force and effect that exceeds intention, but for which we nevertheless need to be responsible. So even though there are a lot of ways and reasons to do a plié, a plié is still a plié. There cannot be a complete free play of the text; each reading is an event of determination. In connecting the theory on *self* with event in this section, we can recall Barthes' idea of text being "close to current biological conception of the living being" along with Derrida's ideas on "responsibility" and get something very much akin to the Santiago Theory of Cognition, which speaks about the dynamic of knowing discussed in the previous section on *Self* (see pages 31–34). A review of this section will lead us to a deeper understanding of the role of interpretation and doing and also its effect on our change and growth. In Chapter Four you will find practical exercises that integrate these ideas in action in preparation for the more advanced practical physio-vocal work in Part III.

Both Barthes and Derrida lay the groundwork for a possible reversal in the order of aesthetic interpretation. It is not that there is some meaning that the artist, writer, or composer then expresses through some medium or disciplinary set of rules. A meaning cannot be divorced from the specific event of its inscription or the materiality and practice of its production. This might be described as an anti-hermeneutic approach.[3] "To be what it is, all writing must, therefore, be capable of functioning in the radical absence of every empirically determined receiver in general. And this absence is not a continuous modification of presence, it is a rupture in presence" (Derrida 1972: 8).

While Derrida and Barthes were prime forces in the discussion of event within the poststructuralist tradition, Gilles Deleuze, who identified as a transcendental philosopher, saw things from other angles. Deleuze also interrogated disciplinary formations that assumed notions of inherent meaning, but his notion of event is notably different and particularly helpful when speaking about practice. This might be because, unlike Derrida and Barthes, he was not a literary theorist.

Deleuze's arguments are not made by a rejection or acceptance of "representation" as a force in the understanding of experience. Like Derrida and Barthes, he argued that there was no given grounding or authorizing foundation by which we act/perform or perceive, but rather that *what meaning is* is created and generated in a between place. But the other side of that concept, and a departure from much literary theory, is that performance could not be understood *as* representation or construction either (this includes those of language, identity, and disciplines). Colebrook summarizes his alternative position: "we can select and assess our values, not by giving them some ultimate meaning, or foundation but by looking at what they *do*. Ask, he insisted, not what a text means but *how it works*." She further explains that "Art, Deleuze argued, is not just a set of representations; it is *through* art that we can see the *force* and creation of representations, how they *work* to *produce* connections and 'styles' of thinking" (emphasis added) (Colebrook 2002: xxxii).

For Deleuze, event is about *becoming*. It is dynamic, in process with both the particular and the whole, happening simultaneously in a live web. In considering the relationship between Deleuze's becoming and his event, we need to understand that becoming for him is not the leaving of one thing and landing in another, but rather a characteristic of every aspect within an event. So for him it is not about measuring event by the change that happens from one to another but that rather we live in a sort of constant production of change-ness, the flow of becoming. Events are events because they live in change, in a constant becoming, as they produce in the flow of becoming.

So if we look at the singing of an arpeggio, as part of a vocal warm-up, as an event, it is in the actual event of the singing of that arpeggio that a *becoming* of sorts is happening. But there is also a becoming that can be measured from one arpeggio to another. It is not the singular event or its relationship to the next that is important but rather its becoming-ness, the *how* the arpeggio *works* in *process*, *through* the *doing*, and the *force* in *production*, both in and of itself and also in relation to the next event and all others.

> **There is no work of art that does not indicate an opening for life, a path between the cracks**
> Signs imply ways of living, possibilities of existence, they are the symptoms of an overflowing (jaillissante) or exhausted (épuisée) life. But an artist cannot be content with an exhausted life, nor with a personal life. One does not write with one's ego, one's memory, and one's illnesses. In the act of writing there's an attempt to make life something more personal, to liberate life from what imprisons it... There is a profound link between signs, the event, life, and vitalism. It is the power of nonorganic life, that which can be found in a line of a drawing, a line of writing, a line of music. It is organisms that die, not life. There is no work of art that does not indicate an opening for life, a path between the cracks. Everything I have written has been vitalistic, at least I hope so, and constitutes a theory of signs and the event.
>
> Deleuze in an interview in 1998 (Bogue 2004: 9)

Deleuze might say that one does not conceive of action and then do or perform it, but rather that to conceive/do and to think/create are constituted simultaneously. We will begin to draw from this dynamic way of considering the field of *Performing* (B), from which the *Performer* (A) and *Performance* (C) emerge simultaneously. In many ways, this way of considering *event* is key to what is meant by the term *integrative* as applied in this book, discussed in greater detail in Chapter Three and then applied in practice in Part IV.

Event as used in performance theory

Now that we have discussed the term *event* as used within poststructuralist literary theory and briefly introduced its usage in the context of Deleuze's work, we are now ready to discuss how the term has been used to understand the workings of various disciplines and aesthetics within performance.

Event has taken hold as a working term within current performance theory to help understand and work with the dynamics among the forces that may constitute a performance experience. These can include media, performance practice, design, materials, space, and audience. Event is often used as a way of bracketing experience in the understanding of functionality, meaning, and perception across aspects within the performance event.

Examining performance as event can be helpful, particularly in looking at the dynamic of the performer/audience relationship, which can be seen as analogous to the inscriber-receiver. The receiver, like the *reader*, can be seen as analogous to an *audience member or spectator* as they experience, interpret, see, hear, feel, and witness, as they are mutually present in a time/place/space as members of a performance event.

You may recall the poststructuralist argument that made no one component the full custodian of meaning. Thinking through the term *event*, we can also come to see that the reader/spectator/audience/experiencer[4] can now be recognized as a meaning-maker too by the very act of their reading/seeing/witnessing/ experiencing. When Barthes stated the following, he was referring to this dynamic. "The reduction of reading to a consumption is clearly responsible for the 'boredom' experienced by many in the face of the modern ('unreadable') text, the avant-garde film or painting: to be bored means that one cannot produce the text, open it out, set it going" (Barthes 1977: 163). This argument can be interpreted for performance as follows: the audience's inability to engage in the meaning, due to a reliance on a passive receiving of supposed inherent meaning, renders the audience's experience dead.

Breaking the boundaries between performer and spectator can return theatre to the notions of a communal event and, in Rancier's words, *emancipate the spectator*. Rancier writes that "Theatre should question its privileging of living presence and bring the stage back to a level of equality with the telling of a story or the writing and the reading of a book. It should call for spectators who are active interpreters, who render their own translation, who appropriate the story for themselves, and who ultimately make their own story out of it. An emancipated community is in fact a community of storytellers and translators" (Ranciére 2007: 280).

When performance is seen as event, it generates a dynamic of meaning toward an aesthetic of the performative where everything is a potential meaning-maker. These meaning-makers include random things such as a sneeze, a tummy growl, an animal pooping on the stage, and also the personal experiences and states of the audience member. For instance, a performance experienced on a first date is different than that same production experienced at a Saturday matinée taken in with Grandma. "There no longer exists a work of art, independent of its creator and recipient; instead, we are dealing with an *event* that involves everybody — albeit to different degrees and in different capacities" (Fischer-Lichte 2008: 18).[5]

When we take this further, we can see that it not only confronts the boundaries between spectator and audience but also between disciplines and all intermedial aspects. Years ago, at the beginning of the journey for the development of the Integrative Performance Practices, I observed that, "This idea of event also has its ramifications for other arts, such as lighting, set design, costume design and film editing. Just as Derrida and Barthes explored the concept that the writing can perform, the stationary arts can also perform, especially if they are rendered active contributors to the dramatic event, (rather than merely depictorial)" (Bryon 1998: 186).

In the Integrative Performance Practice, *event* speaks directly to issues of interdisciplinarity, and in doing so defines a new sense of the *active* within a field of *performing*. This is how my initial inquiry began. "Since it is the *event* that *happens* on the stage through the *act* of *performance*, to choose or be aware of the fields of *operations* that contribute to a happening is essential if the desired effect is to have all these operations working together in a *network* to allow for that event" (Bryon 1998: iii).

Even since the "performative turn" (first mentioned on page 38 in this chapter), we seem to still have difficulty understanding and valuing the *practice* of performing and how the *way* that we practise generates meaning. As we go forward, keep in mind that active aesthetic, liminality (when seen as an aesthetic, to be explained in the next section), and performative aesthetic are different, as we will explore select examples of currently used terminology to unpack the subtle but important distinctions.

We must remember that the wish for an integrative performance practice is not entirely new. A unified or integrative theatre of sorts is an idea that has constantly returned since ancient times; up to Wagner and, more recently, within hybrid and multi-media modes of performance, we have struggled to find a working process that would allow this to occur. Each time, of course, the search has had different aesthetic, political, social, and spiritual motives, along with different vocabularies and technologies. The key point for this book, however, is one that I have stated before: "Crucial to any interdisciplinary integration is what we have yet fully to recognise: the act of players in the act of performance executing the operations of a discipline. In order to begin to understand the disintegration currently in place, the scholarly privileging of theoretical knowledge over embodied knowledge in relation to 'meaning' needs to be addressed" (Bryon 2009: 135).

The final sections of this chapter help to highlight some of this problematic privileging and, with it, the implications of the adoption of certain terms as applied to performance practice(s).

Liminality and the interdisciplinary event

In many ways, liminality is the central concept that defines Performance Studies as a field. Late in the last century, anthropologist Arnold Van Gennep identified three rites of passage: preliminal, liminal, and postliminal.[6] (The word "liminal" comes from the Latin *limen*, meaning threshold.) One might think of it in terms of a "between" state, one of becoming. A commonly used example is that of the adolescent, who has left childhood, preliminal in this instance, but has not yet arrived at the status of adulthood, postliminal in this instance. Adolescence in this way is a liminal state in the ritual of growing up.

Victor Turner, influenced by Van Gennep, extended the use of the term beyond the field of anthropology and applied it to contemporary culture, society, and politics, as influenced by the movements of 1960s counterculture. Within his development of the term, the liminal space could be perceived as a kind of theatre. For Turner, liminality was less about a middle state of transition and more about a lived experience. "Liminal entities are neither here nor there; they are betwixt and between the positions assigned and arrayed by law, custom, convention, and ceremonial. As such, their ambiguous and indeterminate attributes are expressed by a rich variety of symbols in the many societies that ritualize social and cultural transitions" (Turner 1969: 95).

With this movement from *states* within ritual toward ritual as *process*, one can begin to understand how the term was key to the area of Performance Studies. The idea of *liminal rites of passage* has served several functions in the field of Performance Studies. Turner's theorization of the term has been an important point of scholarship in that it has provided a mode of analysis that allows us to view wider *processes* as types of performance.

As we have discussed, theatre was, through the anthropological model, perceived as a way of considering social, cultural, and behavioural events as performance. With the application of liminal theory, boundaries could be seen in terms of a play between a sense of becoming, oscillation, and all things flow. These include the previously discussed boundaries that lie between the audience/spectator and reader/writer and also those once thought to determine identity, such as race and gender.

For theatre makers, liminal thinking brought an intervention to the boundaries that previously helped structure the making of work. It is often no longer clear who or what generates meaning, who or what creates the work, and what dictates the making: is it the director, the performer, the producer, the media designers, the set designers, the media itself, the space, the costumes, the props? This clearly contributed to the range of ways we create work and the new forms that have emerged, such as multi-modal, intermedial, multi-disciplinary, hybrid, site-specific, physically based theatre, devised rather than text-based theatre, and performance art, to name just a few. "With respect to theater, the movement from entertainment to efficacy came via a shift in emphasis from the playscript to the actor's body; in dance, attention moved from formal choreography to movements of everyday life; and in both dance and experimental theatre, there was a shift away from theatrical to environmental spaces" (McKenzie 2001: 37).

Terms like "liminal spaces", "the liminal body", and "liminal performance" are now commonplace in the theorization of contemporary work. However, when liminality is used to discuss the operations of theatre-making as a practice, difficulties can occur.

Susan Broadhurst, speaking of liminal performance, applies the term to select performance constructs in an effort to define a *liminal aesthetic*. Such application of the term goes directly to my concern that many uses of key terminology within performance studies can sidestep the *act* of *performing*, especially in the consideration of interdisciplinary performance practice. In an effort to "formulate an aesthetic theorization" for which "traditional critical equipment is inadequate in its present form" (Broadhurst 1999: 24), Broadhurst states that, "Liminal performances are hybridised and intertextual, and share common quasi-generic aesthetic features, such as heterogeneity, indeterminacy, self-reflexiveness, eclecticism, fragmentation, and a certain 'shift-shape style'" (Broadhurst 1999: 168). Such performances "include stylistic promiscuity favouring eclecticism and the mixing of codes" (Broadhurst 1999: 13). We will see in a moment why in the IPP this categorization presents a difficulty.

In defining the liminal aesthetic, she understandably draws from Derrida's supposition of "undecidables" such as "différance" and "iterability" as crucial in the recognition of process. Where it becomes a problem is when she identifies works such as Robert Wilson's *Theatre of Images* and Pina Bausch's *Tanztheatre* as examples of her identification of the liminal aesthetic. What is really interesting is what she excludes from her definition of liminal aesthetic. Artaud's *Theatre of Cruelty* is excluded because of its "pursuit of an essentialism", and Brecht's *Verfremdungseffekt* and *Epic Theatre* because of an inherent "political agenda". Broadhurst asserts that "Brecht's plays can only be understood, in the sense he intended, by the theoretically informed" (Broadhurst 1999: 11).

The difficulty here is that, within discourses such as this, what is not fully considered is that the *way of performing* any performance piece affects and influences meaning and aesthetic. Brecht's plays can and have been created and performed and experienced in ways that both adhere to and do not adhere to Broadhurst's own stipulations of liminality, as has Bausch's work. The *way of performing* generates meaning over/through and within intended constructions or ideologies of performance. This is where a distinction between a *way of doing*, activated within the field of *performing* (B) as an *active aesthetic*, might be helpful, as opposed to the aesthetic that is traditionally attributed to a quality of the *performer* (A) or of the *performance* (C).

Codified acting — a take on performance disciplines

When Schechner looks at modes of performance that take years of training, such as ballet, Western opera, Chinese opera, and Noh, he calls these "codifed acting", because such disciplines are for him "based on semiotically constructed gestures and movements, songs, costumes, and makeup set by tradition and passed down from teacher to student by means of rigorous training" (Schechner 2002: 156).

He says that in order for codified acting to be mastered one needs to "begin very young when both mind and body are flexible" (Schechner 2002: 158). Somehow Western acting training, no matter how rigorous, is excluded because "one can begin to learn realistic or Brechtian acting relatively late in life because people have 'practiced' daily behavior all their lives" (Schechner 2002: 158).

Putting aside for the moment that to enact "daily behavior" on the stage is a most complex and difficult dynamic to master, there are a few other difficulties here. Regarding needing to start young: most Western opera singers do not begin when they are children; in fact, it is strongly discouraged, since the breath-body has yet to fully develop. However, opera singers still manage in adulthood to train their mind/bodies to sing off the throat with an exacting use of breath, sounding the notes on the page, with libretti acted in four or five languages.

Perhaps the flexible mind/body control is a discipline that can be learned in adulthood as an active aesthetic, whereby a myriad of possible aesthetic "codes" can emerge through many possibilities of sound and movement with emotive combinations. In Part II we will learn how we can make this happen through proven and doable ways of working.

Importantly, if we are to accept that codified acting takes years of training, and requires rigorous exercises and coordination between the mind/body, valued because it is situated as a mastering of codes (which lie outside of our experience of doing and our integrity in the act of doing), well, then, do we not adhere to context? (See Derrida and context, pages 28–29.) If we as performers adhere to the *Performer* (A) doing the *Performance* (C), do we not leave our alchemy? What do we have allegiance to? Where and what is the aesthetic of our doing?

We will in the next chapters rather approach practice, be it an exercise, a musical or movement phrase, or a scripted beat, as part of an *Event*, in full recognition of crossing, colliding, and intertwining sets of variables that include self, discipline, intent, breath, and centre.

On a most basic level, is it not true that in actuality, codified or not, the years of training needed are not about the learning of positions and sequences of dance, or the memorizing of notes and phrasing of music, but rather the *way* in which to *do* these anew each time? It is not the signs and signifiers or the codes of performance that render the learning of these disciplines time-consuming, but rather the act of the doing, the *way* of *practice*. The codified performance emerges out of this *way* of doing, an active aesthetic, not as the performative object of an "actor/performer" activating codes. It is this *way* of *doing*, the *Practice* of the *practice*, that is passed down from teacher to student. It is this that takes the time and requires exactitude: not the learning of codes.

Despite the many efforts to come to terms with *performance* (C), be it a liminal, performative, or codified dynamic, when we start to speak of performance it would seem that the term as adopted by Performance Studies scholarship constrains it in the very traps it wished to escape. Is it possible that *performing* (B) is considered more in the realm of practice and doing, where *performance* (C) is considered more in the realm of analysis, thinking, research, and theory? A thinking/doing, practice/research, embodied/disembodied tension seems to be intrinsic within the field of Performance Studies. (The term "embodied knowledge" as a separate distinction of knowledge within this work is questionable. What would disembodied knowledge look like in the full considerations of the earlier discussions on the mind/body connection, experience as transcending the subject/object, and the autopoietic nature of knowing and learning? See pages 32–34.) However, tensions between thinking and doing are a part of the discussion among performance theorists and practitioners alike.

Thinking-doing/doing-thinking

As a very general take, the history of philosophy is in many ways a history of trying to either reconcile two seemingly separate camps (those of doing and those of thinking), or to marginalize one in favour of raising the status of the other. In her book *Professing Performance*, Shannon Jackson eloquently illustrates this perceived divide as manifest in the roles of "She-Who-Is-Preoccupied-With-Making-Meaning" and "He-Who-is-Preoccupied-with-Meaning" (Jackson 2004: 111). This age-old fight for supremacy or reconciliation has maintained a strange and somewhat false set of dualisms guiding discussions around the status of theory and practice. More recently, a healthy and rigorous relationship between both is developing with the increasing advent of Practice as Research scholarship.[7] However, there is still a tension even among the advocates for Practice as Research about what the balance of theory and practice should be within the modes of delivery of the research in order to consider it rigorous.

> **A box of tools**
> A theory is exactly like a box of tools. It has nothing to do with the signifier. It must be useful. It must function. And not for itself. If no one uses it, beginning with the theoretician himself (who then ceases to be a theoretician), then the theory is worthless or the moment is inappropriate.
>
> Giles Deleuze (in Foucault and Bouchard 1980: 208)

In this book, we recognize that all knowledge, including scholarly knowledge, is embodied. Thinking is viewed as a doing of the mind/body. When we practise, we are discovering, and testing, and witnessing. When we think, analyze, or witness, we are doing practice. With this said, we do not really need to reconcile them as two sides of the same coin constituting each other. It may be more productive to think of theory and practice as both the same and also different. They are both two different types of practice and both two different modes of research.

In a famous discussion between Deleuze and Foucault, the former explains how the relationships between theory and practice are partial and fragmentary rather than totalizing or complete: "...theory is always local and related to a limited field, and it is applied in another sphere, more or less distant from it. The relationship which holds in the application of a theory is never one of resemblance. Moreover, from the moment a theory moves into its proper domain, it begins to encounter obstacles, walls, and blockages which require its relay by another type of discourse (it is through this other discourse that it eventually passes to a different domain)." He further elaborates, "Practice is a set of relays from one theoretical point to another, and theory is a relay from one practice to another. *No theory can develop without eventually encountering a wall, and practice is necessary for piercing this wall.*"

Foucault agrees and declares, "theory does not express, translate, or serve to apply practice: it is practice. But it is local and regional, as you said, and not totalising" (emphasis added) (in Foucault and Bouchard 1980: 205–217).

It is more within this Deleuzian realm, a recognition of a field where things become things rather than represent or constitute each other, that we will continue to examine what it means to make work, explore, and practise as an integrative practitioner. We will do this from the field of *performing* (B), where there is no tension between thinking and doing; in fact, as will be made clear in the next section, they are both emergent properties of this active field that favours no one element.

As we continue towards a practice whereby acting, singing, and dance become one Integrative Performance Practice, terms that you have encountered within this chapter, such as "becoming", "performativity", "liminal", "theory", and "practice", will not be used as such in the studio. However, it is important to understand the journey of such concepts as they have lived within the areas of performance theory and performance studies, since they continue to have lasting implications on our work as practitioners of performance. We will retain one term, though: *Event*. It will become a crucial tool in Chapter Eight in the analysis of text(s) toward the activation of our practice(s) within interdisciplinary work.

The theory in Part I is here to help us reconfigure some of the ways we consider practice and to understand how the framing of our practices in the areas of dance, voice, and acting are continuing to be affected. As we go forward to deal specifically with the issue of integration, we will first briefly review the prior sections, and then move toward science to forefront the importance and effectiveness of *performing* (B) as an integrative field.

NOTES

1 This narrative, which states that Performance Studies took hold first in Chicago and New York, is the commonly told story, evident in the writings of Carlson (2003), Schechner (2006), and McKenzie (2001). There is, however, another take to be found in *The Sage Handbook of Performance Studies* (Madison and Hamera 2006), which focuses on an evolution deriving from speech programmes with elocution and oral interpretation as a source. Regardless, the inherent interdisciplinarity within the field remains the same, as do the complexities inherent in the term performance.

2 To further explain this term "iterable" as Derrida uses it: "My communication must be repeatable — iterable — in the absolute absence of the receiver or of any empirically

determinable collectivity of receivers. Such iterability (*iter*, again, probably comes from *itara*, *other* in Sanskrit, and everything that follows can be read as the working out of the logic that ties repetition to alterity) structures the mark of writing itself, no matter what particular type of writing is involved (whether pictographical, hieroglyphic, ideographic, phonetic, alphabetic, to cite the old categories). A writing that is not structurally readable — iterable — beyond the death of the addressee would not be writing" (Derrida 1972: 7).

3 The idea of an anti-hermeneutic approach to performance and practice for an interdisciplinary performer was first proposed in 1998 in my PhD thesis, *The integrative performance theory: an anti-hermeneutic approach for opera*. The work used the notion of the *event* as a possible bracket for which one can contain a shifting template of dynamics that include all doings, happenings/events, and obstacles in a way that sidesteps status and authority of text(s), including practical devices of "pre-scribed" expression. Part IV of this book draws from the text(s) analysis method proposed.

4 "Experience/er" is a term first coined by Robin Nelson in *Mapping Intermediality in Performance* (Bay-Cheng 2010: 45) In the context of contemporary arts and media, experiencer serves where audience or even "spect-actor" (Boal) prove inadequate. It suggests a more immersive engagement in which the principles of composition of the piece create an environment designed to elicit a broadly visceral, sensual encounter, as distinct from conventional theatrical, concert, or art gallery architectures that are constructed to draw primarily upon one of the sense organs — eyes (spectator) or ears (audience). In her interactive virtual reality installation, Osmose (1994–1996), for example, Char Davies dubbed audience "immersants". Though it might not directly involve touch, smell, or taste in addition to sight and hearing, work that engages an experiencer draws upon Merleau-Ponty's (1962) insight that the body is a medium for perception of the world, and Deleuze & Guattari's (1980) notion of "haptic space" which denies opposition between the senses.

5 Fische-Lichte argues that her idea of event derives from Max Herrman's work, a pioneer in the field of *Theaterwissenschaft* (the study of theatre) in Germany. She praises him for the "performative turn", "which turned from regarding theatre as a static work of art to considering it as a spatial, embodied event, thus opening the way to developing an aesthetics of the performative" (Carson in Fischer-Lichte 2008: 6). This movement developed at the same time as Performance Studies in the United States. Interestingly, in her work she draws from many researchers and practitioners from the US Performance Studies camp to help articulate her particular take on performance as event.

6 See Van Gennep, A. 1960. *The Rites of Passage*, Chicago, IL, University of Chicago Press.

7 For more information on current developments within Practice as Research in the arts, see Robin Nelson's *Practice as Research in the Arts, Principles, Protocols, Pedagogies, Resistance*, Palgrave 2013.

Chapter 3

Towards integrative performing

LET'S AGAIN REVIEW OUR WORKING TERMS: we are people called *performers*, who do something called *performing*, towards an outcome called *performance*.

A	B	C
Performer	**Performing**	**Performance**
Who is doing.	Way of doing.	What is done.

In Chapter One we looked at what it means to be a *Performer* who does this thing called *Performing*. We worked with the relationships between A and B in the above diagram. We examined the various ways *self* (as performer) is considered and positioned in practices of acting, dance, and voice. In Chapter Two, we looked at what *Performing* (B) is, within the current understanding of *performance*. Chapter Two considered the relationship between B and C. There, we looked at ways the *act of performing* is placed within current understandings of *performance*. This brought up interesting issues, particularly in regard to the dynamics of who and what is making or doing the meaning of a work or piece. Most importantly, where does the meaning of a work happen? Is it in you the performer as you do your practice, or is it in the text or construct set out for you?

We now come to the final theory section of the book, in which we will come to understand and establish *performing* (B) as a powerful middle field through which our *performance* (C) and ourselves as *performers* (A) emerge.

But first, let's review what we have learned.

In Chapter One, Who is an integrative performer?, we explored self as performer through the mind/body perspective of the latest neurosciences. We read about the experience of self through phenomenology and as a performative entity; and finally we drew upon select concepts in cognitive studies by examining what it means to know and learn. This chapter aimed to equip us as interdisciplinary performers with the tools to collapse the traditional divides between *performer* (A) and *performing* (B). This is important because, as discussed, what a dancer, a singer, and an actor are expected to be as *self* as they engage with their practice(s) is often different.

In this practice the performer is NOT expected to negotiate between different selves/*performers* (A); neither, as we will learn next, are *performers* (A) expected to negotiate between different performance practices.

There are, of course, traditions, especially those developed since the 1960s, that work across perceived dualisms and towards integration for specific goals. Many of these have drawn from Eastern spiritual, physical, and performance practices. Movement work such as Feldenkrais, Alexander, Bainbridge Cohen's Mind-Body Centering, and other somatic practices have quite clearly worked across the mind/body divide. Performers working in the tradition of Grotowski, Brook, or Chaikin will find voice, movement, and acting fusions applied to chosen aesthetics towards particular types of work. Through the next sections on practice, these examples, along with others in the areas of acting, dance, and voice, will be discussed in relation to particular practical considerations.

However, for the moment, it remains true that an integrative practice that is applicable in any aesthetic, with any director or conceptual dramaturgy, eludes us as Western performance practitioners. Acting, singing, and dancing are still most often taught as three separate disciplines, with three separate practices, trainings, and conditionings. Often, when they are fused within particular practices, they are only possible for that particular production, company, or practice. The IPP has no one aesthetic outcome or politic as a driving force. This book is for the performer in the act of performing, to be used as a tool to take and apply in every and any way wished.

In Chapter Five, for instance, very different breathing practices and different notions of what it means to "be in centre" will be discussed. The differences between dance, voice, and acting, and also those differences within different practices in the same discipline, will be touched on and reconciled toward an integrative practice. We will learn how all performance practice can be acted on effectively as one — as one integrative practice, without compromise to the aesthetics of any as a separate discipline. How this is possible will be touched upon in this last section on theory and, moreover, subsequently proved by your own working through the practice in Parts II and III, culminating in your ability to support and activate your doings within Integrative Performance Analysis in Part IV.

In Chapter Two, What is integrative performance?, we began by looking at the many ways the term *performance* has been taken on by such disciplines as anthropology and literary theory, forming an area of scholarship called Performance Studies. We learned many ways in which this adoption and adaptation has had implications for how the performer and the act of performance is perceived in terms of status as a *meaning maker*, especially in the *act* of *doing* our practice(s). We touched on the ways in which our practice(s) have been viewed or understood within various disciplinary models, and, through the notion of *event*, began to introduce a way to see that a dissolve between *performing* (B) and *performance* (C) is also possible, offering a more effective understanding of what we actually *do* in the *act* of *doing* our disciplines.

So with boundaries between *performer* (A) and *performing* (B) and also between *performing* (B) and *performance* (C) dissolved, we are left with a lovely middle field: PERFORMING, an active and live field from which *performer* and *performance* emerges. But how does this work? What does it mean to see performing (B) as a *field*? To understand, we need to consider the ways thinking about, evaluating, and understanding complex organisms and environments have changed within the last century. We as *performers* have become more complex, as has our performance environment; however, many of the training models for the interdisciplinary performer remain within old linear and compartmental paradigms.

SHIFTS IN THINKING

In the previous section it was discussed how a cultural revolution in the mid to late twentieth century had affected the way in which the arts developed toward hybrid forms as genres were blurred. At this same time, profound shifts in the way we think took hold in the areas of physics, social sciences, behavioral sciences, biology, physiology, ecology, and philosophy. Old, received thinking based on an understanding of a Cartesian mind/body split[1] started to give way.

Further, in line with movements in the hard sciences, along with theoretical innovations in quantum physics, the old Newtonian mechanistic view of the universe based on cause and effect was seriously challenged. The world, its workings, and ourselves within it are now no longer being viewed, in rigorous areas of study, as simply mechanistic and made of elementary building blocks for which we can view the parts as separate objects.

Our practice in terms of universal flux of events and processes

Indeed, to some extent, it has always been necessary and proper for man, in his thinking, to divide things up, and to separate them... if we tried to deal with the whole of reality at once, we would be swamped... However, when this mode of thought is applied more broadly to man's notion of himself and the whole world in which he lives (i.e. to his self-world view), then man ceases to regard the resultant divisions as merely useful or convenient and begins to see and experience himself and this world as actually constituted of separately existing fragments.

What is needed is a relativistic theory, to give up altogether the notion that the world is constituted of basic objects or building blocks. Rather one has to view the world in terms of universal flux of events and processes.

David Bohm in *Wholeness and the Implicate Order*
(Bohm 1983: 2, 9)

In place of the old linear, mechanistic thinking, new conceptual frameworks have evolved that view the world more as a network of regulating dynamic relationships and patterns. Complexity theory, nonlinear dynamics, systems theory, chaos theory, the holographic principle, and emergence theory are just a few. Of course, this book cannot not review all of these (it would be a much larger and different book); however, this book will draw on select concepts from these fields to explain what is meant by integration within this practice. For now, what is most important is that there has been a marked shift in the ways in which we consider parts and wholes. These shifts in thinking can offer very practical implications for how we as performers might see ourselves and our practice(s), especially while working across disciplines.

RETHINKING THE PART, THE BIT, AND THE LOCAL

For now, let's begin by looking at the local, or the parts that make up a whole.

"Local" for you, as you go through the practice, might mean the smallest moment of a thought, an attitude (*Haltung*, page 12). Most performers know that our personal attitude affects the entire; that is, all combinations of body, mind, and action. A "part" as we go forward might be the way you hold tension in your ankle in direct relation to how your breathing operates and, interestingly, your level of emotional availability. The "whole" might be the execution of a physical phrase of movement, or a line of a song, or the emotional journey of a character — and the ways in which that ankle affects it. The little things do have a sort of dynamic that affects what we determine as the big things. The big things, or the *whole*, affect the little things too. Parts II, III, and IV of this book offer a working practice that puts you in the place of a more expanded and intelligent position of choice within your practice as you work across the parts and the whole simultaneously.

You may remember that in looking at the term *performativity* within performance theory, we have already considered self as something that performs itself into self and is performed onto (pages 27–30). In the concept of phenomenology we looked at experience as an exchange that transcends the subject/object paradigm (pages 23–27). The Santiago Theory of Cognition offered a way to think of seeing, knowing, and learning as dynamic exchanges between the self, which is both at the same time distinct and inseparable from its environment (pages 30–34). Finally, at the end of the last section, through literary theory, we took all this further, considering meaning as built not by separate codes inherent in text, gesture, design, discipline, or *any* one component, but rather as entities set forth and also emergent as part of the event, which holds or brackets all these components (pages 40–52).

If you are sensing a theme here, you are correct. I am suggesting that it is perhaps not a linear model, nor an either/or, cause/effect, mind/body, subject/object, theory/practice, or part/whole dualistic dynamic that will bring forth the possibility of effective integration within our disciplines, but rather a different way: leaning towards recognizing things in their *active* doing/performing(s) as part of a *system*. This shifts the thinking away from cause and effect paradigms and toward *correlations*.

But what of these parts and these wholes, or these environments local and global? When working practically, how do we build, make stuff, control and repeat a performance task, with one discipline or many, if it all seems so open and theoretical?

Holographic principle

As we move away from theory and towards practice (between which, as discussed on pages 50–51, there is no tension in this work), an analogy I often use when teaching comes from something called the holographic principle. A hologram provides an effective metaphor for undivided wholeness (*holo-* comes from *whole* and *-gram* from *write* in Greek). Any science buff knows that a hologram projects a three-dimensional image and is created by way of splitting laser beams. It works this way: one beam is bounced off the object to be photographed and a second is bounced off a reflection, colliding with the reflected light of the first beam on its way to the film. The way a holographic film or plate looks to the eye is nothing like the picture of what it will project; instead, it looks like a bunch of irregular ripples, reflecting the collision of and crossing between the two split beams, like the ripples made by two separate stones being thrown into a pond.[2] The criss-crossing of these "ripples" is called the interference pattern, and this is what creates the hologram. Where this gets really interesting is that if you hold a holographic film or plate projecting an image of, say, a hat in your hand and then drop it to the ground, shattering it into pieces, not all is lost. With a hologram, if you were to project a portion of the film you would not see a small part of the hat but rather the entire hat, just faded. The crux here is that all the information from the interference pattern is distributed evenly across the surface, offering a record of the entire image even from a small portion of the film/plate. In essence: the part is in the whole and the whole is in the part. This holographic principle is used in this work in a few ways:

- In Part II, where we learn how to work, we will explore through the concept of awareness that our attention to awareness, even before we execute one step or part of a task, will directly affect the outcome of that entire task.
- In Part III, in the physical exercises, we will learn how the observation of a part of your body will tell you much about the way the entire body will work. We will also learn how the entire quality of the sound you make will be determined before a note has even been uttered. This first step, the very first part in the act of voicing, is the intake of breath. When working with character, we will explore how an entire character can be found in the way in which a simple gesture or even blink of an eye is acted. Throughout, we will also see how the holographic principle recognizes no disciplinary boundary between acting/singing/dancing.
- In Part IV, dealing with text analysis (script/chorography and score), we will learn that the emotive, musical, or movement-based happenings that make up the dramatic event also contain the entire event within them. We will learn how this can help us to make creative choices in correlation with both the text(s) and the practice to support the integrative instrument. It will not so much be a building upon text but rather a designing of an active framework that will render the text(s) a fellow performer in the act of doing. It is in this way that repeatability will be achieved.

RETHINKING THE ENTIRE, THE WHOLE, AND THE GLOBAL

What happens to our understanding of the whole, the entire, or the global when we consider parts as not discrete building blocks, but rather interrelating dynamic elements that help to make up a system as whole? The way we think of the whole may need a little shift.

You may recall the box on page 14 where the term emergence was introduced. Emergence describes what parts of a system do together that they would not do alone, or how collective properties arise from the properties of parts. It speaks to a system's function in that it can describe what something might do in relation to its environment that it would not do by itself.[3]

These processes can include complex organisms such as human beings and also non-human nature systems. For instance, the mind can be seen as an emergent result of neural activity. When thousands of birds flock or fish swim in schools, this can be seen as emergent. Hurricanes can be viewed as emergent from the complex workings of an eco-system. Traffic jams and teen culture fads are among other examples.

We will look at voicing, emotion, and physical movement, especially while integrated, as emergent properties of centre and breath. In this way, you will find that you will not be asked to negotiate or build linearly with more than one discipline or practice; you will do one practice whereby any combination of singing/sounding, acting/emoting, and dancing/movement will emerge.

> **Precise set of acts... becomes in some area an athlete of God**
> I am a dancer. I believe that we learn by practice. Whether it means to learn to dance by practicing dancing or to learn to live by practicing living... In each it is the performance of a dedicated precise set of acts, physical or intellectual, from which comes shape of achievement, a sense of one's being, a satisfaction of spirit. One becomes in some area an athlete of God.
>
> Martha Graham in her biography *Blood Memory*
> (Graham 1991: 3)

Transdisciplinarity

To look at how we might consider new correlations between the disciplines of acting, singing, and dancing to allow for the emergence of an integrative performance practice, we turn to an idea developed by Basarab Nicolescu called *Transdisciplinarity*.

To sing and dance and act within currently taught models of each discipline, which in many ways conflict with each other, is complicated. As discussed in Chapter One, the interdisciplinary performer often has to negotiate among different ways to situate the self in practice. Fundamental aspects of our bodies can be taught and conditioned in conflicting ways. For instance, as mentioned previously, breathing practices within the performance disciplines are often at odds with each other. What it means to work from centre can also be most confusing (see Chapter Five, pages 98–100). The relationship of the dancer/singer and actor to their text(s), be they that of choreography, the score, or the script, is approached in very different ways. The performer's role and when or if they enter the discussion of making meaning at different stages changes, and with that come varying degrees of responsibility. All these conflicts can take the energy away from the work of simply doing the doing of performance and into the sheer challenge of working out how to make it possible: negotiating disparate trainings. For a performer wishing to work from an integrated self within an integrated practice, this has until now been a most complicated challenge.

McGregor, speaking of transdisciplinarity, offers an explanation. "A complicated problem is hard to solve because it is intricate and detailed. A complex problem has the additional feature of emergence, the process of deriving some new coherent structures, patterns and properties" (McGregor 2004: 2).

Transdisciplinarity draws its notion of complexity from the sciences of quantum physics, chaos theory, and living, adaptive systems. Although not hitherto applied to performance practice, Nicolescu's notion of Transdisciplinarity offers a way to think and practise beyond the disciplines of acting, singing, and dancing.

Transdisciplinarity "takes us beyond disciplines by weaving a new kind of knowledge" (Nicolescu 1997: 12–14). The prefix "trans-" indicates that which is at once between, across, and beyond all discipline. "Its goal is the understanding of the *present* world, one of the imperatives of which is the unity of knowledge" (emphasis added) (Nicolescu 1997: 12–14).

This "present" world for the performer might be seen as the site of action where self meets the act of doing in the moment. We will speak more of this in Part II, but for now presence can be viewed, as theorist Cormac Power stated in his in-depth study on presence in performance, as "...a function of theatre — theatre is a place where different levels of presence are manipulated and played with — rather than an (essential) attribute" (Power 2008: 175).

Where Nicolescu is most helpful is in his breakdown of the functional relationships between disciplines and the different models of transferability. As an opera singer you may consider yourself a singer and an actor; as a dancer you may consider yourself a dancer and an actor. An actor needs to be able to move, voice, and act. A musical theatre performer who has to dance, sing, and act to varying degrees is often called a "triple threat", denoting that it takes three separate levels of skill working to equal degrees at the same time. Of course, increasingly dancers are being required to voice and singers to move and dance; however, the negotiation is still in place, and further institutionalized by the separation of departments of study in the academy and apparent in the various classes that the performer needs to attend on a regular basis to condition and train up disparate skills within what is perceived as separate aspects of expression, dance, voice, and acting. Nicolescu's breakdown, although designed to speak to the social sciences and culture, offers a sobering reflection on what we as performers actually do to train.

For Nicolescu, disciplinarity can be defined as one practice concerned with itself. For him, to think beyond disciplines goes to the heart of the previously discussed subject-object interaction (see Chapter One): "the subject cannot be captured in a disciplinary camp" (Nicolescu 2005: 143). In order to more fully explain this, he distinguishes between multidisciplinarity, interdisciplinarity, and transdisciplinarity as follows:

- "*Multidisciplinarity* concerns itself with studying a research topic in not just one discipline only, but in several at the same time. Any topic in question will ultimately be enriched by incorporating the perspectives of several disciplines. The multidisciplinary approach transgresses disciplinary boundaries while its goal remains *limited* to within the framework of disciplinary research."
- "*Interdisciplinarity* has a different goal than multidisciplinarity. It concerns the transfer of methods from one discipline to another. Like multidisciplinarity, interdisciplinarity transgresses the boundaries of disciplines while its goal still *remains* within the framework of disciplinary research. Interdisciplinarity even has the capacity to generate new disciplines, like quantum cosmology and chaos theory."
- "*Transdisciplinarity* concerns itself with what is *between* the disciplines, *across* the different disciplines, and *beyond* all disciplines. Its goal is the understanding of the present world, of which one of the imperatives is the unity of knowledge" (Nicolescu 2005 143–144).

In looking at these definitions and substituting the word "practice" for "research", we can view the disciplines of performance practice in an interesting light. Disciplinarity is pretty straightforward; any traditional dance class, singing lesson, or scene study workshop will offer this type of concentration on discipline, as will the execution of these learned practices performed in traditional formats.

Multidisciplinarity might be likened to a production of Bizet's *Carmen* (for instance), where there are opera singers and musicians, but also a required ballet sequence, traditionally drawing on an esteemed ballet company with skilled dancers. Such a production will also have actors and children, marching and singing. They all will likely affect each other and possibly, in a healthy working environment with time permitted, even learn and grow from their interactions with each other, but in the end each will go back to their own closed disciplinary camps.

Interdisciplinarity is very much a part of the post-1960s lexicon of the intertextual and hybrid modes of production (discussed earlier as performative or liminal aesthetics—see pages 47–49). Barthes stressed that interdisciplinarity is "not the calm of an easy security; it begins effectively (as opposed to a mere expression of a pious wish when solidarity of the old disciplines breaks down)". Barthes refers to this as an "epistemological slide", and opposed this to an all-important "break" (Barthes 1977: 155).[4]

The ensemble work of Grotowski, Brook, and Chaikin, as mentioned earlier, could be seen to fall in this category. New practices are developed, but they stay within the aesthetic boundaries that define the company. This category could also be used to shed light on exciting new advances in intermedial performance such as those of Lapage, Complicite, or the Wooster Group; however, even within these examples, the performers and their practice tend to serve the construction of the interdisciplinary event while negotiating their practice(s) from either trained conditionings born of a home discipline or a disciplinary aesthetics trained in via a company grounded in an interdisciplinary practice bespoke for their work.

The concept of transdisciplinarity offers a most exciting proposition for the artist who wishes to develop a practice that allows them to work *across*, *between*, and *beyond* the disciplinary boundaries conventionally set in the practices of acting, singing, and dancing. It is from this methodology that the Integrative Performance Practice was developed, acknowledging that the part is in the entire, that sound, movement, and emotion are emergent, and that the performer and the performance emerges from a central field of performing. This middle field acts as a fulcrum of activity with a most specific, workable physical centre, a cohesive practice of breathing, an articulated practice of attention allowing, through one practice, any choice of discipline, multidiscipline, or interdisciplinary aesthetic to emerge. It provides an effective model, an active framework by which knowledges and processes become mutually interdependent.

ACTIVE AESTHETIC

The active aesthetic lives within the field of *performing* (B) as a quality of the *way* the *doing* of a *process* is *practised* in *action*. It is from this active field that the aesthetics of the *performance* (C) and you as *performer* (A) emerge.

We mentioned earlier in this chapter that active aesthetic differs from the usual use of aesthetics, as applied to performance and the performer, in that it is concerned with the steps before the product or outcome is usually evaluated. By engaging with the active aesthetic you can witness or evaluate the *way of doing* in process, the qualities within the *activation* of *generating* a *process*.

An active aesthetic does not offer a way of evaluating what is done or who is doing it. It does not evaluate the *performance* (C) or the *performer* (A). It rather offers a way of witnessing qualities of the doing of what is done and who is doing, the way of doing. It lives in the field of *performing* (B).

The active aesthetic privileges a field of doing. We use action-based words to allow for the re-activation of a process in the present. The language used within the work recognizes that expressive products or outcomes such as emotions, gestures, shapes, tone, and timbre are all symptoms of doings. We do not do the sound/steps/emotions. A *performer* (A) does not do the *performance* (C) but rather an active, live, and present set of doings that result in the emergence of notes/steps/emotions. This goes, too, for the activation of a text, whether that text is a score, piece of choreography, script, or some combination of these.

The active aesthetic shifts the ways that we consider the interaction with the text(s) toward a discussion allowing and requiring choices in full consideration of how one *does*, rather than how one *represents*, *shows*, or *depicts*. It is a place of responsibility whereby the performer fully recognizes that "meaning" *happens* in the *act* of performance rather than being situated in the text to be passively transferred. It is also a place where we respond not as puppets but *partners* with texts and with the conceiver's concepts (e.g. composer, scriptwriter, choreographer, director, set designer) of the production as a performance event.

Most importantly, in Part III, which will take you through key elements of the practice, you will learn that it is through the active aesthetic that the entire voicing, moving, and emoting self can meet its full potential. This works partly because if we are not doing the doings of singing, acting, and dancing but rather a practice that allows the emergence of singing, acting, and dancing, there will be no competition or negotiation, but rather an integrative instrument working towards an integrative outcome.

Not much more can be said about this without some doing. It is an *active* aesthetic, after all. However, you will find that I will refer back to key concepts, so you may want to remind yourself how such concepts as the holographic principle or the Santiago Theory of Cognition work, for instance. Choose what you need when you need it, and dip in and out of the practice and theory section to design your own level of comfort integrating the two aspects. However, it really is all doing/saying — saying/doing the same thing.

NOTES

1 See pages 17–19 for a more detailed discussion on Descartes, which includes the fact that this received thinking around his stance on the mind/body has been oversimplified and his stance was not as hostile to an integrated self as some have supposed.

2 For more detailed information on how this actually works, and also how this hologram is used as an analogy in quantum theory, see David Bohm, *Wholeness and the Implicate Order* and Brian Green, *The Fabric of the Cosmos* (pages 481–485). For how the holographic principle is used as a way of understanding memories and the brain within neuroscience and cognitive studies, see Charles Hampden-Turner, *Maps of the Mind* (pages 94–97). For conversations about the East/West approaches to mindfulness and the holographic principle, see Stanislav Grof, *Ancient Wisdom Modern Science* (pages 167–179) and Yuaso Yasuo, *The Body and Self-Cultivation and Ki-Energy* (pages 52, 101). For

a popular explanation that covers all bases, albeit a little bit new-agey, see Michael Talbot, *The Holographic Universe*.

3 For a good overview of the various discussions across philosophy and science with respect to emergence, see Bedau, M.A. and Humphreys, P.E. *Emergence: Contemporary Readings in Philosophy and Science*, MIT Press, 2008.

4 Barthes did not want to suggest some conscious decision to re-ground theory on a new foundation. Instead he sought to challenge the very notion of foundation through the event of structure. Once one takes the idea of structure seriously, one has to recognize that knowledge and learning are the effects of movements that are not within the realms of decision and knowledge.

PART II

Working in the field of performing

Chapter 4

Centre, presence, and the initiation of task

IN THIS SECTION we enter the domain of the studio. As a result, you will find that there is a change in tone. Although we will work within the critical framework introduced through theory in Part I (Chapters One, Two, and Three), we will here transfer those key ideas into a studio-based vocabulary as we unfold new skill sets.

As this is a non-linear practice and not a technique, you will find that you will later be able to enter into the work from many different angles. I do, however, recommend that you read and do the foundational work in this Part before you skip around in the exercises in Parts III and IV, some of which will require a grounding in practices that are shared in exercises before. This will be stated in the section on "preparation" at the top of the instructions of each exercise. But first, let's learn a little about how to work within the Integrative Performance Practice (IPP).

DOING A TASK

This is the most important lesson you can learn within this practice. It is more important than any other tip, approach, theory, or practice that you will encounter. It is key because the doing of a task is the practice of your practice. It is where the discipline of your discipline resides. It is through your attending to the doing that the quality of what is done will be determined. It is also through your attending to the doing that you bring your entire potential to a task. It is where you will integrate the performer (you, your entire acting, voicing, moving self) through the field of performing towards performance. This is why in this particular practice this step is not overlooked, skipped, or assumed; it is a primary, crucial, and integral condition of the work. It is also not a thing that is *mastered* but a process that requires a constant returning to.

So what do we mean by *task*? The task is what we have chosen to do in the moment. It can be an exercise in class, such as an arpeggio, a plié, or a sensory exercise. It can be an action on the stage in the act of performance, such as the crossing of the stage, a lifting of your partner, or a cadenza. When you are working with a director, conductor, choreographer, or teacher, it is what you *agree* to do. When you are working alone, it is whatever you determine or choose to do. At the end of this chapter we will learn a tool called *Conscious Practice*, which is particularly helpful in solitary practice. At this particular junction, "intention", "motivation", and "purpose" are not factors in deciding what a task is. We will return to the idea of "intention" in Chapter Seven when we speak of acting as a discipline. For now, however, task is what you do. It's more local, and simply about the *way* of doing something, not the reason why.

So what are you actually doing?

One of the first structures I take a group through when I conduct a workshop is that of a simple task of sounding. It does not matter which country I am in or what combination of trained actors, singers, or dancers there are in the room; the results are strikingly similar. (Review reading exercise on page 13.)

In the workshop, as we learn a little about each other, we start with a simple task. I often invite the group to stand around the piano and I make sure that we all understand that we are simply going to sound an arpeggio. I make sure we all know what that means, and that we all understand the task. I explain that we do not need to make it beautiful or of any particular style; just sounding the pitches as best we can in this moment. I play a simple chord that would sit comfortably in anyone's range, then I play the arpeggio and the chord again. I say, "Okay, let's sound". I play the chord again (which indicates quite successfully that this is the moment to breathe in preparation) and then I say "Freeze!" before anyone can sound. While in our freeze, I invite us all to look around at each other and to notice bodies, faces, breath placement, energy, and anything else. We invariably giggle at the absurdity.

It is striking what a bunch of *stuff* we have in the room at that one moment. It is as if all the artists, open just moments before in readiness and curiosity, shift into certainties, habits, obligations, stories, histories; lots of thoughts, lots of feelings, lots of… *stuff*. There are various combinations of strange "singerly" faces (the tensions of which don't help the act of voicing at all) and even some hands raised as if the turning of a hand might will the sound to do something. Often there is a shift back onto the heels as a result of taking in an enormous amount of breath. For some, there is just a bearing down and a lifting of the body's centre into the chest in such a way as to allow them to make as little sound as possible while "looking" like they are singing. Sometimes there is an intensity that comes over a person's eyes, a *performance* persona, eager and ready to "exhibit" their skills. There can be "good student" stances that have more to do with pleasing than with sounding. There can be hiding, checking, proving, testing, showing, placing, auditioning, trying, wanting, and wishing, but very rarely is there simply preparation for simply sounding. *All the things that lie outside of the field of the task* — in this case, to sound a note — *we call stuff.*

What is meant here by *stuff*? It sounds a little colloquial, but the word, as ambiguous as it may be, is chosen on purpose. Some refer to this as "baggage" or "damage", but such terms give *stuff* great importance, can engender defensiveness or shame, and tend to generate narratives. Importantly in this work, we work to resist placing a value on our *stuff* (either positive or negative). It is the task that remains important, not the *stuff*, and the value of the work is in attending to the task, not the *stuff*. We purposefully keep this term general so that it is easier to *witness* our stuff without the attachments that come with judgement and diagnosis (more on this in a few paragraphs). Simply, *stuff* is the extras that are present when you are doing a task. We will learn in the next pages how to integrate your stuff, or release it, so that it ceases to be superfluous accompaniment to your tasks.

So let's return to that piano — what are we *actually* doing? (A good sense of humour about oneself is really helpful here.) Standing around a piano in itself can do a number on some of us; the idea that we are in a workshop and there is a group dynamic can also contribute to generate stuff. The act of sounding can be an exposing proposition. Standing in front of a piano and singing arpeggios might be something we have done many times before, making us return to past patternings, techniques, or values. All this can contribute to an unintentional redefining of a task. Changing the task is fine when it is a choice: however, *when we are not aware of our stuff, the task can be hijacked.*

> Insanity: doing the same thing over and over again and expecting different results.
>
> Attributed to Albert Einstein

This initial exercise does not have to be that of sounding; it can be the task of saying a line from a text or as basic a physical task as picking up a scarf from the floor. Really, it can be anything. The enquiry remains the same. What is the doing of the doing? What are we actually doing when we think we are doing the task? The exercise helps us to begin to enquire: what did we believe we *agreed* to do? Are we aware of our agreements? What contributes to them? Being aware of what you bring to a task will enable you to respond to the task from a place of responsibility.

Some ways in which we confuse the task

Often in the act of practice we let the task *do us*. Some teachings and practices even inadvertently encourage this; clocking hours and hours of scales or barre work, or just saying lines without an awareness from self with conscious connection to the task, can be dangerous, because *what you practise you get good at*. Practising well is so much more important than practising long and hard. Most importantly, by remaining unaware of what you actually practise, you can practise in damaging habits that can take years to unlearn. What's more, *there is no such thing as not doing*. You are always practising, learning, and developing the you: the you that is the artist. What you actually practise is what you actually get good at! (Review Part I for discussions around self and practice through the lens of neuroscience, phenomenology, performativity, and cognitive studies and further how these relate to our place in the construct of what is now deemed Performance (C).)

Sometimes we can find ourselves double-tasking. In the above example, a person *trying* to sound at the same time as *pleasing* the teacher will produce a different performance/outcome than one simply *sounding*. After enough repeats of such behaviour, this person will condition their living being, the artist, their self, into one that is quite excellent at *trying* and *pleasing*.

As we learn new practices, the impulse to double-task can present a challenge. We are understandably concerned as we learn both the correct technique and a chosen artistic action, and we can forget about the doing. It is for this reason that this book chooses the language in the exercises with great care to work to minimize this tension. Further, in Part IV, when we start to work with text, choreography, and music, we will learn how to integrate our technical and artistic needs into one simple action that allows the emergence of plural outcomes.

But first, this chapter is about sharpening the ability to work effectively, on your own terms, and in a way that helps to pattern in the integration of your physical, vocal, and emotive self as an instrument.

Witnessing vs judging and diagnosing

To witness is to notice. When we witness, we take gentle note of what is happening as it happens. It is light in touch and also peripheral in energy. If, for instance, we have a task of walking across the room and picking up a coin, we might notice that we are "performing" walking rather than just walking. We might witness that we are affected by those watching, that there is an affectation to our walk that we do not usually have. We might witness that we are hearing the clock on the wall tick, that there is a tension in our jaw and that we have stopped breathing. We say to ourselves when the time comes, *isn't it interesting*, when I was walking I was *doing this* and *doing that* rather than simply putting one foot in front of the other walking to the coin in the middle of the room. *Isn't it interesting* I feel self-conscious. *Isn't it interesting* there is tension in my jaw. *Isn't it interesting* I stopped breathing until I got to the coin and then took in a breath… *Isn't it interesting.*

It is in this way that witnessing allows us to attend to the experience of doing the task: the phenomenon of the doing with respect to the intentionality in the task. (Review pages 23–27 on phenomenology.)

What witnessing is NOT is judging. As in, "Darn, I am doing it again, I have it wrong". It is also NOT "Great, I am doing it, this is right!" or any variation of these, either verbal or non-verbal. To be in the flow of the doing is to do the doing of the task, not the doing of judging your progress or watching yourself do the task. This is why witnessing is not watching with intent but noticing with an "isn't that interesting" soft sort of humour.

What witnessing is also NOT is diagnosing. As in, "Okay, I can do this better, I just need to relax my foot". Or, "Almost there now, breathing, put one foot in front of the other". Or, "God, I am never going to get this right", or "That's it, keep on going, this is it, your foot's relaxed now". If you are busy directing yourself and teaching yourself and diagnosing yourself, that is the doing. It will yield its own results, but not the result of performing the performance task, of simply picking up the coin.

Some worry that if we are not judging and diagnosing that we lose a sense of discipline. This practice draws a very strong distinction between discipline as punishment and discipline as practice. Within these pages there is an exacting and challenging practice; however, its work resides in the active aesthetic (see pages 60–6 in Part I, Chapter Three), in the process of doing, and therefore the discipline is to continually return to the task, not leaving the task to make a new task of judging or diagnosing. What witnessing does is to allow an avenue for reflection and mindfulness without losing the integrative self in the act of doing.

So witnessing is simply that, a noticing. Let go of any sticky impulses to tell a story, to attach to a feeling, to justify a position, to go down a track of thoughts, to go into any "zone". Go into the doing of the doing as it unfolds in the present moment with a commitment to the task and a curiosity that only goes as far as "Isn't that interesting". Of course, if at any moment you are unsafe, you can then leave the task and take care of yourself; but often we leave the task for reasons of ego, fear, control, or habit, reasons that for the most part were not a part of the task that we agreed to engage in. It is this dynamic that makes performing one of the bravest professions when engaged in with integrity.

As stated in Part I, it is in the field of performing, the doing of the doing, that the alchemy of our work resides. It is crucial to spend time and attend to this field, since it is here that the meaning of our work as performers is born.

Witnessing allows you to be kind to yourself as you learn. It keeps you curious and in growth rather than grounded by judgement and boxed by diagnosis. It allows you to be able to respond to an observation. It keeps you safe and in a position of response-ability (the ability to respond) at the same time, and it gives you information to reflect on so that you can work out how best next to organize your practice. (For a reminder of this type of reflection and its important role in a learning process that takes us beyond habitual patterning, see The Santiago Theory of Cognition, pages 31–34.)

What is really important about this work is that it's okay if there is stuff. In fact, this is what makes you the individual artist that you are. This work is not about getting completely "clean" or neutral, without negativity or tension. It is not about beating you into submission to one technique that will negate others (this would presuppose a particular aesthetic judgement, and this is about an active aesthetic, not an aesthetic (review pages 60–61). Who is without stuff? How interesting would we be if we were? It is, however, important to be cognizant of your stuff, to claim your stuff, and to witness so that you are present and able to make wider, deeper, and more varied choices with your entire vocal, emotive, and physical self as you master the practice and your instrument. This is not therapy, but it can be therapeutic. This is not religion, but it can feel spiritual. This is about the performer in the act of performance, you as an enabled integrative performer capable of an integrated outcome.

Thoughts/feelings/awareness — Who's doing the doing?

Witnessing can be quite a challenge when we are in the habit of thinking that self is determined through the act of thinking or the act of feeling. Both judging and diagnosing require the functions of thinking and feeling. For some this might be radical, but: you are NOT your thoughts: neither are you your feelings. We HAVE thoughts and feelings.

Try this:

At this very moment, can you witness your feelings? In a moment, I will ask you to notice your feelings. These feelings may be sensations in your body, a felt sense in your being, or emotions. They can also be non-verbal feelings that words may not be able to convey. Take a moment now. Notice any feelings you may be having.

Now let that go. Let's try another thing:

In a moment I will ask you to witness any thoughts that might be coming up. Notice the language, the rhythm of your thoughts, the nature of your thoughts, any consistency... They may even be slightly non-verbal, a thought gesture for instance, as in the way we can direct attention to certain areas of cognitive understandings or attitudes. (See *Haltung*, page 12.) Take a moment and notice your thinking, your thoughts.

Great. Did you allow yourself to do the task of bringing your awareness to your thoughts and your feelings without judging and diagnosing? What did you witness? What was interesting?

The point here is simple. If you are aware of your thoughts, and if you are aware of your feelings, then by very definition you are NOT your thoughts or your feelings. These are things you do or have. This leaves the question: who is doing/having the thinking and who is doing/having the feeling?

The answer: it is your awareness. (It will be the same answer to "Who does the doing?" when we do a doing without too much "stuff" — *meaning things that lie outside of the agreed task* — taking over). Doing the doing from your awareness is an integrative performer's first and continuing lesson. It is the kernel of the practice and its challenge presents itself to varying degrees for different people at different times. For instance, sometimes an artist who comes primarily from dance, when asked to sound, may go to thoughts and feelings to negotiate unknown territory; likewise, the practised singer might go to habitual thoughts and feelings when asked to sound, if that is the way they have practised in their practice. Challenges take some of us out of awareness; they take others of us directly to a field of awareness. Whatever your patterns, they are about witnessing and returning to awareness with every new task and every new breath.

What does it mean to work from awareness?

Doing from awareness means to do from a more integrated self. At this first stage, integration is initially about having access to more of your instrument. Many of us confuse *focus* with *awareness*. On the face of it, it may seem subtle, but in action there is a most important distinction for this practice. Many exacting physical practices have a tradition of using focus as a tool for discipline. Sports psychology promotes focus and some dance, singing, and acting pedagogies promote focus as a quality of determination and commitment. The discipline of this work does not lie in focus, as focus works directly against the process of integration.

Try this:

In a moment I am going to ask you to do the task of focusing on your big toe. (If you are left-handed, focus on your left big toe; if you are right-handed, focus on your right big toe.) Here focus is not a visual instruction, meaning it is not necessarily important to look directly at your big toe. Now for half a minute focus focus focus on your big toe. Take the time and do it now...

Focus.

Now let that go.

For most, what can be observed in the focusing is that their breath has stopped and they lose awareness of the rest of their body and the space around them, including things behind them. Often the tongue gets rooted at the top of the upper palate, and all thoughts and feelings are directed to one place in a sort of tunnel vision. Often people find they need to look at an object of focus. With all of this going on, we will not be in readiness to do anything other than focus on the big toe. I have done this little experiment in auditoriums and in workshops in many countries and, strangely, regardless of cultural differences, the effects are the same.

If we instead draw our *awareness* to that same toe (and this does not mean to "think" toe toe toe, or "feel" the toe, but to *go* there, to allow your awareness to go to the toe), something else occurs.

Explore for about a half a minute what it is to bring your awareness to your left big toe. Do it now…

Okay. For most, this is quite a different experience. We breathe; we have a body, arms, legs AND a toe. There is an environment in which we are working. We are more open and receptive.

Awareness does not disintegrate, hone in, or separate the task from the self or the space within which we are working. Doing the doing from awareness is key.

All tasks within this practice are designed to be activated from awareness. We will witness thoughts, feelings, focus, and any other stuff that takes us out of awareness and transports us to another task. This is not an easy challenge, and the next few pages offer exercises to hone this discipline.

Exercise #1
Who's working?

Simple task from awareness

This is a good exercise for learning what it means to *do* a task *from* awareness. Its main point is to help clarify: who's working? Is it from your thoughts, your feelings, or is it from your awareness that you are doing the task? Who is doing the task?

The first preparatory step strengthens one's ability to locate awareness by drawing awareness to different parts of the body and then to awareness itself. This exercise is best done after a reading or discussion on: witnessing vs judging and diagnosing (page 68), thoughts, feelings and awareness (page 69), and awareness rather than focus (page 70).

In this structure, you will begin by sitting cross-legged on the floor while slowly allowing your awareness to go to different parts of the body. Give yourself the time you need, and allow your awareness to sit where it is for a moment before you shift your awareness to the next location. It is important to note that this exercise is not meant to be trancelike or zone-y. We are not aiming to achieve any heightened state. We are simply about the discipline of doing the doing as a practice.

Notice anything that comes up; if you find that you are drifting into thoughts or feelings, witness and return to awareness without judgement or diagnosis. If you are doing this on your own, do not stress if you go off script; what is important is that when you draw your awareness to a part of your body, you *go there* with your awareness, rather than focus on the place, think about the place, or visualize the place. This ability to *go there* with your awareness will become your saving grace as we move to more advanced work requiring the articulation of subtle muscular systems within the breath-body.

Preparation: Wearing comfortable clothing, sit with crossed legs on the floor in a relaxed position. Put an object that you can pick up easily with one hand within an arm's length away from you on the floor (water bottle, hat, scarf, or pencil are all good contenders). You may wish to pick the object up, put it on your lap and then put it back in place in front of you just once to "rehearse" the movement and get it into your body.

Step 1. With your eyes open and in a soft gaze, allow yourself to breathe while gently scanning your body, noticing any tensions, breathing, allowing yourself to release any tensions you may be witnessing. Continue to breathe and allow yourself to release any thoughts. Once you are ready, draw your awareness to:

- Your right knee
- Your left knee
- Allow your awareness now to go to...
- Your right ear
- Your left ear
- The top of your head
- Your forehead
- Your throat, front and back
- Your chest and upper back body
- Your solar plexus and middle back and sides
- Your lower belly, sides and lower back
- The base of your pelvic girdle
- Bring your awareness to the top of your head
- Bring your awareness to your awareness

Step 2. With your awareness toward your awareness, coming from awareness, slowly and deliberately put your hand out in front of you and pick up your object and bring it to your lap. The task is to pick up the object and put it on your lap.

Step 3. Witness if you stayed in your awareness through the motion. If you did not, when did you leave awareness? Did you return to awareness?

Note: Most people find this simple motion very challenging; often, we notice that halfway through, rather than simply picking up the object, we were watching ourselves. Some find that they go to "performing" picking up the object rather than simply picking up the object. Some find that they zone out during a certain stage of the action. Some find that they think, "I got it, I got it", which of course is thinking, not picking up the object. For others, the move away from awareness can be a subtle pull away to "check in", rather than to trust oneself in the flow of the doing. All of these belong in the category of "isn't that interesting..." (review page 68).

Step 4. Once you have done a little reflection, you can reset and begin again, and when you have learned to pick up the object from awareness, picking up the object and putting it on your lap, you can pick it up, take it to yourself and then put it back down.

Tip: Giving helpful feedback. When we are invited to observe a colleague at work, it is most important that we steer away from language that professes to tell them what they are doing, but rather speak from the first person, in as much detail as possible and with a spirit of enquiry. For instance, it is not helpful to tell someone, "When you picked up the bottle you totally lost it, you left your awareness". Rather, "I noticed that when your fingers touched the surface of the bottle there was a change". Not, "Your mouth was really tight", but rather, "I saw some tension in your jaw when you initiated the movement". Also, be open to the fact that their experience may be different from your observation. That in itself will be of interest to the enquiring practitioner.

Working in groups: This can be done with a group of any size in a circle, with a facilitator speaking through Step One, poising the group to pick up their objects after they have drawn their awareness to their awareness. After the basic premise is understood, the group can take turns doing it one at a time while being watched (this presents another challenge). Those watching can then also witness what they observe. It is interesting for those watching and those performing to see how they are perceived when they are doing the task from awareness and when they leave awareness.

Every habit is a bad habit

What a horrible thing to be told, when so often as performers we work to attain excellent habits within our work. What can be meant by such a statement? I first heard this from a spiritual teacher, Sri Swami Satchidananda, at an ashram in Virginia where I spent a few wonderful summers as a teenager. At the same time, I was doing intensive training as an actor at the NYC High School of Performing Arts, learning physical concentration, emotional availability, and presence exercises in various forms. I was very proud of the "good" habits that I had been cultivating while practising and living in my everyday life. Although this work is not about an avenue towards spiritual enlightenment, "every habit is a bad habit" is a profound statement that resonates with the ideas discussed in Chapter One to do with Phenomenology, Cognitive Science and Performativity.

How can brushing your teeth, eating properly, or exercising be a "bad" habit? How can connecting to breath before making a sound, connecting to centre before doing an extension from the leg, or being simple and true while delivering a monologue be a "bad" habit?

Well, it is simple: as soon as any action becomes a habit, we are no longer doing the doing again anew each time. We dilute the presence in the act of the task. The task can become automatic and we can lose awareness or go to focus. It can become the Performer (A) doing the Performance (C) of the task. We leave the field of Performing (B), our alchemy and the power of our work. As you will learn when you work in this way, even though this may feel counterintuitive to start, we lose energy for the task when we go to habits; whether good or bad is irrelevant.

Staying in the discomfort — the noble struggle

A thing about habits is that they are comfortable. In many ways, working in the field of performing (B) is not exactly comfortable, although it can be pleasurable. To allow for the new conditions that unfold in each and every moment both within and without as we do a doing again for its first time can be uncomfortable, especially if we are working to de-pattern ourselves out of ingrained habits.

I am not advocating that we all need to "torture ourselves for our art" (partly because habitual torturing of self for one's "art" tends to offer its own type of "comfort"). I am saying that comfort is not the aim within the field of performing. This can get confusing when habitual barre work, unconscious reeling off of scales, and saying lines by rote can "feel" as if we are doing our work; however, when the work is about staying within an active aesthetic in the field of performing, then a habitual way of practice is not what you are looking for. In this work the discipline resides in the *way* of doing, not in an unconscious repetition of doing something over and over again for hours. Remember, we get good at *exactly* what we practise, which includes unconscious practice conditioning in disintegrating habits. Instead of coming from habitual repetition, here we do the doing — again, we do not rest on our laurels, but rather bring forward what we have in the here and now to the chosen task in this moment. We engage consciously with our current body/mind self, meeting the performance task in an active rather than passive way of doing.

This can be uncomfortable because there is perceived risk involved (but no more than if you work in the habitual way, if you really think about it). But again, it can also become very pleasurable when we learn to trust that we are dynamic and able to engage with the experience of the doing each and every time. It is also quite freeing when we realize that each pass through an exercise or performance task offers a new opportunity to do it better, be more present, and engage in a way more connected to a task from a more integrated self. This takes bravery; the returning to the doing of the doing, as opposed to repeating what felt comfortable or relying on habits, is the *noble struggle*.

It is not about "getting it"

So often when learning a technique we work to "get it". Getting it for the singer might mean that moment when we sound a note for the first time completely off the throat; for the dancer, it might be executing that move in a way that feels so balanced and easy that the effort was little but the physical result was buoyant; for the actor, it might be that moment that we really believed we were that character in that moment for a few beats. We "got it". We got it!!! YAY — but how do we repeat it? It can be a reason for celebration and even a moment where the mind/body begins to re-pattern itself into expanded possibilities — but only if we can do that doing again. "Getting it" can make our teachers/directors/choreographers really happy and us happy, but we are the practitioners. How do we become custodians of our own alchemy? How do we repeat what works? Can we?

Repeating the feeling of when we got it rarely works more than once, because instead of doing the task we were doing when we "got it", we will be doing the task of *trying to repeat a feeling*, which takes us out of the agreed task.

Doing the doing anew each time, witnessing and returning to the task in each and every moment, is key to this work.

Working with felt sense

In this work, witnessing one's *felt sense* becomes a most useful tool. Felt sense in this context is a term that denotes the sensory experience of the aspect of self that we are bringing awareness to at this moment. It does NOT need to be rational. For instance, my felt sense might feel dark and gooey. It might feel heavy, fragmented, orange. It could also be metaphorical, such as floating, filled with water, rigid like a bar of metal, like a strobe light. In fact, it is helpful not to create too much narrative but to just notice such things as the consistency, colour, rhythm, or position of a felt sense. You can have a felt sense in relation to an exercise, in this moment now, in relation to certain people, or in relation to situations. Most of the work around felt sense is about attending to the felt sense of the aspect that you are choosing to draw attention to at that movement and just letting yourself *be* there. This can be uncomfortable but is part of the noble struggle of witnessing without judging or diagnosing, which is the first stage of allowing for change.

Working in the "crispy" presence

A most crucial point of what is meant about doing a task from awareness is that it is in NO way likened to a trancelike state, or any state of being or feeling for that matter.

Often for those coming from more dogmatic performance practices or trained in companies with set ideologies, there can be a conception of awareness and presence as a heightened state. In this work it is not. "Present", in this context, is not a state of being aligned to devotion or sacrifice but a way of doing that includes the doer and the doing as one system available to itself in the unfolding present moment. In this work you aim to be both responsible and able to respond to the external and internal stimuli as one. This work is about the performer in the act of performance, on their own terms, in and of the world.

As a result, we are NOT aiming for the *being in the flow* sort of feeling that invariably gets a little bliss-like or zone-y. Although this type of felt sense can be comfortable, as previously discussed, it is not the aim of this work. We will find that bliss-y, in-the-zone, trancelike states are not only unhelpful, but can be unsafe, especially as we enter into the work in Part III.

Presence can be a difficult thing to communicate, and getting present in preparation to work may require an entirely different approach from one day and one moment to the next. When working with artists, I refer to the quality of presence that we are working with as a *crispy presence*. This term is chosen only to distinguish the *felt sense* from a trancelike state or a zoning out and has proven helpful. However, this is not to be confused with "alertness", which is more aligned with "focus". As discussed earlier, focus as opposed to awareness can cause tension, narrow the field of availability and disintegrate the instrument (see page 70). In fact, often it is helpful for the "A" student-type practitioner to approach a task like a "C" student (it's a serious challenge for some to soften their *trying hard* and *good student* tendencies). For each artist, and in each moment, a personal balance needs to be struck in the act of doing the chosen task.

So in discussing presence in relation to this work, we never speak about optimum, heightened, or focused states, as we cannot *do* states (states, like emotions, are emergent); rather, presence here is spoken about in the service of the *way* we *do* a task from *awareness* in the unfolding and constantly developing present moment. Witnessing, coming from awareness and working from a specific centre aligned with your breath-body (the subject of Chapters Five and Six) will make this possible, repeatable, and even enjoyable while releasing newfound availability from your most integrated physical, vocal, and emotive instrument.

The "company" we keep?

As mentioned earlier, we all have stuff, which in part helps to make us interesting and individual. *Company* and *stuff* are related but slightly different in that stuff is *what you bring to the task*, and company will have more to do with how your stuff plays out in the doing of the task. When our stuff — be it tensions, thoughts, feelings, or even more subtle behavioural patterns such as needing to please our parents or teachers as we work, or overcoming feelings of failure — when our stuff lies outside of the doing of the task (meaning if it is not integrated or let go), it then accompanies us in the agreed-upon task and can change it. It becomes *company*.

In the exercises within this chapter you will have become aware of some of the things that accompany you as you practice. This company can come in the form of thoughts, feelings, attitudes (see Haltung and the box for Gestalt in Chapter 1 on pages 12 and 13) or even unvoiced assumptions. You may have also noticed that when you leave the field of awareness this inhibits your ability to *witness* any company you might have. When we cease to witness the things that accompany us, these things have a tendency to take the task away from what was agreed and towards new tasks. Most people discover that even with a simple task of picking something up or walking, both tasks that we have been doing for most of our lives, a whole lot of things that might fall out of the field of the chosen task tend to accompany us. This takes us out of working in the flow of presence in the act of doing the task.

What sort of stuff do we bring to the work? What things accompany or disrupt a task? — and I choose the terms "accompany" and "disrupt", rather than "get in the way of", "hurt", or "contaminate" because there is no pure product that we are aiming for, but rather a clarity in the way of doing the task. It is through this clarity that the active aesthetic, our way of doing, will be determined. As mentioned in Chapter One, with the IPP we do not aim to psychologize, cleanse, free from negativity, make pure and natural, or clear the artist of stuff before engaging in the act of doing. These actions tend to become tasks in themselves and are often the defining characteristic and determining aesthetic of the practices that embrace them.

The following exercises will offer some ways to learn the differences between "getting it" and "focusing" and a particular practice of awareness. They are designed to hone some new "muscles" towards working within the active aesthetic in the flow of presence and to help you define what your own noble struggle might entail as you witness the company you keep. This foundational work will be very important in Part III when we encounter some exercises that may at face value feel familiar to some, but are very specific towards the conditioning of an integrative instrument that is able to sound, move, and act to full potential.

Exercise #2
Vipassana walking meditation

> Little do ye know your own blessedness; for to travel hopefully is a better thing than to arrive, and the true success is to labour.
>
> Robert Louis Stevenson in *Virginibus Puerisque* (Stevenson 1911: 371)

In the Vipassana walking meditation we will practise attending to the doing of walking, which helps to discipline the mind and the body, connecting and integrating intention with action. We will draw awareness to the action of the feet and attend to the moment-by-moment experience of movement that will be broken down into deliberate steps as you execute the task of walking. Here you will allow your inner talk to connect directly to the doing of walking. If you witness that you are drifting away from the task of walking, you will acknowledge and return to the doing of walking. This can feel silly at first, but trust the process and it will provide new insights into the nature of your doing while engendering a deeper sense of presence within the flow of the task.

As in Exercise #1, we are not aiming to achieve any heightened state. This is likely to be slow — very slow — and often people manage only a few steps their first time.

Preparation: This is best done in bare feet in a space that will allow you to walk a little distance. A hallway, stage, or rehearsal studio are all good options, and the fewer visual and auditory distractions, the better.

Step 1. Begin by standing, breathing, and standing, simply standing. Let your arms rest by your sides, your face be soft and your gaze gentle and straight ahead throughout. Note that you are "standing", "breathing", "standing".

Step 2. Before moving, and while noting "standing", observe your readiness to walk, noting the acting of intention: "intending to walk".

Step 3. At the same time as you do the action, very slowly and deliberately, silently note the action.

"Lifting" as your heel leaves the floor.
"Leaving" as your foot releases contact with the floor.
"Moving" as your foot moves through the space.
"Placing" as your foot makes contact with the floor.

Step 4. "Pausing" — and then repeat step 3 with the other foot.

Tip: You may find that there are days when other things cloud the task. This is a wonderful opportunity to understand your process in the doing of a task. If, for instance, you find your attention leaves the act of lifting the foot, but rather goes to checking on yourself, simply pause and note "checking" and return to "breathing" and "standing" and start at step 1 again. You may find you go to "sensing frustration"; return to "breathing" and "standing" and continue from awareness rather than from thoughts or feelings. There are times an outside stimulus distracts us; note this too — "hearing clock", "pausing", "standing", "breathing", "lifting" ... "thinking about lunch", return to "standing", "breathing"...

Step 5. When you are ready to turn and walk back, remember to note "intending to turn", "pivot", "turning", "turning", "turning", "standing", "breathing", and "lifting"... and then back to steps 1–5.

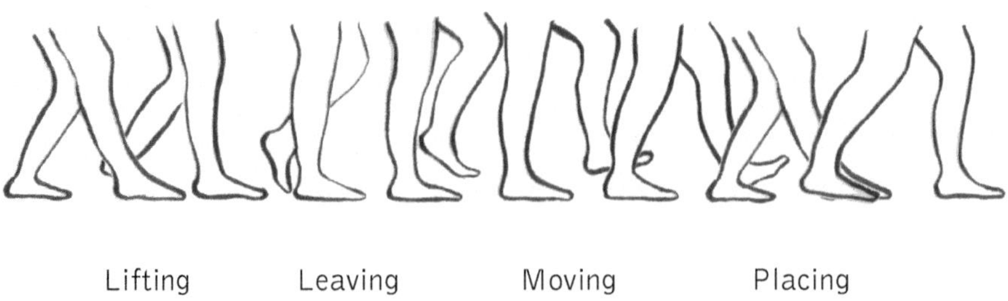

Variations: The basic premise of this meditation can be used in any action. Cleaning up the studio or sweeping the floor in preparation to work is useful, as it helps to prepare the space and the artist for work at the same time. If there is a particularly challenging task within a work, be it vocal, physical, or emotive, the basic attending to the doing of the task in this way can help to integrate the task with the doer and the doer with themself through an attending to the task in the present, with all that is available through the action in the now.

Recognizing company

In order to make choices about the integration or releasing of some of the stuff that we bring to the work, it helps to acknowledge that we have *company* in the first place. It could be: "Oh gosh I am tense today, isn't that interesting", "I just realized that for the last three minutes I have been doing a lot of judging, Hmmm?", "Ouch, my tooth is really killing me, attending to the pain is directing me away from the scene. Interesting", "I feel so excited that I got that role, that I am working from my excited *feeling* and not coming from my awareness, isn't that interesting".

The most common elements that can accompany our tasks can be broken into various physical and/or thought patterns. As you will recall from the first chapter, the mind/body construct can go deep and be practised into us over time as a result of our science and our culture, within our family paradigms, through former trainings, consciousness, and within the subtle webs of interactions that make our societies what they are.

As we work, we will aim to witness the *phenomenon* of doing the task. A quick review of the section on phenomenology will remind you about how this attending to experience can help to reconfigure the way we think about our practice and further integrate subject (you) and object (task) (review pages 23–27). In the section on neuroscience we learned some good news about how we are capable of changing our brain wiring to adopt new notions or re-pattern and reprogramme our mind-body through the innate plasticity of the brain. A review of the section on consciousness studies, with particular attention to the Santiago Theory, will remind you of the ways in which we are a system. We are a complex system structurally coupling with all that we encounter, never fully leaving ourselves but able to grow and change beyond the patterns, when and if we attend to the doing from awareness (review pages 30–34).

Sometimes it helps to make apparent some of our company, but without shame and blame, and with a healthy sense of "isn't that interesting" — witnessing vs judging and diagnosing, sitting with it, perhaps, in the discomfort and letting it be. By making the invisible visible, the unconscious conscious, the unfelt experienced, we can then begin to make choices about what we bring to a task and what the task is.

Direct your life

Until you make the unconscious conscious, it will direct your life and you will call it fate.

Attributed to Carl Jung

There are lots of lovely ways to greet our company. What is important for this work is that when we begin to make some of our company visible we resist pathologizing, therapizing or going into stories around it, especially in the process of practice, conditioning, and making work (unless, of course, that is what the work is about). This is not to brush away the fact that some of this work is likely to reveal some profound and personal aspects of self that might be well worth exploring further in therapy for the purposes of introspection, healing, and personal growth. However, this is not the purpose of this work. In the next two exercises we explore witnessing and widening awareness of the *stuff* we bring to our work, in the service of a greater understanding of the self, towards the integration of our present instrument, toward meeting whatever task is at hand.

Exercise #3

Drawing your body

Preparation: Find blank paper (without lines) and things to draw with. A variety of colours and textures are helpful (such as crayons, markers, pens, pencils, and maybe paint if you have the time to clean up). You will work in silence and privacy. (If working in a group, find a corner to draw where no one will comment on your work. Do not chat with others while you are drawing.)

Tip: This can be done before a warm-up or after to reveal differences in one's physical felt sense and body image. Usually it is done in warm-up clothes, but doing it in costume can also render interesting results and reveal information helpful for character work. Just note that whatever you are wearing is likely to affect the results, so make a conscious choice as to what the enquiry is and frame the exercise from there.

Step 1. Put *one* of the below questions to yourself and begin to draw. Each question is a totally new exercise and should be given time. Some options could be:

- What is the felt sense of my internal image of my body?
- What is an image of my body in this moment?
- What is the felt sense of my body when I sing?
- What is the felt sense of my body when I dance?

- What is the felt sense of my body when I act _____ role?
- What is the felt sense of my body when I am in ______ class?

Step 2. Reflection
This is simply about noticing what we have created in relation to how it reflects the felt sense of your body. The purpose is to illuminate what the drawing has revealed about your experience in your body. If you are working alone, spending time really seeing what you have created and connecting that to your own experience can be interesting. Journaling about your discoveries can also be helpful.

If working in groups, you can share your pictures. It is important for the viewer not to create a story around the drawing or create meaning. Simply state what you see, in the spirit of enquiry, rather than judging or diagnosing, and ask simple one-sentence questions. Make sure you allow time to really listen. Helpful questions might go like this: "It is interesting to see that you have made the throat very long in proportion to the rest of the body, can you share more about this?" or "I see a spiral that gets bigger at the top. Is this your felt sense when you sing? What is that like?"

Exercise #4
Cognitive distortions

This can be used as an ongoing life exercise and is an excellent tool for witnessing as well as part of a studio exercise. It is a valuable way to put a name to some of the mental company and stuff that most of us have. Dr David Burns, noted cognitive therapist and behavioural researcher, presents an effective way of categorizing some of the subtle thought patterns that can take us out of the present moment and derail a task.

In the Vipassana walking meditation, Exercise #2, we noted "lifting", "leaving, "moving", and "placing" as the breakdown of the task "walking". When we noticed other actions (feelings or thoughts) that had entered the task, deflecting us from fully attending to the act of walking, we simply noted what we were doing when we left the task, e.g. "thinking about dinner", then returned to the task, "standing", breathing", "lifting". We will use the categories of cognitive distortions in a similar model. These help to note the thought distortions that often take us into places that are not the agreed task. As creative people, we are delightfully prone to making up stories; it is the gift and the curse of the talented performer. Here we learn a way to effectively discern the difference between helpful thoughts towards the task and when we have left the task. The aim, of course, is to note and work your way back to the practice of the practice in the now, and witness and release some of the habitual practices of thinking that keep us from learning new things and developing new skills.

It is best to read this exercise in its entirety before applying it.

Step 1. Below you will see ten categories of cognitive distortions as defined by Dr David Burns. Become familiar with them, and gently and with humour consider, without shame and blame, judging or diagnosing, but rather with an enquiring, "isn't that interesting" mindset, which ones you have a tendency to employ.

- **All-or-nothing thinking:** You see things in black-and-white categories. If your performance falls short of perfect, you see yourself as a total failure.
- **Overgeneralization:** You see a single negative event as a never-ending pattern of defeat.
- **Mental filter:** You pick out a single negative detail and dwell on it exclusively so that your vision of all reality becomes darkened, like the drop of ink that discolors the entire beaker of water.
- **Disqualifying the positive:** You reject positive experiences by insisting they "don't count" for some reason or other. In this way you can maintain a negative belief that is contradicted by your everyday experiences.
- **Jumping to conclusions:** You make a negative interpretation even though there are no definite facts that convincingly support your conclusion.
- **Mind reading:** You arbitrarily conclude that someone is reacting negatively to you, and you don't bother to check this out.
- **The fortuneteller error:** You can anticipate that things will turn out badly, and you feel convinced that your prediction is an already established fact.
- **Magnification (catastrophizing) or minimization:** You exaggerate the importance of things (such as your goof-up or someone else's achievement), or you inappropriately shrink things until they appear tiny (your own desirable qualities or the other fellow's imperfections). This is also called the binocular trick.
- **Emotional reasoning:** You assume that your negative emotions necessarily reflect the way things really are: "I feel it, therefore it must be true."
- **"Should" statements:** You try to motivate yourself with should and shouldn't, as if you had to be whipped and punished before you could be expected to do anything. "Musts" and "oughts" are also offenders. The emotional consequences are guilt. When you direct "should" statements toward others, you feel anger, frustration, and resentment.
- **Labelling and mislabelling:** This is an extreme form of overgeneralization. Instead of describing your error, you attach a negative label to yourself. "I'm a loser." When someone else's behaviour rubs you the wrong way, you attach a negative label to him: "He's a goddamn louse." Mislabelling involves describing an event with language that is highly coloured and emotionally loaded.

- **Personalization:** You see yourself as the cause of some negative external event, which in fact you were not primarily responsible for.

(Burns 1980: 42–43)

Note: The above were originally designed to identify "self-defeating" patterns that can lead to depression. Because of this, they all read from a negative point of view. Here we use them not as a diagnosis of self-defeating patterns but simply as a way to note distortion habits that take us out of the agreed task. Because of this, you could turn most of these around to more positive language and they would still be distortions. For our purposes, and in the case of performance practice, it is just as important to note and return to the present even if it takes you away from positive thinking. We can use positive thinking to distort also. For instance, if you win a vocal competition and decide then that you are better than all around you and deserve special attention and decide now to show up late and disrespect your colleagues, well, this seems like a case of *Magnification.* Likewise, if at an audition someone comments on how much you touched them and cries with sincerity at your monologue but also mentions that you are a little short for the role and you then quit your day job thinking you have won them over and will get the part, this could be a case of *Jumping to Conclusions* or *Filtering.*

Step 2. When you are doing a task next and find that you are coming from your thoughts rather than your awareness, consider which of these distortions to note; witness "Isn't that interesting, I am ***labelling***", "Isn't that interesting, for the last fifteen minutes I have been using a lot of ***should statements***".

Step 3. Witness what effects the distortion has had on your felt sense of your body; are you holding tension in your mouth, for instance? Does your forehead feel tight? Are you breathing from a higher place in your torso? Could your face soften?

Step 4. Breathe and return directly to your awareness (which is non-verbal). Continue to do the chosen task from your awareness.

Let it go — Let it go — Let it go

With Ex. 3, *Drawing your body*, we begin to notice some of the less verbal or articulate aspects of our felt sense within our body. With the *Cognitive distortions*, Ex. 4, we can make conscious the patterns of behaviour that are also in the body but can be recognized in more verbal or articulate models. Both are there to help make the invisible more visible so that we can distinguish between what we want to integrate into the chosen task and what is superfluous. What do we do when this kind of stuff arises and becomes company in our work? The next exercise is a little tool to help release these as they arise and before they become "sticky", meaning before they create narratives that lie outside the task at hand, feelings that might take us out of awareness, or habits that might muddy our task. "Let it go — Let it go — Let it go" is a tool that helps to release the aspects of self that can take us down paths that lead us away from the moment, disintegrating self, which in turn will take us out of the agreed task. This is a tool that you can use as you work when you sense a little whiff of your stuff. It is also helpful language that can be used by a facilitator (e.g., teacher/director) while working to assist artists toward returning to the task at hand after the previous concepts of this chapter have been taken in.

Exercise #5

Let it go — Let it go — Let it go

Preparation: This exercise takes no preparation. It can be done anywhere. It can be done with the below as a sort of inner monologue, and it can also be facilitated.

Step 1. Read the below (or have someone read it to you), giving time between ideas to witness what is here in the now and then release it.

The moment that just transpired is now ... gone.
...the last breath you took...gone...it is now the past...
...your feeling about that now is past... gone... there will never be that again.
...Gone. That moment....gone.
...let that feeling you are having now go....
...that "trying to get it" ... gone...
that indefinable thing ... gone ... Let it go.
The beginning of that thought ... Gone.
The act of noticing ... gone ...
that...gone.
The feeling in your body is now of the last moment ... the next will come ... gone... let it go
... the words you just read, gone. You will never be the you that read them like that again...that you ... gone ... let it go ...and it ... let it go.
Each moment is different.
Interesting idea?... idea...Gone...
...that moment of reading the words and the way your brain fires when you see something for the first time: gone ... gone ...let it go ...
...the visions that you are seeing, gone.
...that breath, gone.
Let it go.
...whatever is now, let that go, gone.
This moment. That moment. Let it go....

Let every moment go and allow yourself to live in the flow of the presence.
...and that gone too.
...let it go.
Let it go — let that go — let it go.
Let it go — let it go — let it go.

Step 2. Stop reading, you get the idea ... For a few moments put down the book and play with letting it go. No need to go fast, try this at a gentle sort of walking pace. Witness what is with you, in you, outside, and around you; what you see; what you feel; what you think; your felt senses. Witness and let it go, over and over...

Step 3. Now play with letting it go before you can even label or settle on what "it" is. Let the act of constant letting go become the energetic dance ... and from moment to moment, without letting anything stick, let feelings, thoughts, the beginnings of feelings, the beginnings of thoughts go, let that go, let that go, let it go.

Step 4. To end: Breathe; bring your awareness to your body, your breath; gently stretch and notice your felt sense; witness any thoughts and breath.

Tip: What many find when doing this is that what is left is simply awareness. No stuff, no company, no narratives, and no comfortable habits. It can be weird. It can also be a wonderful way of experiencing living in the flow of presence. A "crispy" non-trancelike presence, active, not passive. This is a helpful tool to reorganize an integrative self toward the task at hand, and a wonderful release of superfluous tensions/thoughts/habits/energy. The script can be modified to suit the room, the situation, or the artists' patterns; however, the basis is about the dance of letting go, not any particular aesthetic.

Exercise #6

I am, I want, I need, I feel

This exercise, developed by Eric Morris and found in his book *No Acting Please*, has been a part of my tool kit as a performer and a teacher for over twenty years. I quote it here and also offer some variations that help to make it more a part of an integrative practice tool. Read this entire exercise, original and possible variations, before deciding how you wish to proceed. In my experience, explaining this while moving through the space is best. When I teach it I start it by walking and speaking clearly,

"I Am____, I Want_____, I Need _____, I Feel ____" (repeated over and over with new inserts each time). I encourage students to do this while also taking the space, as this invites a bold and immediate response from the practitioner. If we start too quiet and still, the tendency seems to be a cerebral and guarded response rather than one immediately responsive to the impulses that may arise.

Original exercise from *No Acting Please*

This is done aloud in a stream-of-consciousness fashion, but very rapidly, so that you don't have a chance to reflect on or to premeditate what you say. The purpose is to surprise yourself with what comes out. Start every sentence with one of the four statements, not necessarily in that order. For example: I want to do this exercise ... I am tense ... I need to be good ... I need to be seen ... I feel self-conscious ... I feel my fingers ... I need money ... I am what I am ... I feel foolish ... I want to laugh ... I am laughing ... I need love ... I want to know what I want ... I feel full ... I need space ... I am running out of things ... I am looking at the floor ... ! The exercise is purposefully designed to channel your impulses into the format of "I Am, I Want, I Need, I Feel." When you respond to the specific line of self-questioning, your awareness of the moment-to-moment realities becomes clearer. The important element is the impulsiveness of your response. If you take a beat to think about the response, you might just be filling the blank with your conditioned thought rather than your real feeling. It is important to remember that if you go blank, say the first thing that comes to your mind no matter how illogical or nonsensical it may seem. You may repeat "I Am____, I Want_____, I Need _____, I Feel ____" many times, but encourage yourself to go back and forth between four statements.

(Morris 1979: 28)

Possible variations:

- Following the above, this structure can be further developed by letting the words that follow the "I Am____, I Want_____, I Need _____, I Feel ____" be replaced by sound and movement. Much of what we are, want, need, and feel is beyond words and can be expressed in spontaneous sound and movement.
- This can be done with an entire class working at the same time, allowing a certain sense of anonymity. It can get noisy, but the group dynamic can also be encouraging.
- This is also a great exercise to do individually in private in preparation for practice.
- This can be done as a solo with an audience as an advanced exercise for learning how to be "private in public".

MEETING IN THE MIDDLE

Meeting in the Middle is something you can do with a partner, in groups, and also with a task. It is a way of finding and exploring the contact point between you and another element within your task. We will learn it in relation to a partner. I first developed this exercise twenty years ago in Melbourne with a group I put together called the Mercurious Ensemble, experimenting with performance practices as part of devised work.

Meeting in the middle becomes increasingly important as you wish to expand your witnessing beyond the self. It will become an invaluable tool for creating safety and greater awareness when we work with others, especially while doing catches and assisted leaps in Chapter Five. It is also key to ensemble work and devising practices in that it reconfigures the field of awareness to include a workable contact point that will allow for the integrity of a performer while engaging with any other element within the chosen domain of the task. One can meet in the middle with another artist, a prop, a part of scenery, or a piece of technical equipment when working in multi-media performance. It is a way of operating with whatever is at this moment considered "other", making it/them a partner.

In the following exercise we deal with something akin to an aura-like energy field, and it can be tricky; however, it is not a concept used without precedent. We will work with an intangible quality that we carry beyond our physical body that creates a kind of personal energetic kinesphere. It is something often experienced as a felt sense, in this case emanating from self and in relation to other. The idea of working with fields of awareness that lie outside the realm of the measurable and physical is not new in the performing arts. Michael Chekhov spoke of radiation (Gordon 1987: 181) and this exercise was developed as an organic extension of what is commonly taught as Stanislavsky's "Circle of Attention", the origin of which is briefly documented as "creative circle" by Mel Gordon (Gordon 1987: 62). However, the creative circle or circle of attention exercise worked with the performer creating an energetic awareness of attention as a circle about three foot in circumference around the actor's self, then extending it out to the entire stage/room, out to the town, continent, planet, and back again to self. *Meeting in the Middle* evolved by manipulating the field of attention in relation to *another*: exploring the *crossover* of *contact*; finding a point of Meeting in the Middle; and cultivating a common contact of awareness that includes other and self.

Exercise #7
Meeting in the Middle

Preparation: Both participants will have centred themselves through Ex. 10, *Three-part breath*, and have a practised understanding of what it means to come from awareness as opposed to focus. This is in many ways an advanced awareness exercise. It is helpful if the practitioners know how to witness their *stuff* and *company*, as explained earlier in this chapter, and have done Ex. 5, *Let it go*.

Requirements: Two people, standing facing each other with about two and a half feet between.

Step 1. As you stand and face your partner, witness any felt senses you may have in your own body, notice and release any "stories" or cognitive distortions. Let these go. This is about just being in the here and now, seeing and being and breathing while standing in front of one another with awareness of self and self with other. At this stage no verbal or gestural reflection is required or even helpful.

Aside: Often when students first stand and face each other there can be giggles, some discomfort in being seen and seeing, witnessing and being witnessed. It is not uncommon for verbal comments, movement, shaking out of tensions, or tightening in some idea of "focus" to spring out initially. Witness these. "Isn't that interesting". This is all "company". However, in this we are aiming not to "comment", judge or diagnose our experience but rather to let this moment be. The wish to create a narrative can be strong; however, this is not what this particular task is about.

Step 2. As you stand in front of your partner, imagine a subtle plumb line smack in the middle between you. Do you meet there? Does your energy extend beyond the line more toward their person? Does it stop before the line closer to your own front body?

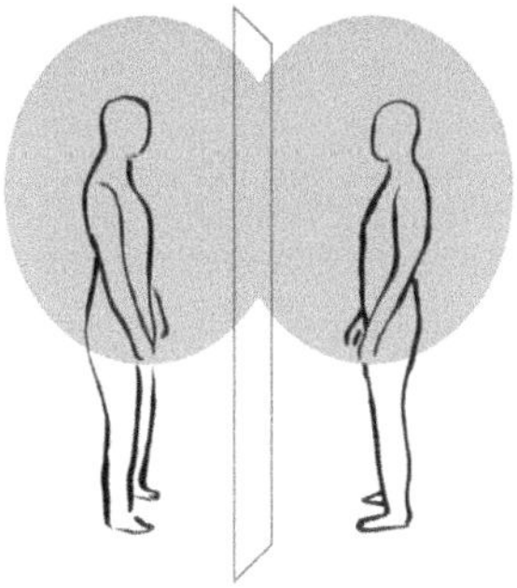

Tip: If there is a third person or a facilitator in the room, they can slowly sweep their hand across the space directly in the middle of the two bodies, to help the participants to orient their observations in relation to the middle.

Aside: We all meet challenges, things, people, and tasks differently. As we learned in Chapter One, this can be cultural-, gender-, and/or family-based. It is also changeable in different environments and in relation to different stimuli and, importantly, possible to shift. As a generalization, those who have learned that "getting on top of it", "taking charge" and "covering all bases" is the most effective way to engage with a task might find they gravitate to a place in front of the middle line. Conversely, those who have learned that being "polite", "cautious" or "waiting" is the most effective way to engage might find their energy stays closer to their own body and behind the middle line. Of course, these are generalizations, and there are as many reasons for one as for the other.

Step 3. While breathing and witnessing self and other, work to "meet in the middle". At first it is common for the two to miss each other, with either little overlaps (both overshooting each other) or with gaps. One way to think of it is as playing with expanding and contracting your own energy field. Having a third person witnessing can help to make this clearer. It is invisible but strangely very apparent. You may wish to have little discussions about where you sense the other is, using a hand to cut the air and using as few words as possible. Give this some time and notice, rather than judge and diagnose. When two finally meet in the middle many feel a little "jolt"; some can experience it as a really quiet and peaceful union. Have fun with this.

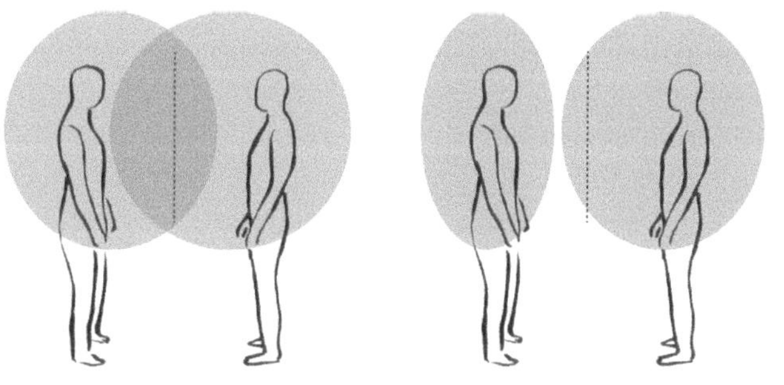

(Stopping at Step 3 the first time through this exercise can often be enough. Once this becomes clearer, progress to step 4.)

Advanced or Step 4. As a next step, we will play with expanding and contracting your own energy field to the middle line and other lines of your own choosing. Both partners can play, one at a time, with shifting the line. While the first partner aims to keep their line in the middle, the second will experiment with bringing their energy way forward (three inches in front of the partner's face) and then bringing it back (three inches from their own face). Both will witness what this experience feels like. As the one shifting you may ask: Where am I more "comfortable"? Do I have any accompanying tensions I can release? How does each position (front of line/behind line) affect the quality of my awareness? Where do I feel more connected, safe, present? As the person who is holding the middle line, you may ask yourself similar questions in relation to what it is like to be "passed through" and engaged with at the different positions.

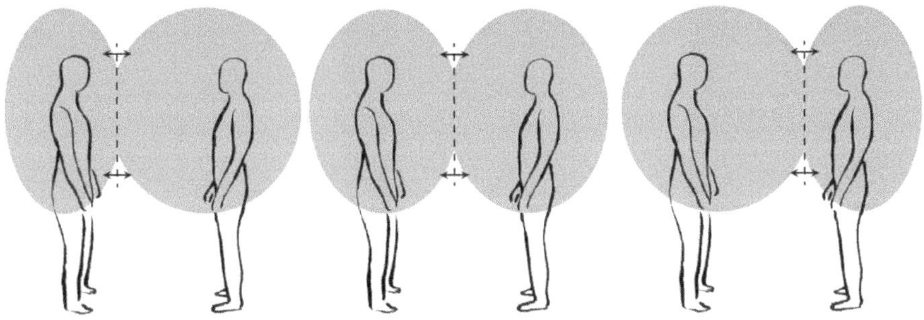

Uses and variations: You can Meet in the Middle with a challenging task, meaning not pushing it or engaging with too forward an energy, or leaning back and waiting for it to give to engage. Meeting in the Middle is an energetic concept that manifests in the entire self.

You can Meet in the Middle with more than one person; it is very effective as a way to help ensemble groups to coordinate movement in unison. It can also help to create an optimal improvisation environment where the acknowledging and taking forward of ideas/movement and sound can happen in such a way that the core of the impulse does not get overshadowed or hijacked by individual impulse but remains and grows as a collective.

Meeting in the Middle is a wonderful tool for working in dance, physical theatre, or circus, where much partner work can be dangerous if there is not a subtle yet acute awareness of the other's body in balance and motion.

CONSCIOUS PRACTICE

All the concepts and exercises in this chapter are designed to offer a tool kit towards working mindfully and in a way that puts the practitioner and their practice at the centre of their work. In short, it has been about the *way*, the active aesthetic. In this chapter we have learned about witnessing, awareness, felt sense, cognitive distortions, the company we keep, the noble struggle, and meeting in the middle.

In Part III we will learn many tools that will show *what* to do to engage an integrative physical/physiological and emotional centre that makes the most economical use of the integrated breath/body, making it possible to sound, emote, and move at the same time without compromise to a chosen aesthetic or production requirement. However, before we learn *what* to do, it is crucial to establish the *way* to work. It is through the *way* that we really integrate the instrument/self within any task. It is through the *way* of doing that we begin to take responsibility for our practice and be able to respond to the requirements of our practice as we are increasingly asked to work in expanding styles of direction or choreography, uses of emerging technologies, within different renderings of texts and among varying hybrid disciplinary configurations.

If you recall, earlier we noted that "There is no such thing as not doing", and further, that *whatever you do, you get good at*. If we practise unconsciously singing scales, doing hours of physical repetition, or learning lines by rote, who is working — thoughts, feelings, or awareness? Are we doing the exercise, or is the exercise doing us? Who or what is making the choices? What is being learned, conditioned, or practised in?

> **The easy beautiful**
> The difficult must become habit, habit easy, and the easy beautiful.
> Attributed to Prince Sergei Volinski (Moore 1984: 2)

A good way to keep track of your practice(s) can be found in the *Conscious Practice Journal*. This tool will help you to stay accountable and in doing so help you in the journey of taking in new skills; it also helps you to evidence and reflect on the actual effects of your time in practice. It can be a good "temperature taker" in working out whether you really understand the function of that exercise that your teacher/facilitator or perhaps this book has been asking you to do. It's surprising how often we do what we are told and do not really understand what we are doing when we work alone. Doing a task, over and over, hoping that inspiration will arrive out of the blue, is both frustrating and, arguably, irresponsible. The Conscious Practice Journal puts you at the centre of your work; it's about the integrity of you, the practitioner, taking responsibility within the field of performing which is the alchemy of your own art in the making.

WORKING WITH THE CONSCIOUS PRACTICE JOURNAL

This is not so much an exercise, but rather a meta-exercise. It will hold all the exercises that have been introduced and all yet to come. The explanation to follow, however, is written in the style of the exercises for consistency.

Preparation to work: Create your space for practice and carve out a dedicated amount of time to work. Turn off all phones, computers, and anything that might distract you from your tasks. Wear clothing that is dedicated to your practice (no street clothes or ornamental jewelry). Some find it is helpful to create a ceremony by lighting a candle, using scents, or simply walking around the space clockwise before you begin and then again counter-clockwise when you finish. Ceremony can help to mark this space and this time for this practice.

Diagram: Below is a sample diagram of how you might map your practice. You can fill it out in any way that speaks to you. You may have only one task for the session or you may have ten; regardless, you will always have the first step "Objective for the session", the steps following the set tasks titled "Reflection on today's practice", and "Thoughts for next session".

Objective for the session:		
Task	Intention	What am I witnessing?
Reflection on today's practice:		
Thoughts for next session:		

Step 1. After preparing yourself and your space to work, scan your body, witnessing (rather than judging or diagnosing) any sensations. Notice any tensions and draw your awareness to them; breathe, and allow any changes to occur. Notice any thought patterns or positioning that may be occurring; attend to these by simply drawing your awareness to any felt sense that accompanies them. Allow any changes to occur. Shift between these for a few moments and take a soft touch inventory of what may be accompanying you in your work today. Accept this in readiness to begin.

Step 2. Planning the session (a+b+c)

a. You will start by looking at the bottom of the chart from the day before in the section, "Thoughts for next session". You might find that you coached yourself towards a better quality of working, such as: "In practice today I was obsessing about how the director did not give me good feedback, I found myself working in focus rather than awareness with thoughts intervening in each task. Tomorrow I will start with a Vipassana walking meditation, before moving directly into the monologue/step sequence/aria — I will then practise witnessing my cognitive distortions and practise letting them go before moving on to bigger challenges". You might find that you noticed a particular challenge in the scope of the work, such as a musical phrase, a challenging step, or the dropping of character at a certain section of text, and made a suggestion to yourself about the logistics of the session: "After warm-up start in section _____ instead of the beginning. I seem to be losing awareness and practising in unwanted stuff in this section. Work from point _____: at the start". Look at whatever you wrote and take note of it as you work out what your tasks are for the day.

b. Objective for the session. Here you decide what this session is about, what you wish to achieve. Your notes in "Thoughts for next session" will help to remind you of your last session. You can then choose to build from there or go in another direction. (You may have had a lesson or rehearsal that solved the last session's problem and you may be onto another area.) It is important NOT to be general in this section or the next. Your objective will not be "to practise for two hours". What are you practising towards? Give yourself an objective, a way of doing, not a what to do. Make it active, not passive. Toward what purpose are you practising at this time, now? To work on your awareness in action? To explore the way the character's physical being might respond to the new choices of action that the director gave last night? To isolate your iliopsoas so that your leap to the right is even with your left leap in the pas de deux? To work through the cadenza so that you don't glitch on the passagio on the way up after that octave leap? Each of these objectives would have at least four very specific tasks aligned to them.
c. Decide on your tasks and their intentions. You can either plan all your tasks in advance or go from task to task as you notice what is needed. (If you plan your tasks in advance you may need to deviate briefly to accommodate things that might arise.) Here you set your task and then its intention. These are very different things and it is in their very difference that you will find the key to what "conscious" is in this practice. For instance, a task "to sing through my vocal range in arpeggios" is fine, but unless we are more specific, we are in danger of having the exercise do us. What do you want the doing to be when you sing through these arpeggios? The possibilities are endless; one can sing through the range in arpeggios to stay connected to breath throughout, or to work on the break between f-c in preparation for the melismatic passage in the aria, or to align the higher harmonics with the notes toward the bottom of the range. Likewise, barre work and sensory work will also have very specific reasons attached, based on what the objective is for this practice. We work with purpose, witnessing and aware of the doing of the doing: the intention of the task towards the objective of the session.

> **Be specific!**
> Generality is the enemy of all art!
> Attributed to Konstantin Stanislavsky

Step 3. "*What am I witnessing?*" and "*Thoughts for next session*" work in similar ways, the only difference being that the former is more immediate and will help you practise critical yet helpful reflection in the flow of your process. It can also help you make decisions about what you might do as a next task. So if your first task was to do "sensory work" towards the intention to "make more real for yourself the person you are speaking to in the monologue" in preparation for your audition today, and you find that you are noticing "at one part I lose complete belief in my action and stop owning the lines and it is making me tense", then you witness and write what is happening, your felt sense and any of your cognitive stuff that may be present. Your writing this might shift something for you; or you may decide that a relaxation exercise with the intent "to shift your felt sense and connect to your awareness" might work best next; or you might decide that you need more energy in the work and that doing the "I am, I want, I need, I feel" exercise with the intent "to both warm-up and get more present with what is available to me now" is best. "What am I witnessing?" helps you to reflect and also make choices about the way you will work towards the objective of your session, taking into account the state of yourself in the moment.

> **Details!**
> God is in the details.
> Attributed to Ludwig Mies van der Rohe

Step 4. To end, reflect on the entire session by witnessing (remember, not judging or diagnosing) what happened in this session in relation to your objective. Make helpful suggestions for your next session. Then reverse any ceremony you may have had to start mindfully, ending this practice before you enter into your everyday life.

Terms we have learned that will be taken forward into Part III are:

- Task
- Witnessing
- Awareness
- Felt sense
- Cognitive patternings
- Company
- Noble struggle
- Meeting in the middle
- Conscious practice

PART III

Integrative Performance Practice

Chapter 5

Working from the integrative centre

IN PART III WE WILL LEARN THE FUNDAMENTALS of the integrative breath-body, capable of sounding, moving and acting — even in the most emotional roles, complex choreography, and virtuosic singing — without compromise of either expression or technical exactitude. Some of the exercises may seem familiar on the surface, but it is most important that you read the detail and resist any habitual patternings and overlaying of past trainings. Stay curious about the differences in this work. As is true with the learning of any new practice, bringing former approaches into the new work without fully understanding the differences between the old and the new can muddy the effectiveness of the new opportunity. It is helpful to recognize former assumptions and habits as part of your *stuff*, as defined in Part II. This may mean we need to *witness* and acknowledge past trainings that have worked within our respective discipline(s), but *note* (a term first learned in Ex. 2, Vipassana walking meditation) when former experiences become *company*. There will be familiar terms and perhaps even familiar requests for movement, but in this practice the task, the doing of the doing, will be most specific.

Part II offered a clear way of practising that will help make the rest of the content within this book effective. In the spirit of all the work in Part II, go forward with a sense of curiosity, compassion for yourself, and an unwavering commitment to return to the doing of the doing. We will start with the most mystifying yet important element present within all the discipline(s) of acting, singing, and dance: that of centre.

A sense of centre is fundamental for the performer and is a central part of all acting, dance, and singing techniques. What is meant by centre is not practised or articulated in the same way across the disciplines, or even within disciplines, and as a result can be confusing in its ambiguity. Good news: in this practice, the centre is exact! In this work you will learn to use one exact centre for the explicit reason that the key to the effectiveness of this practice is that the integration of everything — your breath, all physical movement, and all emotive action — initiates from and connects to one centre. Centre in this work is at the perineum, which resides at the bottom of the pelvic floor between the anus and the genitals.

With each new task you will return to the perineum; with each inhale and exhale you will connect with the bottom of the pelvic floor; and with each movement you will move from this centre. This will both happen as a point of awareness and have beneficial psychophysical and physiological implications for those wishing to integrate their dancing, singing, and acting self. This will prove key. We will learn that in the IPP centre is a physical and emotional integrator of your instrument. We will strengthen muscles that support the use of this centre and learn how to release muscles that keep us from accessing it. We will learn to sound and move and act, as one, from one centre.

Many of us will need some training and practice to get closer to centre. Many of us have practised in a sense of centre that is slightly higher, engendering certain tensions unconducive to the exacting use of the breath-body in full motion. The first exercises in the chapter will help to isolate and activate centre, which will assure the integration of your emotive breath-body. Before going into detail about how to work with the exact perineal centring, the next section aims to demystify what can be a confusing subject. Let's examine how this centre may contrast with other notions of centre that you may have come across.

CENTRE, WHICH CENTRE?

If you have been practising dance, voice, or acting it is very likely that you will have come across ways of using some idea of centre. You may have even been taught the importance of using centre to balance, coordinate, and increase flexibility and breath control in the body. You may have experienced the way a centre can encourage a sense of calm and readiness. Perhaps centre was referred to as the core, point of centre, or centre of gravity. You may have been asked to engage your centre, move from centre, go to centre, or just get centred.

Centre is not new. It has long been recognized in the East as part of ancient practices in various meditation, chant, dance, and fighting forms. In Butoh, a traditional dance-mime form from Japan, a "power centre…could be imagined as a ball of steel in the centre of an [sic] triangle whose apex is the anus and whose other two angles are the corners of the pelvis at the level of the navel" (Azuma in Barba 2006: 40). In Kathakali, the highly stylized Indian dance-drama, centre is at the "root of the Navel" or *Nabhi Mula* (Zarrilli 2000: 93).

In the East, since there is no philosophical or practical tradition of a mind–body split, centres are about a sort of *dance of energy* as released through the breath-body, promoting a harnessing and readiness, poised and in flow. This "energy" is known throughout the East as Ki (Korea), Chi (China), Qi (Japan), and Prana or Pranavayu (India).

To varying degrees and in different guises, this notion of centre has been adopted and adapted by Western practices.

In somatic approaches to Western mind-body centring or mind-body integration, notably within the work of Irmgard Bartenieff and Bonnie Bainbridge Cohen, centre is seen as having primal roots connected to the embryonic experience. In this type of work the site of centre tends to revolve around the navel. Hackney, writing about the Bartenieff Fundamentals, speaks of "Core-Distal Connectivity" (which is a similar concept to Bainbridge Cohen's "Navel Rotation"). Hackney states: "The pattern of Core-Distal Connectivity is a comforting reminder of primal beginnings within your mother's womb, when the life support system poured directly into your body at your centre. Your navel is but a residual scar of separation from this lifeline of the umbilical cord… 'Core Support' for limb-torso connections is available to us expressly because those internal body connections have already been explored and strengthened in actual movement while in utero" (Hackney 2000: 69). Erkert explains Bainbridge Cohen's similar "Navel Rotation" through this visual: "Picture a starfish and imagine taking all food, all sustenance, through the belly button… There are six limbs all connected to this core: the head, tail, arms, and legs" (Erkert 2003: 46). Both of these practices have in common the idea of the navel or belly button being centre. For our purposes, a focus on the navel has a tendency to engage the short muscles in the abdominal wall, which will get in the way of diaphragmatic movement and impede the type of breath that is needed when voicing and engaging in extensive movement at the same time. Sustained sound will tend to jiggle or glitch in line with jumps and bends.

In treatises on acting we find that centre can be described in various ways. It can be "located in the middle of the belly" where "The natural progression of the breath goes freely from the middle of the belly outward to the periphery in all directions" (Lugering 2007: 49). The breath centre can reside "deep within the body, in an area roughly three finger-widths below your navel" (Benedetti 1997: 19) and also in "the region two to three inches below the navel" (Zarilli 2009: 26). Again, you will notice that all these are quite a bit higher than the perineal centre.

Voice trainings can be similar to acting trainings in the articulation of the placement of centre, but with a focus in service of "breath support". Sometimes the East is invoked, especially where it is perceived that these traditions "link personal strength and acceptance to a physical focus centre in the lower body…placed one and a half inches (or the three middle finger-widths) below the navel, and one and a half inches (4cm) inward toward the spine" (Shewell 2008: 265). Kayes beautifully articulates a largely received understanding of how breath action works around this centre through the imagery of a "diamond of support" in which the top is the sternum, the bottom the "pubic arch" and centre the navel (Kayes 2004: 33–34), and asks that you "make sure you are moving the centre of the belly towards the backbone when you make the sound and that you are able to recoil at the end of phrases" (Kayes 2004: 124). We will learn that with the IPP such movement will *happen* but is not a *task*. It is not something we *do*. This is because the drawing in of the stomach can create tensions in the abdomen that will create glitches in the sound and loss of harmonics during extended movement. The perineal centre will allow more flexibility in the intercostals (lower ribs) and the sternum (chest plate) while in full motion without impeding the diaphragm, whereas a drawing in of the navel will not. Any movement of the stomach towards the back body on the exhale will be the symptom of and come after an upward-moving action of the perineum. In this work we do not move or draw the abdomen anywhere. Also, we do not think of breath in terms of *breath support*. Since singers tend to learn to sing while standing, an "architecture of support" is often *built* in this position only. There can be a tendency to *protect* this support while in motion, creating tension. Instead, we will learn a *dynamic alignment* that is directly supported through the perineal contraction.

In dance, Erkert points out that a class is often "a ritual that hunts for the ever-elusive centre, and the dance teacher builds a maze to support the search" (Ekert 2003: 44). The centre in the IPP, while closer to the low point of centre in modern dance, is still lower than often taught. For instance, in Martha Graham's technique the contraction part of the contraction/release sequence becomes the dynamic through which centre is established. This is often taught as a movement stemming from the feeling of being punched in the lower belly, or from the percussive exhale that happens in a laugh or a scream, resulting in a "natural" curvature of the spine with a hollowing of the lower belly. This, however, will still be too high for the integrative practitioner, as this approach presents difficulties for sounding due to some of the abdominal tension that can again impede the diaphragm when moving from this understanding. This is not to say that dancing ballet and modern dance or even acrobatic work while singing is impossible; in fact it is more than possible. The approach to movement, however, will be slightly different.

Similarly, with Pilates, which many modern dancers use to condition, there is a "scooping" of the lower belly or drawing of the "navel towards the spine" (Siler 2000: 20). Although with good training this is not considered the same as "sucking in your tummy", even done correctly this creates difficulties in the complete release needed of the pelvic floor on the intake.

Eric Hawkins' dance technique presents a practice of centre that can be perceived as lower than that of Graham. In his work, movement starts by "initiating and controlling movement from the body's pelvic centre of gravity; swinging the legs from high in the hip socket to activate lightness and freedom finding the body's midline through the spine's four curves — cervical, thoracic, lumbar and sacral" (Stern 2007). For an excellent articulation of this type of centre Eric Franklin's book *Pelvic Power, Mind/body Exercises for Strength, Flexibility, Posture, and Balance* is really helpful.

We have taken a little journey through the different ways in which performing practices currently consider centre. At least one of them is likely to be familiar, and if you are an interdisciplinary practitioner it is likely that more than one is familiar to you. It can be confusing, and can also sometimes feel like the places that you are being asked to access are somewhat vague. Here, we will work from one centre that integrates not only your mind-body but your acting, dancing, and voicing self. Interestingly, this approach tends to work in concert with the approaches described above; it's just a little more specific, and starts the action of centre a little sooner in the doing of the task.

THE POWER OF THE PERINEUM

The perineum sits at the bottom of the pelvic floor between the genitals and the anus.

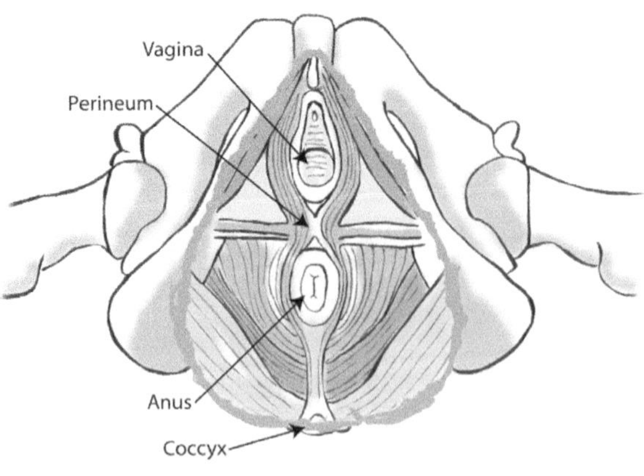

In this work, the perineum is the centre: the place from which we initiate all movement and the place that we directly connect to with each inhale and each exhale. We literally return to centre at every breath in this work, with a slight perineal contraction in an upward direction on the exhale (or when voicing).

When first learning this, it can be a challenge to isolate the exact location of the perineum. It is important that this contraction is not too far forward (as in the sensation of trying not to pee) and not too far back (as with an anal contraction). It's in the middle, the centre of the pelvic floor. Also important is that this action of contracting upward is not confused with a lock or simple tightening of the pelvic floor. Rather, what you will be working towards is a drawing up of the perineum as if creating a plumb line through the centre of the body up and out through the top of the head. This up and out is KEY!

When working from the perineum is done correctly it will allow an exact engagement with the iliopsoas muscle system (which we will speak about in detail shortly), allowing the release of superfluous tensions in an economical use of the skeletal, muscular, and fascial systems in the act of moving and voicing. This action will engage the long muscles in the abdomen while allowing the shorter muscles that can impede diaphragmatic movement to remain flexible. This engaging of the long muscles will lengthen the torso and encourage a lengthening of the neck. You will find that this lengthening will be key in maintaining the integrity of vocal tone in physical positions that bend the torso. The feeling will be that of support, length and lightness, with at the same time a sense of groundedness.

A perineal contraction may be something you are familiar with, as it is often used by dancers, especially while being lifted. It will help to create more height and also make the person being lifted feel lighter. For yoga practitioners who have practised Moola Bandha (root lock), this is very similar; however, in this practice this is not a lock but a drawing upward. Moola Bandha is the practice of stimulating the perineum, which corresponds directly to the root chakra in the yogic tradition. (We will discuss the perineal contraction and yoga practice in more detail in the next segment on chakras.)

In this work we observe an initiation from the perineum as centre. When centre is sited at or below the navel, as previously discussed, especially in somatic practices, it is often considered as a source for connecting to a centre, aligned with an *embryonic*, *womb*-related *primal* experience. This does not work well for the integrative performance practitioner, who requires a centre that does not track directly to a personal narrative, but rather needs to operate from a place where witnessing the self in and of the world in a non-trancelike way is essential.

Connecting to the root chakra via the perineum might be what it means to work as an adult; it might be what it means to take responsibility for your practice rather than relying on what can present as "comfortable" (see page 74). Regardless, what has been discovered in the years that this work has been in development is that in order to work in a truly integrative way, sounding, moving, and acting as one, initiating with awareness from a lower place is crucial. This is not to say that the riches of the navel (with all the corresponding implications) are not to be accessed; they are essential, but are engaged as a *symptom* of the perineal contraction, supported as an integral part of your practice. The event of the practice here is just larger.

EXPLORING THE METAPHOR OF THE CHAKRA

In this work we will use the chakras as a way of exploring aspects of our experience as it aligns with the body. We will use it as a metaphor. Empirical academic rigour regarding chakras as a way of "measuring" the experience of the body is not the aim here, but rather an understanding of received thinking around this powerful aspect of Eastern practice, which has often been invoked and woven into the various vocabularies of performance disciplines as a way of measuring and engaging with the more subtle aspects of our creative, experiential system.

The most widely used chakra system in the West is the same one familiar to yoga practitioners. It comes from the Hindu tradition. There are, however, other traditions, such as the African shamanic tradition, that of traditional Chinese medicine, and the Tantric chakra model, in addition to Egyptian, Tibetan, Incan, and Cherokee systems. (For a more complete comparison of the traditions of "chakraology" and a more involved look at scientific research in this area, Cyndi Dale's book *The Subtle Body, An Encyclopedia of Your Energetic Anatomy* is a good place to start.) The Hindu tradition claims anywhere between four to twelve chakras, but the most modern derivative of the chakra system outlines seven chakras. Chakras are as old as humanity, and the term translates from Sanskrit as "wheels of energy" or "wheels of light". In the Hindu tradition, they correspond to the endocrine system and intersect with the main branches of the nervous system.

The system of chakras speaks not only to places in the body, but to experience, energy, our thoughts, our feelings, our spiritual experience; in short, the phenomenon of being in and of the world as an energetic being. When speaking about chakras, we are not just speaking about anatomical aspects of the human form but exploring an understanding of the flow and awareness of the more subtle and often esoteric aspects of our energetic system.

The diagram offers a summary of information collated from a plethora of sources over the years. Information on the chakras and their corresponding attributes are not hard to find; however, what is shown here is some of the information that has proven helpful to the performer during the twenty-some years I have been developing this practice. It is not so much meant to be referred to as an authority, telling you who you are or what you are doing, but rather to serve as an accompaniment to your instincts and observations about your *company* and your strengths as you explore and notice how you respond to various tasks within your practice.

It is often interesting for artists to discover that there is a connection between the Manipura Chakra, located in the solar plexus — where the diaphragm sits — and our sense of self and our ego. We do tend to hold our breath and block this chakra when at our most insecure about how self may be encountered. Singers often find it liberating to discover that the Vishuddha or throat chakra is related to the right to speak, self-expression, and creativity. The Svadhisthana Chakra, located between the genitals and the lower abdomen, is a seat of emotions and a great gateway for flow and movement. The perineal centre is situated in the first or root chakra, the Mulahara Chakra. It is basic and tribal; it deals with safety and fear, belonging and self-preservation; it connects to the adrenals and is a major integrator or disintegrator of your entire system. This is but one reason why, in this work, we return to it at each and every breath, and why it is where we determine centre to be.

In yogic practices the contraction of this root chakra is called Moola Bandha, and is known for its profound benefits, which transfer quite nicely to the performer.

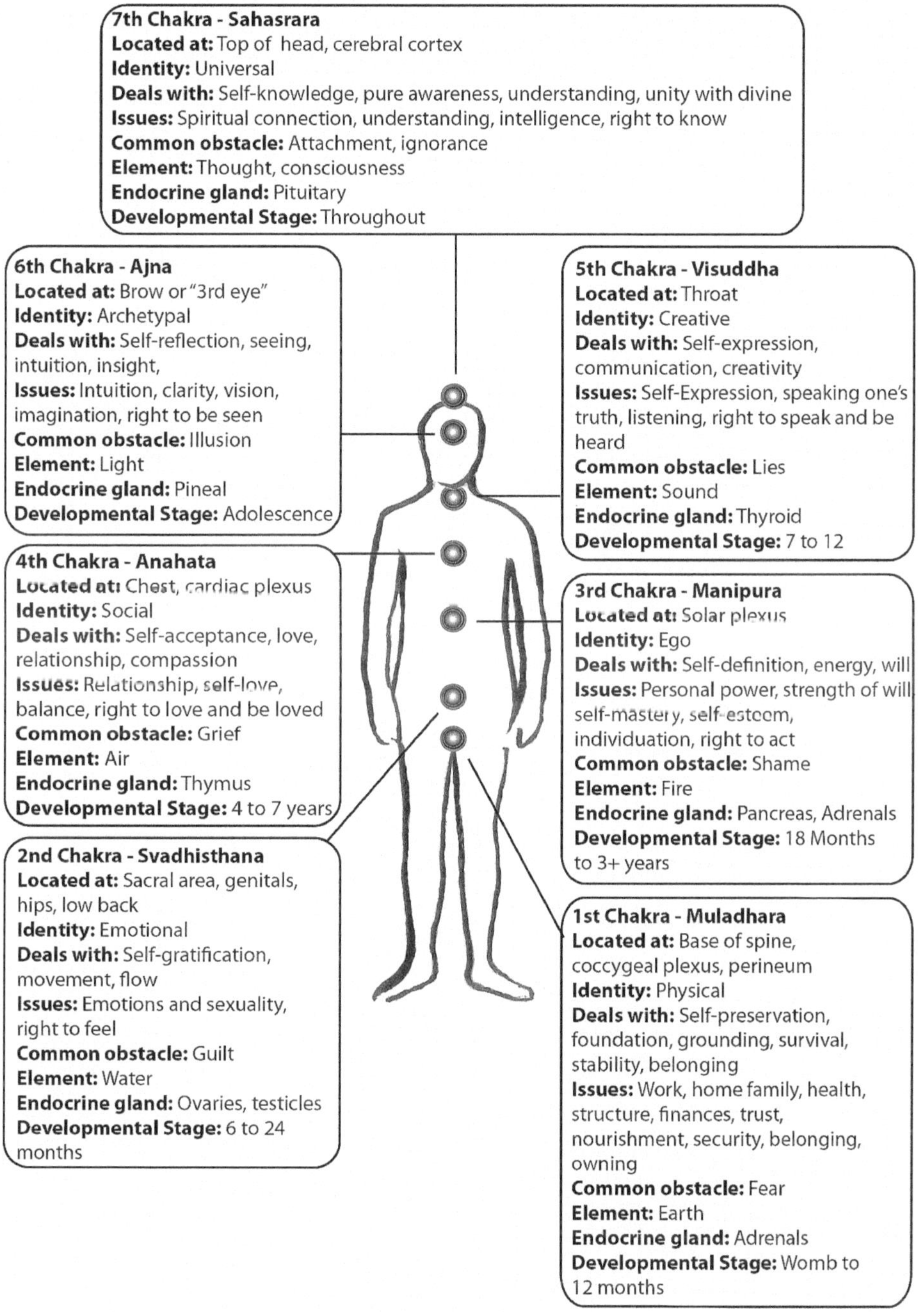

Bandha translates as *lock*, but in action it is more like a contraction, not a stuck action. The practice of this bandha is known to regulate nerves, calm the mind, connect one to their entire breath-body, and both ground and lighten. This happens by the stimulation of the parasympathetic nervous system, working together with the endocrine system.

Swami Buddhananda explains the profound effects of the perineal contraction known as Moola Bandha. It "stimulates both the sensory-motor and the autonomic nervous systems in the pelvic region. When Moola Bandha is performed, stimulation activates parasympathetic fibers emerging from the pelvic spinal cord. …The overall effect of stimulating both parasympathetic and sympathetic nervous systems is to rebalance these two major components of nervous activity in the body. This has very definite repercussions on the hypothalamus (responsible for the complete endocrine system) which relays its information to the whole limbic (emotional) system and the cerebral cortex (outer layer of the brain)" (Buddhananda 2000: 3).

Exercise #8

Isolating the perineum

This exercise serves to help distinguish the exact placement of the perineum on the pelvic floor. When starting to work with the pelvic floor, some confuse the urethra, the anus, and the perineum. This sequence helps us become more familiar with all the bits down there.

At first, it is best to do this in a firm chair without cushions that allows your legs to sit at a 90-degree angle.

Step 1. Sit on the chair with both feet on the ground. Put your feet in line with your knees and your knees in line with your hipbones. Plot an imaginary line from your tailbone at your back (coccyx) through the perineum to the front of your body at the pubic bone.

Step 2. Gently and slowly rock back and forth on the chair along this imaginary line, tilting your pelvis back (this will gently round your back as the imaginary line makes contact with the chair, finishing at the tail bone) and then forward (which will create a gentle arch in your lower back as you tilt your pelvic floor towards your pubic bone). Continue this gentle rocking back and forth, drawing your awareness to the base of the pelvic floor along this line. As you rock, notice as you pass through the middle, between the pubic bone and the tail bone.

> Note: as you explore this movement note any extra "concentration" muscles that you might be employing. Is your tongue free? What is happening with your jaw? Are you breathing? Can you release your legs a little? Are you hooking in your stomach muscles? Your back muscles? Can you activate this movement from a lower point of centre that will allow less tension?

Step 3. After you have explored this movement, isolating its action as low in the body as you possibly can, come to neutral. This will be in the middle, not too far forward and not too far back.

Step 4. In this neutral position, exhale completely in preparation, inhale as low in the body as possible at this time and then, on the next exhale, contract the place behind the central point. It will be as if you are trying to prevent passing wind (farting). Release this completely on the next inhale. (Repeat if you need to isolate this feeling.)

Step 5. In the neutral position (and you may wish to move back and forward again to release any tensions from Step 4), exhale completely in preparation, inhale as low in the body as possible at this time, and then, on the next exhale, contract the place in front of the central point. It will be as if you are trying to prevent urinating (peeing). Release this completely on the next inhale. (Repeat if you need to isolate this feeling.)

Step 6. In the neutral position (and you may wish to move back and forward again to release any tensions from Steps 4 and 5), exhale completely in preparation, inhale as low in the body as possible at this time and then, on the next exhale, draw the central point in an upward direction. This will be the perineum. Release any tensions around the anus or the urethra.

Step 7. On the next inhale, release the pelvic girdle and, on the exhale, gently engage the perineum, drawing it up as if following a plumb line up through the innermost vertical centre of the body, plotting a path from the perineum out the top of your head.

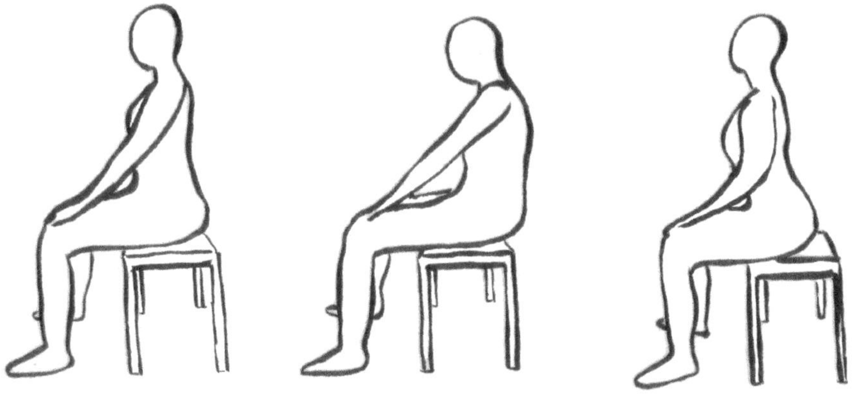

Variations: After this action has been learned, steps 1—7 can be done while sitting on the floor; after that action is understood, trying steps 4—7 in any position helps to find a dynamic alignment.

INTEGRATIVE BREATHING

In this practice breath, centre, and movement are inseparable and considered concurrently. Because of this, there are a few commonly used terms that we do not use. In the IPP, we refer to the *breath-body* rather than breath control or breath support. We think in terms of a *dynamic alignment* rather than posture alignment or core support. When considering what happens with respect to facial resonance when voicing, we consider *directional energy* of the breath rather than placement. These will be learned in detail in the coming pages.

Clearing up some of the received thinking around what one does (as a task) and what happens (as a product or symptom of doing a task) is also important. For instance, the term "singing from your diaphragm" has no place in this work. We do not *do* anything with the diaphragm: it moves as a symptom of a set of actions.

The diaphragm is a large dome-shaped muscle that attaches to the front of the body at the sternum, at the sides around the lower ribs, and at the back at the spine (seventh through twelfth ribs). It separates the upper chest (heart and lungs) from the abdomen (stomach, intestine, etc.). We will explore how the diaphragm moves up on the exhale and descends on the inhale. (For those interested in a more comprehensive breakdown of the anatomy of the body, Blandine Calais-Germain's *Anatomy of Movement* is a good resource.)

What is sometimes confusing is that the diaphragm, although the primary muscle of respiration, is not something most of us can *directly* affect. If you could, then when you got the hiccups you would be able to tighten or relax the diaphragmatic muscle and stop them. As any of us who has spent time holding our breath or drinking water upside down knows, we do not have *direct* control of our diaphragm. The reason why instructions such as "use your diaphragm" or "breathe from your diaphragm" or "sing from your diaphragm" are counterproductive is that if you try to *do* anything in that region you are not likely to directly affect the diaphragm; you are invariably going to cause tensions in the abdomen or solar plexus which will do the exact opposite of what you are aiming toward. These tensions will stop the full movement of the diaphragm.

A similar clarification can be found in the understanding of what it means to inhale. In this practice, most action or *doing* of a task happens while voicing or on the exhale. On the inhale, we will aim to *get out of the way*. As a result, we do not use the term *inhale* as it seems to indicate for most a drawing in of breath. Drawing in of breath tends to work directly against the low point of centre and causes tensions that will impede movement, eat up oxygen (giving us less breath), and adversely affect our tone when we sound.

Rather than an *inhale*, we refer to the intake of breath as simply that, an *intake*. The intake happens as a symptom of a slight movement sideways of your intercostals (lower ribs), which happens naturally as a response to your body being ready for new oxygen. This little action from the intercostals creates a vacuum effect (think of what happens when a hatch in a submarine is opened: water rushes in and fills the empty spaces). When this little space is created, air comes rushing in, the lungs fill with air and the diaphragm is displaced downward, which will in turn displace the organs, releasing the bottom of your pelvic girdle and expanding the lower abdomen and back body, allowing them to move out. At the same time as the diaphragm releases downwards due to the increased volume in the lungs, the ribs will expand and the sternum (breast plate) will rise. This can all happen without you doing much at all. This is how you stay alive when you are asleep. In fact, trying to *do* anything at this juncture is most likely to tighten the muscles in the body that hold the ribs and sternum, in addition to the abdominal muscles that house the soft organs in the belly. Holding in this way will create less space for the air to flow, since the holding of muscles will require oxygen, which will result in less breath for voicing. It is simply counterproductive. So there is no "pushing out of the belly" on the intake, no "drawing in of breath", no "directing breath to the back body": basically, you get out of the way. It is worth witnessing if there is any holding happening that might be blocking the breathing mechanism; it is not easy if you are holding for control, out of fear, because of habit, to protect, or in connection with any of the issues corresponding to the above diagram of the chakras.

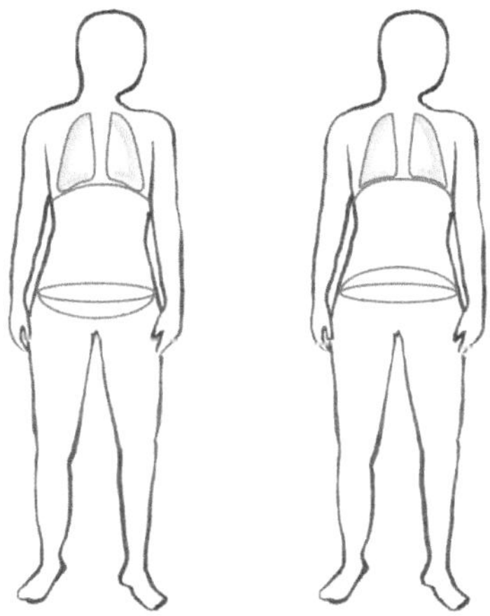

Intake Exhale

Exercise # 9
From inhale to intake

This exercise is designed to help you experience what it feels like to get out of the way on the intake. It can be a challenge, so be kind to yourself and anyone you are working with and remember to witness rather than judge or diagnose. It can be helpful to do this after Ex. 6, *I am, I want, I need, I feel*, with the sounding and moving variation as preparation. As you progress through the practice, let yourself return to this to observe your progress; much of the coming work will profoundly support your body's ability to get out of the way on the intake.

The physical character of this structure is quite fast. It is a swinging action into a forward bend, and there is likely to be a pause in this position (it is in this pause that the kernel of this exercise resides). After a slight expansion (which can be very subtle) from the lower ribs in your back body, you will come to stand as the air rushes in. *We are aiming not for a controlled inhale, but a rebounding intake.* Read all the steps before doing the exercise, as they come in quick succession.

Step 1. In the standing position, do a little jump and land, releasing any residual habitual tension. Allow the landing to settle your body in what feels like your most balanced and poised standing position in this moment. Scan your body, witnessing any tension, and release where possible. Let your arms simply hang and your tongue, jaw, and face relax. Let your knees remain soft and unlocked. This little jump-and-clear action has been playfully termed by my students the *Etch-a-Sketch,* after the toy made by Ohio Art Company. It's an analogy for the fact that you need to give the toy a "shake up and down" to erase.[1]

Step 2. Exhale completely in preparation (and by this I mean completely; with breath, the more you use, the more you get, so be generous).

Step 3. On an intake, raise your hands above your head. (This will create space in the ribs and sternum, encouraging a more generous amount of air to enter your body.)

Step 4. On the exhale, let your body swing over with legs bent into a forward bend. Let all the air out; when you think you are done, continue on an AAAAHH or a SSSSSSS: you will always have more. Let more air go, let all the air out, and when you think you are done, let even more out. Continue to release the air out further; trust that your body will take care of itself — this is not about control.

Step 5. Drawing your awareness to your back body, stay out of your way, witness any movement and LET your body release the intercostals (when you do you may feel a little jut outward in your lower back body). Let your body fill with air on its own. As you fill with air (you will not inhale), come to a standing position with hands at your side at the same time as the intake.

Notice — Etch-a-Sketch — and give it another go, experimenting with how much you can get out of your way on the intake (step 5).

Working in partners: It can be helpful to work with someone, with the partner cupping the lower ribs on the back body from Steps 3—5. Be sure to use the flat of the hand, as fingertips can tickle or give the wrong messages. Also, do not be afraid to use a little pressure, especially when the person is bent over, as it is this pressure that will help make the jutting out of the ribs apparent. If you are the holder of the ribs, be sure to use productive language in any feedback.

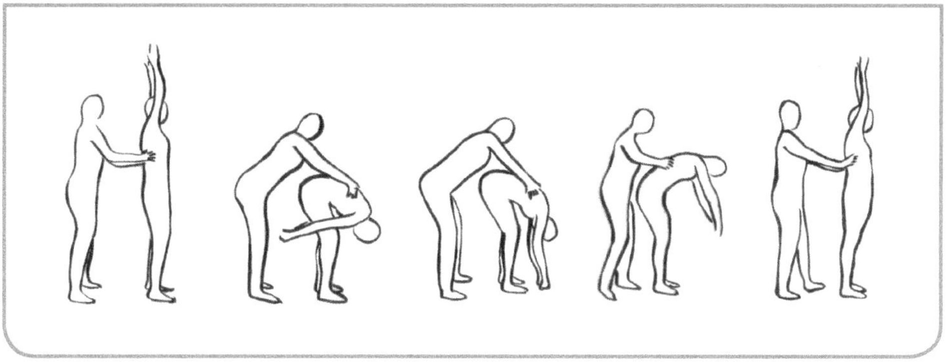

SUSPENSION

Next, we explore the space between the intake and the exhale. It can be helpful to explore this while moving. For instance, the action of the intake can correspond to the raising of your hand upward, and the exhale with bringing the hand down again. Try that a few times, where you let the movement of your hand match the intake of breath on the upward movement and the exhale on the downward movement. Explore this until you get the sensation that the hand and breath are one, until it is as if the breath is moving the hand.

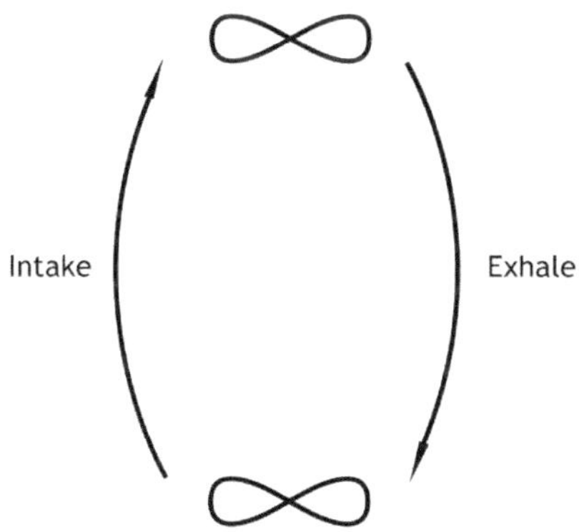

What happens at the top of the lines, in between the intake and the exhale? Do you have any tensions, or are you holding? What happens at the bottom of the lines, between the exhale and the next intake? Is there a grabbing?

In this work what we are aiming for is a *suspension* between breaths. A suspension is not a holding, a grabbing, a saving up, a locking, or even a stopping. It is alive! Keep the place between the intake and the exhale alive! You can move and smile and chew in a suspension. It is a dynamic pause. Some have described it as having the quality of a balloon or a floating feel; however, that tends to work more for the top of the lines between the intake and exhale.

We need to also have a suspension between the exhale and the intake which for some can feel scary, as the illusion that one won't get oxygen or sustenance can take over. So as you explore this, notice, witness — do you have company? Breath is in many ways about trusting yourself.

When I teach this I often need to gently tap the top of artists' heads, or I suggest "take your hat off" (see top chakra in chart), as people can bear down between the breaths when they forget to suspend. Everyone is a little different. Explore and witness your own patterns.

As you begin to explore the places between and to create safety there, consider what might happen to the imagery of the lines. Is the suspension, the place between, like a dotted line, a fluid dance, or something completely different? As you get more comfortable with the suspension, see if you can chew and stick your tongue out during the suspension. Once you begin to trust more, can you roll around on the floor or jump up and down during a suspension? Eventually in this practice, the intake, the exhale and the places between will become a simple breath-dance, without glitches, grabbings or superfluous tensions. This breath-dance will always initiate from the perineum.

Next, we learn how the perineum works in the act of breathing. We will also work to understand the isolation and independence of the relationships among the perineum, the intercostals, and the sternum. You may find that what is asked on the exhale is the reverse of other breathing practices that you have encountered. One function of this "reverse" breathing pattern, as stated previously, is to connect to the perineal centre at each intake and exhale. We will learn others later on.

Exercise #10
Three-part breath

Now that we know that the anatomy of the breath involves a coordinated dance of the diaphragm, ribs, belly, and pelvic floor, this exercise at first helps to isolate the elements of the breath-dance and ultimately serves as a foundational conditioning exercise towards the coordination of the constant perineal connection that is required for the ability to voice, act, and dance as one.

Preparing to work: Working from *awareness* as part of your Conscious Practice, lie on the floor in constructive rest position: legs bent, feet on the floor, arms by your sides with palms up. Check that your feet are in line with your knees and that your knees are in line with your hip bones. Gently draw your chin towards your sternum to allow your neck to elongate. Release your shoulders, tongue, neck, and jaw and let your body rest as it makes contact with the floor.

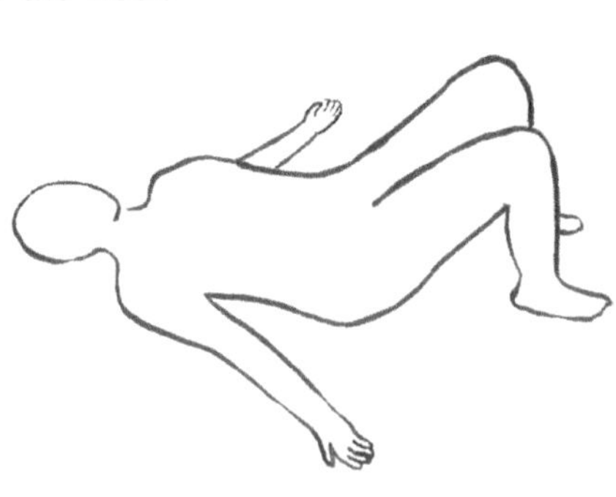

Tip: Many people, when learning this position, proprioceptively misjudge their alignment. Find a partner to check that your feet and knees are indeed in line with your hip bones and not where you feel your hips are. This specific alignment will become more important as we learn to release the psoas and work with the full breath-body towards more advanced movement.

Step 1. Exhale completely (all air out) and then allow the air to enter your body when you sense it needs it. (Return to Ex. 9 if there is any confusion about the action of the exhale.) Repeat this, working towards allowing your body to breathe you!

Step 2. This step can be done by gently placing your hands with one resting on your lower belly and the other on your sternum (chest plate), or with both hands resting on your intercostals (lower ribs): it is good to alternate after a few cycles. In either case, let your hands be heavy and your arms relaxed. Here the task is to establish three parts to your intake breathing. After a complete exhale through your mouth, intake through the nose releasing: ONE — your perineum and lower belly will release first; TWO — your ribs will then release outward from the back, front, and sides; THREE — your sternum will gently rise. Three parts, in that order, on the intake. Exhale through the mouth and work on this isolation on the intake. Notice how it affects your exhale as you get better at the isolation of the three parts.

Step 3. This step is the key to a constant connection with the perineum. Exhale completely, following the instructions in Step 2, but this time on the exhale release your air on an even flow of a "sssssssss" like a snake. (Be mindful not to unnecessarily tighten your tongue, jaw, or neck.) On the initiation of the "sssss" (exhale), allow your perineum to draw upwards (or contract upwards) towards the top of your head. This will hollow your lower belly as a symptom. This perineal action, in connection with your lower belly hollowing, will be considered ONE. As you continue to "sssss" in an even flow you will notice your ribs start to draw in towards your spine — TWO, and lastly your sternum will release downward — THREE.

Clarification: So here it becomes clear that the three-part breath starts and ends with the perineum contraction. It is important to note that the "contraction" is not a locking or drawing in on itself, but rather a drawing upward as if in a plumb line through the vertical centre of the body out the top of the head. When I teach this, I often make a slurping sound as if through a straw to indicate the action, and it seems to make more sense than words.

Putting it together: So, in constructive rest, alternating where you wish to place your hands to help isolate the three parts: exhale completely, then on the intake, ONE — release your perineum, pelvic girdle, and lower abdomen; TWO — your ribs will then release outward; THREE — your sternum will then rise. Suspend the breath (rather than hold) and then on a "ssssss", ONE — draw in or contract your perineum (this will hollow your lower belly first and then your upper belly); TWO — your ribs will release in toward your spine; THREE — your sternum only at the end will release downward (so work to suspend it up and not collapse). THEN suspend and ONE your perineum and pelvic girdle will release... and the cycle continues and you condition your pelvic floor, stomach, intercostals, and chest to be flexible and dynamic, engaging with the three-part breath. Most importantly, you will at first be learning to isolate your perineum and maintaining a constant connection to this as a physical and breath centre. In the following work you will see that every sound and movement will initiate from the perineum.

Reminder: As you work with the drawing in/contraction of the perineum it is important to remember its actual location. It rests between the genitals and the anus. This is really important and can get fuzzy for the beginner and even the more practised as we grow and change. So, in short, the contraction will *not* be an anal contraction or the sort of action you do when you need to keep from peeing. It is in between. This is crucial, as initiating from too far forward or back rather than the centre of the pelvic girdle will have a domino effect right up the body and will affect sound, movement, and integration of the nervous system.

THE ROLL

Because breathing and moving are considered, learned, and practised as one in this work, we will go directly to the most important exercise in this work, the roll. We will return to the roll throughout the book as a marker, letting you experience how each and every exercise helps you move further and further into the exactitude of the integrative instrument.

> Note: It is not recommended to do the entire roll if you have ever had a head or neck injury, are taking stroke medication, are pregnant, or are having a heavy menstruation. As with all exercises, check with your doctor if you have any concerns. For those who will not be going upside down, working with partners can help to achieve similar results. Instructions for this adjustment can be found in the following section under "partner assists".

The roll can take time to perfect and is different each day. It can be challenging, perhaps because it passes through every chakra; for some, it is because the idea of going upside down can be disorienting and feel ungrounding (however, we maintain grounding through the perineum). It can be challenging because until you learn to trust that it is the breath that will do the work, shifting to thoughts and feeling and *trying* rather than *doing* can take over. It will be especially helpful to remember the concept of "let it go let it go" as expressed in Part II. Also, it is most important to remember that you can *never* repeat the roll: we do the doing anew each time. *There is no getting it.* Remembering to *witness* is key, as is working in *conscious practice* and clarifying your task.

This exercise is, ironically, not about the shape of the roll but rather the way of doing the roll. Whatever the resulting aesthetic may be, it will come as a symptom of the active aesthetic, the way of doing, and the attendance to the task (this of course is true of all performance tasks, be they a sung phrase, a line in a scene, or the execution of a physical sequence). You will see this roll used for different tasks as your skill progresses and the exercises get more advanced. You (A) are not doing the roll (C) but rather you are doing a doing that will bring about a roll.

What is important is the practice of the practice, the way in which you attend to the task. This is the gold that will help you to achieve the task here. In time you will be able to go from rolling to standing, to leaping, to lifting, and back down to a roll while singing and acting a phrase of music at the same time without compromise to either aspect of expression. You will accomplish this because rather than doing all these things at once, you will be doing one thing, initiated and connected to centre from the part of you that is your awareness. But for now, and at each time, it is the roll where we begin to fully know what we have brought to the work today, and where we begin to work with our integrative instrument in the now.

The roll is an integrative performer's best friend. It is both a profound exercise and a simple task. Through the roll you can witness where and in which ways you might be leaving self in the act of a task. You can witness where you may be resisting movement in the body. You can witness when thoughts or feelings take over from awareness (review Chapter Four, specifically pages 69–86), creating resistance in the act of doing from a centred self (review Chapter One for a more in-depth discussion on what we mean by self in relation to practice). Together, these observations will help to reveal qualities in the practice of your practice or the active aesthetic. The discoveries you make will help to identify issues that impact every aspect of your work. This clarity will allow you to make effective adjustments toward better integration, quickly and effectively, as soon as the very next breath.

Having worked through what it means to act in presence while witnessing rather than judging and diagnosing (pages 68–69) as part of a conscious practice (pages 90–94) we start with our first challenge, which engages and tests every muscle while moving from centre.

> Before enlightenment chopping wood, fetching water.
> After enlightenment chopping wood, fetching water.
> Buddhist Saying

Exercise #11
Rolling from centre

Preparing to work: Make sure that you have a safe and soft floor below your body. (A yoga mat is a good option.) Prepare to work from *awareness* in line with the *Conscious Practice* work. Sit with your feet in line with your knees and let your body hang over your legs in any way that feels both released and supported by your centre.

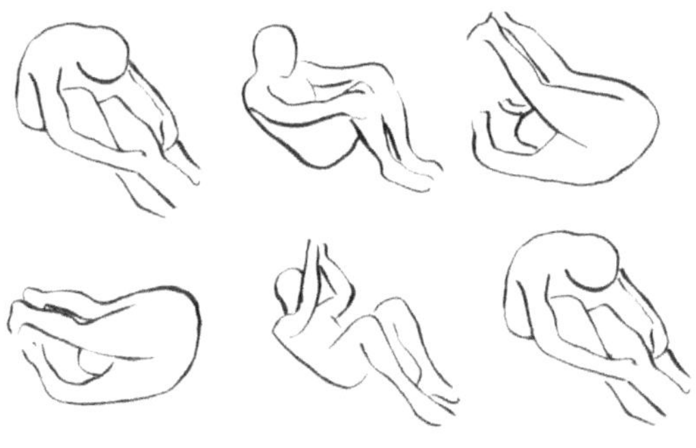

Step 1. Simply roll back while letting your arms go over your head. Your feet may or may not touch the ground behind you. Roll back to sitting. Notice what that felt like, if there were any tensions, thoughts, feelings. Let that go and move on to the next step.

Step 2. In the starting position, practise your three-part breath (Ex. 10). Remember that every intake releases your pelvic girdle and every exhale has a gentle contraction of the perineum upward while you release your body over your legs. Both the intake and exhale begin with an action in the perineum. With every exhale let your body connect further into the actioning of centre. Allow your jaw, tongue, hands, to let go and your head to be heavy.

Tip: Let this starting position take as long as you need it to. You know you are ready when you get to the stage where you can maintain a constant awareness of the action of the perineum through both the exhale and the intake. Remember that awareness and focus are two different things (review pages 70–1) and that awareness is not about engaging with thoughts or feelings (page 69). Some people find it helpful to visualize a thread from their perineum up through the inside of their body out the top of the head on the exhale, both lengthening and releasing over their legs as they stay connected to the perineum. On the next intake, the perineum will release and the process can begin again. It will be the action of the perineum through breath that will help you to maintain awareness to centre. It will be the breath's connection to the perineum that will initiate the movement in the following step.

> Breathing and body are one. Breathing and mind are one. Mind and body are one. At the time of observation, mind is not an entity which exists independently, outside of your breathing and your body. The boundary between the subject of observation and the object of observation no longer exists. We observe "the body in the body".
>
> Thich Nhat Hanh (Hanh 1990: 48)

Step 3. Once you are ready, exhale completely, emptying your body of all air, intake in preparation and on the next exhale voice an "ssss" (with as little tension in the lips and jaw as possible). This will create a gentle pressure, helping to engage your perineum with a contraction upwards. At the same time, release your centre backwards, rolling the perineum over so that your arms and legs flip over your head (see figure on page 116).

Clarification: This task is not about doing the shape or aesthetic of a roll. Rather, the rolling will come as a symptom of the active aesthetic or the doing of the roll as described in the steps. The task is to draw your awareness to centre through your three-part breath, connecting to the perineum, and then rolling the perineum over on the exhale. This will result in an integrative roll (and lots of other wonderful things soon to be explained). Simply doing the doing can feel very vulnerable, in contrast to picking up our comfortable patterns of "showing", "dancing the shape", "getting it right", "checking" or "giving it a go". But none of these is the task. To do simply from awareness can feel like risking your life. This is why the life of the performer is such a brave one. Witnessing (see page 68) the things that get in the way and returning to centre through the doing of the doing is the noble struggle.

> A bit of advice given to a young Native American at the time of his initiation: "As you go the way of life you will see a great chasm, jump. It is not as wide as you think."
> Joseph Campbell (Campbell 1991: 298)

Step 4. When your legs are over your head, you can continue the exhale on a "ssss", letting the perineum flip back and drawing your body back to the sitting position. In effect, this creates the back (legs over head) and forward (arms over legs) movement as one phrase through one long exhale. Or you can break it into two steps where you suspend with your legs over your head having exhaled completely, intake in your three-part breath with legs over the head, and on the next exhaled "ssss" let the perineum, through the action of breath, take you over to sitting again. Try different breath patterns, witnessing how to best support yourself to stay connected to the perineum through breath from awareness.

Some helpful language: Let the breath move you — Let everything flow from centre — Centre is the motor from which your arms and legs will flow — Allow your body to release backwards, staying connected to the perineum throughout as your arms go over your head and your feet follow as a symptom of the perineal action.

Steps 2, 3, 4: Do the roll multiple times. With each intake and exhale a new opportunity to return to centre through the three-part breath connecting to the perineum is available to you. Let your torso, then arms and hands, then thighs, then legs and feet ribbon out from the centre. Each roll is a chance to get closer to your optimum centre of the day. This is how we begin the practice.

REFINING THE ROLL — MIRROR TENSIONS

The roll gives us much information. One of the most interesting things is that you can often see what is going to happen in someone's roll even before they begin to move. As the roller is in the starting position, an astute observer will note a subtle holding in the torso, where the roller will begin to initiate the movement. This tension will be mirrored in the legs directly. The higher the place of initiation in the back body (as they roll back), the further towards the knees in the thigh will engage (as the legs go over the head). There is a mirror tension in relational distance from centre to the legs and centre to a corresponding place in the torso. See figures below which illustrate the concept of corresponding tensions.

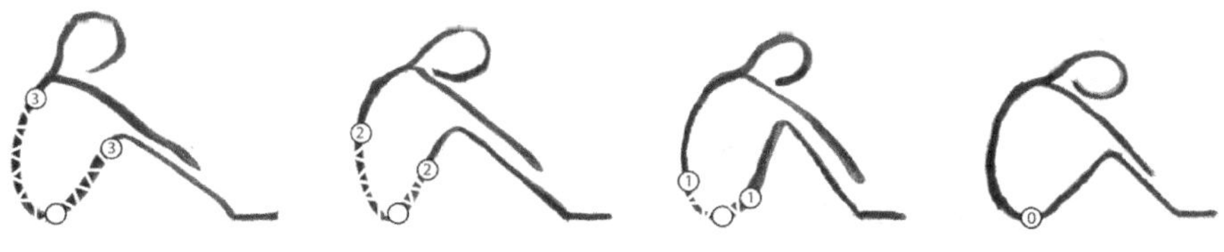

In looking at the diagram we see that if you initiate the roll from between the shoulder blades, you are likely to tighten and initiate from the legs at about 3 inches below the knee to bring them back over (shown as 3). Correspondingly, if you initiate from the solar plexus, the middle of the thigh will engage (shown as 2), and if you initiate from the navel, the area in your thigh approximately three inches below the crease will engage (shown as 1). To roll from centre is to roll from zero-to-zero. It will feel shockingly easy and strong at the same time, as it uses very little muscular engagement but makes use of the body's natural balance. Rolling from this centre also tends to be conducive to working from awareness rather than focus and tends to be accompanied by less inner talk. The reasons for this may be explained by the action of the perineal contraction and its relationship to the parasympathetic nervous system.

It is our goal to initiate from closer and closer to centre, so that each roll is simply a flip of the perineum with both the torso and the legs ribboning out from there.

This movement will be fuelled by the three-part breath with its corresponding perineal contraction. (Review Exercise 10, *Three-part Breath*, page 110). Rolling in this way will take the least amount of tension possible. Bringing your awareness to centre each time is key. You do the doing anew with every roll. We do not copy the aesthetic, meaning the look or feel of a roll that may have once worked before, nor do we imitate a roll that we have seen another do successfully; rather, we doing the doing again — awareness to perineum, three-part breath, and roll — in *awareness*, rather than focus, and simply *witnessing* what we may *let go* before the next roll begins. Review the previous sections if any of these terms as understood in this work are not clear.

Initiating from the perineum, letting the breath move you, and maintaining awareness of this centre in motion will allow a release of the tongue, jaw, and throat, and elongate the torso, so that even while upside down you will be able to voice with no discernible difference in tone. (In fact, often singers find that when they learn this, aspects of their previous technique get better, partly because you cannot outsmart the exactitude required of this type of integrated breath and motion.)

To test this, roll back and pause with your feet over head (feel free to use a pillow or bolster if this is difficult at first, you can place it at your feet if they do not yet make contact with the floor). You will be able to tell where you rolled from just by observing your sound. The lower towards centre that you initiated the roll, the freer the throat, tongue, and jaw will be. If you roll from the zero point you should be able to sing ANYTHING in this legs over head position, using ANY pitch or dynamic without ANY discernible difference to tone or harmonic than if you were in a standing position. The further away from centre that you initiate the roll, the more blocked the sound. At 3 it is hard to get anything out.

Once this process is learned and trusted, you will be on your way to go from standing to sitting, to rolling, back to sitting, to standing, and then leaping WITHOUT any glitches, or compromise of line, tone, harmonic, or articulation of sound. This is not a trick, and it is not possible to "get" it, but rather it is a practice that you learn to do anew each time as part of an active aesthetic.

On paper this can sound simple. In reality it is often difficult to unlearn physical and emotional patternings that lock us into certain places of initiation, keeping us from the perineal centre. Returning to the Chakra diagram (page 103) may give you some clues as to what may be accompanying you, especially if you have a pattern of holding in a similar place each time. For instance, the solar plexus (Manipura Chakra) or the navel (Svadhisthana Chakra) can be a challenge to release at the beginning of the roll. Looking to their chakra attributes can sometimes offer keys to what might be getting in the way of the release downward to the perineum (Muladhara or Root Chakra). In addition, all of the exercises in Part II are specifically designed to help unlock old patterns, with rigour, economy, and kindness.

So, as you may be discovering from the prior exercises, when the legs hook in as the initiator of the movement rather than allowing the breath to engage the perineum as the initiator of movement, we will find corresponding tensions in the torso. Likewise, when a part of the upper body hooks in to do the work, be it the solar plexus, chest, or stomach, rather than connecting to the perineum as the initiator of movement, this will create glitches in the sound, disconnect us from the breath-body, and invariably connect us to thoughts and feelings rather than awareness. The following offers some helpful tips to aid in the release of superfluous tensions or patterns of holding that may be getting in the way of trusting yourself to reside in centre.

Exercise #12

Partner assists for finding centre

Assist #1

Step 1. One partner lies on the floor in constructive rest position: legs bent, feet on floor, arms by the sides. Check that the feet are in line with the knees and that the knees are in line with the hip bones. The person standing, with their point of centre as low as possible and knees soft, places the tips of their toes on the tips of the toes of the partner lying on the floor. It will be helpful if both can do a few rounds of three-part breath in their respective positions and *meeting in the middle* with the task and the partner before moving on to the next step.

Step 2. When both parties are centred, the person on the floor lifts their arms toward the person standing, from awareness, making sure that their centre remains low and using the least amount of muscle possible to lift the arms. The person standing, while maintaining a low point of centre, will take the other person's arms with a firm grasp to the forearm from underneath. From here they will both keep soft eye contact throughout, and *meet in the middle*. (Review Ex. 7.)

Step 3. From here, the person standing, with knees bent to support the back, leans back gently, lifting and supporting the person lying on the floor in releasing the torso as they are gently lifted off the floor and suspended. Gentle jiggling can help; a little swaying of no more than a few inches sideways or up and down can help to let the person on the floor begin to experiment with the idea of being completely held, giving the standing partner all of their weight. Releasing any and all stomach or chest muscles and shoulder tension that they may be in the habit of engaging is their task. The aim is to give the standing partner all of their weight.

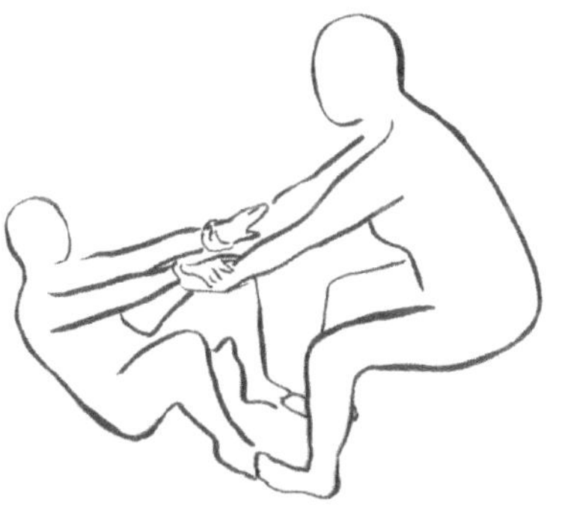

Constructive feedback: In giving feedback to the person working to release, the person standing might notice how much the person is releasing or holding. They might say, "I feel 50%, yep, ok now it feels more like 75%. When you laughed it felt more 30%, yep 50%..." Keep the feedback about what you witness, with language that is not judgemental or telling the other person what they are doing or who they are. So "I feel", "I notice", not "you did, you are".

Assist #2:

Step 1. Begin with one partner on the floor in constructive rest and one partner standing at their feet. With bent legs, the standing partner clasps their arms under the knees of the partner on the floor. The standing person will then lift their partner's legs and lower back off the ground (supporting their own back by working from centre).

Step 2. The standing partner can very gently pulse in small motions up and down or sideways, helping the person on the floor to release muscles in the lower back and stomach that have a tendency to hook in. As the person on the floor is being moved, they will draw their awareness to centre as they witness any tensions and releases.

Step 3. The standing person, when settling their partner's body back to the floor, will gently elongate the torso by drawing the legs towards their own body as they lower their partner. The standing partner then places their partner's legs and feet back into constructive rest and gives them a moment to experience any changes that may have occurred.

Tip: For both of these, an interesting thing about meeting in the middle with partners is that one person's centring can affect the other's. So if the standing partner in these assists has their point of centre very high, it will be almost impossible for the lying down partner to release their centre. The standing person will have the sensation that they are likely to "fall over" the lying person. So it is crucial for both practitioners to work from centre and from awareness.

SOUNDING WHILE ROLLING

One way to witness where you might be holding and getting in the way of releasing down to the perineal centre is to make a continuous sound as you do the roll. This can be done as a scale or a continuous drone somewhere comfortable in the vocal range. As people are first learning, saying the alphabet in a continuous tone while rolling might be less intimidating.

Witnessing what happens to the quality of the sound will let you know where you tend to hold. The sound actually will glitch at the exact place where the torso meets the ground, letting you know where you are protecting or holding. This, interestingly, corresponds to the chakras, and it is worth looking at any correlations that might be present.

Sometimes the tension initiates in the legs, especially with artists that have trained in circus or dance. If this is the case, the sound will glitch in the corresponding distance away from centre in the torso when that part of the back meets the floor. (See Mirror Tensions, page 117.)

When a place of holding or a habitual place of initiating is witnessed, we treat it as a *physical passagio* (meaning passage). The passagio is a term that is used in vocal training; it is the place in the vocal range where the head voice and the chest voice meet and can often present a challenge due to the vocal glitch that can occur in the untrained singer. In voice, one learns to go through it smoothly by using the breath. Here we do the same.

Breathing from centre throughout the entire roll will release these tensions and also abolish the physical and vocal passagio with one action. If there is a glitch, it most often corresponds to a moment when the practitioner loses awareness or that type of "crispy" presence mentioned in Chapter Four.

What is key here is letting the three-part breath, with its continuous connection to the perineal contraction on the exhale (which will eventually be concurrent with sounding), be the impulse for the movement. Sounding with the three-part breath while rolling is an excellent way to begin any work day, as it helps with our basic personal inventory towards a conscious practice. What's here today, how might I work with it?

A more advanced roll (more advanced as it produces a greater challenge in isolating the perineum as centre) is the sideways roll. It, too, helps us to witness what other areas of the torso or the legs tend to get in the way of the perineal centre in motion. As the eventual goal will be to be able to move in any direction and in any combination of styles from the perineal centre with the three-part breath, this is a good next step.

Exercise #13
Sideways roll

This exercise is a way to work towards a more exacting isolation of the perineum as centre in movement. It also unapologetically exposes our habitual patterning that takes us away from this centre. Most practitioners find this a good way to check in with where their body's centre is. It can feel easy some days and present a real challenge on others.

At first the sideways roll can seem like a physical impossibility. It is not. It might feel odd and even emotional to re-pattern away from the habitual controlling muscles of the upper torso, arms/shoulders or the legs and hips. It helps to practise *witnessing.* It can feel like a leap of faith to trust in the momentum of centre. It can be helpful to remember that you are already on the floor: there is nowhere to fall. There is, however, ego to lose and control to release. The fear that can arise is real, but also an illusion. (Review pages 69–70 on thoughts, feelings, awareness.) Preparing to work: Working from *awareness,* you will lie on your back with your legs straight and your arms above your head with palms up. Allow yourself to release as much tension as possible as you breathe. Notice the weight of your arms and legs as they lie across the floor.

Step 1. While lying in this extended position, practise a few rounds of the three-part breath. You may notice that with your arms above your head and your legs straight it may take a few cycles to really release the pelvic floor on the intake and contract it on the exhale. Once you find your best centre for the day, you can change the "sssss" of the three-part breath to a simple exhale with relaxed mouth.

Reminder: In preparation to move and throughout all movement a synergetic connection between the breath and the body is key. You will notice I refer to the breath-body throughout this book for this reason. You will also recall the neurophysiological implications of this mutually interdependent relationship from Chapter One. I often say, "Let the breath 'move' you". The breath in connection to the perineal contraction initiates all movement, voice, and action.

Step 2. Once you have a good connection to the perineum throughout both the pelvic release on the intake and the perineal contraction on the inhale, you are ready to begin. The task here is to initiate a spiral movement from the perineum that will roll your body over on to your stomach. The challenge is to let the perineum, in connection to your exhale, drag your upper body and lower body through the roll and flop over onto your stomach. Notice and immediately release a leg or thigh that wants to hook in and lead. Notice and immediately release an arm or shoulder that has a compulsion to hook in and lead. It may take quite a few re-starts.

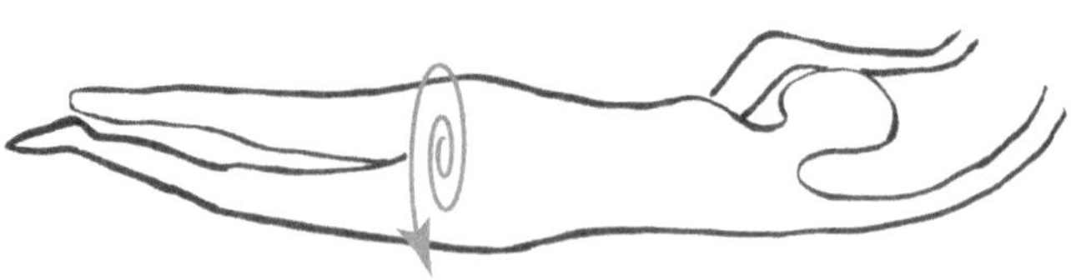

Suggestion for partner work: The partner sits on the floor in front of the direction that you are turning toward. As you isolate the perineal contraction and spiral toward your partner, they can cradle one hand on the lower back in line with the perineum and gently pull to assist this movement forward. With the other hand, as a leg, or shoulder hooks in, they can gently tap it to enhance awareness of the hook in (interestingly, this is not always evident to the person doing the task).

Step 3. Mastering the sideways roll from the back body to the front body can take some time. For most, it is the easier option. After step 2 is attained, repeat the entire exercise, but this time starting on your stomach. With arms above your head, legs straight, connect to three-part breath, and on the exhale, in line with the perineal contraction, spiral onto your back with legs and arms dragging rather than helping or hooking in.

ILIOPSOAS — A PHYSICAL KEY TO INTEGRATION

The iliopsoas (pronounced il–ee-o–SO-az), which from here we will shorten to psoas (SO-az), is a system of muscles that, when working properly, actually integrates the body/mind on many levels and with a myriad of concurrent actions. Many practices in dance and movement work with locating this muscle system as a way of accessing centre in the body (see discussion on various centres, pages 98–100); however, in practice the psoas is quite elusive, since it is hard to "feel". Unlike the feeling of a foot, or the upper palate, the psoas is very difficult to find proprioceptively. (*Proprioceptive* is a term that relates to stimuli produced or received relating to one's perception of a position or of movement within the body.)

When you do engage the psoas properly, the general experience is one of balance, an elongated torso, a release of the abdominals, and an expanded sense of the breath. The more exacting the engagement of the iliopsoas, the less extraneous tensions result, allowing for a more integrated expression of the emotive, voicing, and moving performance self. For this reason, the way in which we use the psoas is crucial to an integrative performance practice and is engaged with in a most exacting way.

On the simplest level, the psoas is a hip flexor that balances and lengthens the body, supporting the swing of the leg when walking. It also supports internal organs, aids in the flushing of fluids in and out of cells, and determines the quality of balance and movement up the entire spine. Further, the condition of the psoas correlates directly with emotional reactions, especially in relation to our fight or flight mechanism, and therefore affects awareness, breathing capacity, and sexual pleasure, along with tensions in any and all parts of the body, as well as the ability to access and release down to the perineal centre crucial to this practice. It is truly a multi-faceted muscle system.

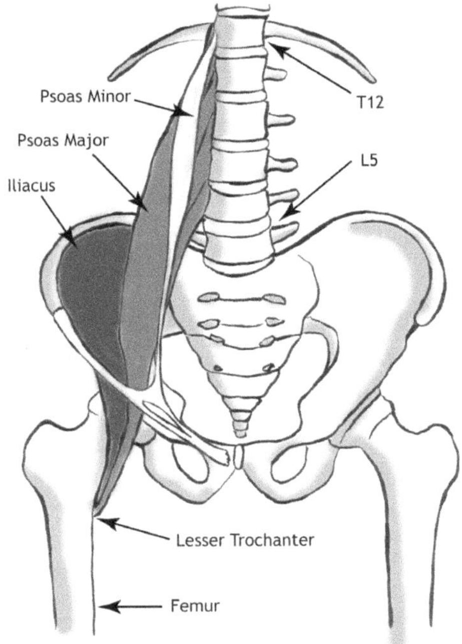

The iliopsoas muscle is composed of two parts. The iliacus and psoas muscles are joined to each other laterally along the psoas tendon on either side of the lumbar spine. The iliopsoas originates anterior to the transverse processes of the T12 to L5 vertebrae and inserts into the lesser trochanter of the femur (see diagram). The psoas minor is slowly disappearing, with some people missing it on one or both sides. This is hypothesized to be attributed to our sitting more than standing, and also our standing rather than resting in a semi-flexed position.

The psoas connection is important for the integrative practitioner working in constant contact with the perineum through the three-part breath. Franklin refers to the psoas as a "hotline between the pelvic floor and the diaphragm...the space retainer and mediator between these two important systems of muscles" (Franklin 2003: 66). As we learned in Ex. 10, *Three-part breath* and Ex. 11, *Rolling from centre*, the pelvic-floor-to-diaphragm connection is key to a lengthening and release of the body in motion and when sounding without compromise. This relationship between the psoas and the pelvis are further made clear in Liz Koch's *The Psoas Book*, an excellent resource for those wishing to learn more about this elusive yet profound muscle system. "For muscles to be supple the skeleton must fully bear the weight of the body, and the pelvis must be free to move. This allows the muscles of the pelvic floor, which are similar to the diaphragm, to be free to relax and 'drop down'. (sic) allowing sensation to circulate freely. The floor of the pelvis and genital/anal area are then experienced as open, vulnerable, and alive" (Koch 1997: 41).

For some, the first experiences of truly engaging the psoas can be akin to a feeling of blankness, less effort, and even a profound emotional release. It is difficult to access an exacting use of the psoas system when coming from thoughts and feelings and/or judgements and diagnosis; likewise, when connected to the psoas such *company* has a tendency to naturally quiet down. This is often because many of the superfluous tensions that we have learned into the body and that we think are needed to stand, sit, breathe, and walk, to be who we have constructed, are actually not needed, and have rather been patterned or performed in as part of our physical *company*. Many of these tensions are directly connected to our ego or constructed (dancer/singer/actor) self. To let go of the extra tensions, some of which we have become quite attached to, can be confronting and also liberating. Working in *conscious practice* while *witnessing* sensations as they arise with *awareness* is very helpful. The psoas IS the physical system synergetic with *awareness* as practised in this work. Further integration can be accessed equally from both. Importantly, EVERY exercise in this practice can be approached as both an awareness exercise and also a psoas exercise.

As in the previous discussions on awareness, engaging with the psoas is not something to "get": one only engages with it in the *flow of presence* by doing the doing again as part of an *active aesthetic*. There is no one position, sequence, or combination or quality of movement that, on the face of it, will reliably let you repeat access to the psoas, in much the same way that we have learned that awareness is NOT a feeling to be retrieved. However, a constant returning to centre through the three-part breath, connecting to the perineum from *awareness* with each and every intake and exhale, will engage the most precise possibility of the psoas, especially after the following work on isolating it and releasing tensions that may be in the way. (Review Chapter Four if the terms *awareness, company, conscious practice,* and *witnessing* are not clear.)

SPINE AND PSOAS, VERTICAL ACCESS

In returning to the diagram above you will see that the psoas is connected to the lumbar spine on both sides. Years of teaching this has brought to my attention an understandable confusion about where the spine sits. The little bumps that you feel down your back (while rolling for instance) can lead some to think that the spine sits at the back of the body. Rather, these are small bony protrusions called transverse processes that sit at the left and right side of the vertebrae. The spinal column actually sits more towards the centre axis of the body. This centre axis is a vertical centre while standing, or the plumb line from the perineum out the top of the head in any position. (See diagram below.)

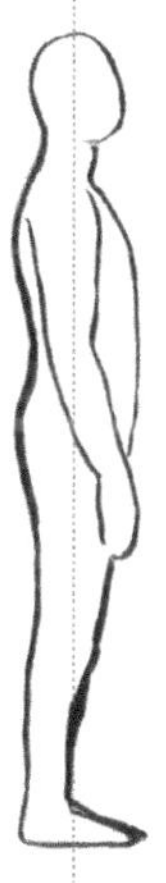

This line can be accessed on an exhale with a perineal contraction upward from the bottom of the pelvic girdle out to the top of the head. One of the important functions of the psoas is to lengthen and create space in the torso against the action of gravity through this vertical axis. When the psoas is activated and isolated, lengthening goes along this internal midline axis of the body as opposed to lengthening up the front body or the back body.

This internal lengthening while standing is not the type that proprioceptively derives from the front body, often associated with a military type of "attention" posture. That type of lengthening necessitates the tightening of the chest muscles and shortening of the back. Conversely, this internal lengthening is not a rigid lifting in the back body that necessitates a holding in of the stomach and tightening of the jaw. Both of these examples impede the three-part breath and also make it impossible to access the pelvic release on the intake, and directly affect the tone and harmonics available while sounding on the exhale. In trying on these front and back lengthenings, it is interesting to return to the chakra diagram to note which energetic centres get engaged, overextended and/or closed down with each extreme or subtlety. In Ex. 18, *The sweet spot (exploring vertical alignment)*, we work directly on this vertical axis. Some may wish to skip forward and then revisit it again after learning the foot and leg relationship to psoas, coming next. With this said, each person's optimal psoas alignment is different — different because we have individual bone structures, muscular consistency, and fascial organization. Some of us may have had injuries, necessitating a valid "new normal" of optimal balance, and some of us have birth anomalies (the lack of the psoas minor mentioned earlier being one example). The action of the psoas can also be different from time to time. Hormonal shifts including menstruation or pregnancy, menopause, and/or transitioning treatments can affect the psoas system, as can emotional trauma, injury, nutrition, medication, and basic health concerns. Again, it is for this reason that "alignment" is not a term used in this practice, but rather *dynamic alignment*, a more kinesthetic awareness of balance in motion, with motion understood also in non-motion, as a buoyant stillness rather than "positioning", "placement", or "posture". So as we go forward to explore and investigate the psoas, your personal psoas system, every exercise is a task of constantly returning to your most optimal engagement with the psoas.

There is no perfect way to begin to explore the psoas, partly because each person is different. It is likely that one exercise (especially if it is your first) will be a challenge. Don't write it off. Return to it the next day after you have worked through others. The one that gave you such trouble could be the one that reveals the most knowledge next. This book will offer many ways to explore your psoas, but, as mentioned, all the exercises to follow (and arguably the ones previously) can be seen as psoas exercises. Other excellent books to find psoas exercises in are Andrea Olsen's *Body Stories* (Olsen 1991: 87–91), and the aforementioned *Pelvic Power* by Eric Franklin, and *The Psoas Book* by Liz Koch.

We will start with an exercise, which in the sequence of work in this book logically follows the *Three-part breath* (Ex. 10) and starts on the floor. The *Hip thump* (Ex. 14) is an exercise that will become your best friend in proprioceptively helping to remember the relationship between your feet and legs as you move further into the more advanced work of leaping and catching. Often artists doing more advanced work in the IPP, finding they have lost their optimal psoas connection, drop to the floor to do a little *hip thump* in order to remember what the psoas connection is while standing. When learning this practice artists often get frustrated that we are "still on the floor", but later they completely appreciate why.

Exercise #14
Hip thump — plotting the path towards psoas

This hip thump exercise is one that I encountered initially while doing an interdisciplinary yoga teacher's training certificate under Don Stapleton. I highly recommend his somatic exercises for harnessing the body's own wisdom and expanding an artist's ability to access and witness the body/self. I have radically modified his version, which originally aimed to "mobilize and synchronize movement in the neck and pelvis" (Stapleton 2004: 101–109), toward *a way to exactingly isolate the psoas and release the superfluous tensions in the legs and groin that tend to impede a balanced dynamic alignment in the pelvis.*

When I teach this exercise I often start by showing practitioners what it may "look" like when they do the movement (just so they don't have to turn their heads to check if they are doing it "right" or go to thoughts as they work). This exercise is really about an internal experience and not about the shape of the movement. The tasks that you are instructed to do bring about the movement as a symptom, so it is often helpful to have a sense of what that may look like so you can let go any thought of "choreography". This exercise can take a good three quarters of an hour when done with full integrity; however, the basic movement is that we will press into one foot, which will lift one side of one hip off the floor while the other just dangles. We will switch feet, and eventually we will press into both feet and the entire pelvic girdle will lift off the floor. Of course, none of that will be what the exercise is about because the choreography is not the task. (See diagram for clarification.)

Preparation: It is important that the practitioner has read through the sections in Part II, which will help to distinguish between "thinking" about a part of the body or "picturing" a part of the body and bringing *awareness* to that part of the body. It is also important to have worked through the differences between judging and diagnosing and *witnessing.* A review of *Let it go* can also be helpful. Knowing the *Three-part breath* is essential. Steps 1 A—C will be done on one side and then the other side. **Do not alternate sides.** It is helpful if the facilitator reiterates which side is being worked on, since in the flow of the work practitioners can forget.

To start: Begin by lying on the floor in constructive rest position: legs bent, feet on floor, arms by your sides with palms up. Check that your feet are in line with your knees and that your knees are in line with your hip bones. Gently draw your chin towards your sternum to allow your neck to elongate. Release your shoulder, tongue, neck, and jaw and let your body rest as it makes contact with the floor. Let yourself breathe, accept your body just as it is now and go to your awareness. Witness how your body makes contact with the floor.

Step 1.

A. Press into your (left) foot, plotting a path from the big toe up through the **inside** of the arch, continuing past the **inside** part of the ankle and up to the mid-**inside** of your calf. As part of the three-part breath, intake, and on an exhale release the pressure.

This is as far as we want the pressure to have its effects at this point. Moreover, we want to work to keep all the outer leg and groin muscles out of the way. The task is to press the inside of the foot, initiating from the big toe, plotting a path into the inside of the ankle and into the middle of the inside of the calf with nothing else hooking in. Do this a few times, witnessing what else wants to hook in. Do you contract the buttocks? Abdominals? Jaw? Interesting. Let that go and try again. Do you hook in the outside of the thigh? Let that go.

Again, press — big toe — plotting the path through the **inside** of the arch in the foot — through the **inside** of the ankle — into the **inside** of mid-calf — and stop. Intake, and on the exhale release — and again, big toe, inside arch, inside of ankle, inside of calf up to the middle of the calf... release. Witness the jaw? The tongue? Release. Let it go! You are already on the floor, there is nowhere to fall. No need to protect. You are safe.

B. And again, still on the same side: big toe, inside of arch, inside of ankle, inside of calf, this time continuing through the inside of the knee and into the inside mid-thigh. What can you release here while keeping the pressure on the inside? Is the outside of the leg hooking in? Pelvis? Jaw? Knee? Isolate the inside of the leg up the mid-thigh. Inhale in preparation: 1, 2, 3, and on the exhale — let out a voiced — Hah! — release. And again: toe, arch of foot, ankle, shin, knee, mid-thigh — and inhale — release, and again...

C. Still on the same side: big toe, inside arch of foot, ankle, shin, knee, through the length of the inside of the thigh, and now into the inside of the inside of the crease in the groin, across into the back of the spine where the psoas connects, pressing, pressing, pressing (here your buttock will lift off the floor as a symptom of the pressure from the big toe and the path up the inside of the leg), inhale 1, 2, 3, and HAH! Release (and this is where the hip thumps to the floor). And again: big toe, arch, ankle, shin, knee, thigh, INSIDE — let go of the outside — let the other side completely hang off the inside of the opposing leg — crease back INSIDE — let everything else release, isolating the inside action of the leg from the big toe through the inside of the leg in the crease and connected to the back — inhale in preparation and 1, 2, 3, and a voiced HAH! Release. And again (at least three times, each time working to really isolate and learn to trust that the outer leg and the buttock and stomach muscles are NOT needed).

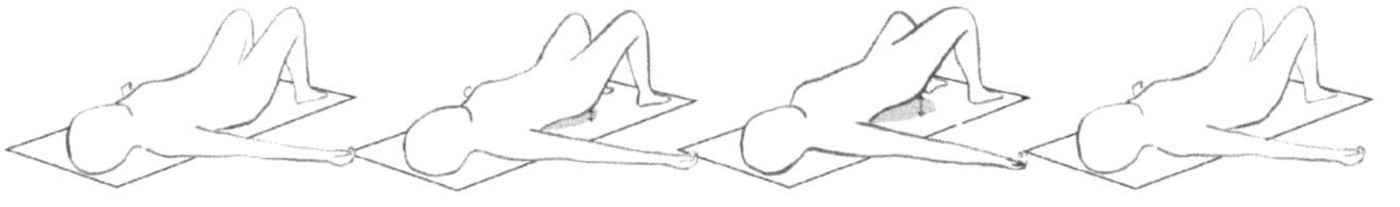

After the first side is finished, take a moment to notice any differences in the length of the spine or the contact that the (left) foot might be making with the floor. Witness, allow any sensations to occur and bring your awareness to the other (right) foot. Each side will be completely different; that is normal. Continue fresh without expectations, entering the task with awareness.

Switch sides and repeat Step 1 A—C.

Step 2. Pressing into both big toes at the same time, the insides of the arches, the insides of the ankles, through the insides of the knees, up the insides of the thighs, into the inside creases in the groin, lifting from the big toes to the back, pressing, inhale 1, 2, 3, HAH! And again, isolating and witnessing each time. Do this at least five times.

Step 3. On the last time, with both legs, hold at the top of the lift (with the buttocks poised in the air) and gently jiggle, initiating from both big toes, plotting the path as you pulse up the path plotted through the inside of the legs, creating a bouncing, bobbing effect of the pelvis in midair that will gently release any tensions in the back. Do this with a voiced AAAAAA, which will also jiggle and may create vibrations in different parts of the body than you are used to from other exercises. (Again, do not endeavour to make a type of sound; let the breath and voicing take its own sonic, vibrational shape.)

To end, bring the pelvis back to the floor in rest position and do a few three-part breaths. Notice any changes in your back, your feet, and the length of your body.

After you finish the exercise, when you do get up, press into the inside of the foot, plotting the path from the big toe up the inside of the leg through to the inside of the crease to create the action of standing. As you walk next, do so mindfully, with awareness of the inside of the foot and its relationship to the psoas, pelvis and length of torso. We will learn a more exacting way to do this transition to standing in the exercise after the next. But first, standing.

Exercise #15
Bridge to leg lift conditioning

As you get the hang of the *Hip thump* you will find that other muscles can hook in in addition to the essential ones needed for plotting the path through the big toe up the inside of the leg. It becomes apparent which extra muscles get in the way of isolating the optimal psoas alignment. The outer side of the outside thigh and also the short muscles in the stomach tend to engage unnecessarily. Letting go of these habitual tensions and then strengthening the psoas, along with the longer muscles in the abdominals, will aid in a long vertical alignment and also make it possible to execute the three-part breath in any position. The bridge to leg lift is a conditioning exercise to help with this.

Step 1. Just as in the final part of the *Hip thump*, press into the big toes of both feet, plotting the path up the inside of the ankle, the inside of the shin, the inside of the knee, then thigh, through the inside of the crease of the back — this pressing will as a symptom lift the pelvic girdle off the floor.

Step 2. With the pelvis off the floor, while working from *awareness*, intake with the three-part breath, and on the exhale raise one leg with the perineal contraction while maintaining the inside action of the other leg on the floor. Do NOT shift to the outside of the leg for a false stability. Let the perineal contraction help to stabilize the pelvis so that it remains as still as possible. On one breath, raise the leg, lengthen it and place the foot back on the floor, plotting the path through the big toe up the inside of the leg.

Step 3. Intake with the three-part breath and repeat on the other side.

DYNAMIC ALIGNMENT

So far in this chapter we have discussed a most precise site of centre. In the IPP we work with the perineal centre actioned through the three-part breath both on the intake and the exhale, isolating an exacting use of the psoas system. This breath, perineum, and psoas relationship provides the foundation of what we will now learn as *dynamic alignment*. Dynamic alignment allows the performer to move and sound in extended ways without superfluous tensions or compromise to the breath that could adversely affect aesthetic possibilities of dance and singing. Dynamic alignment is based on a consistent connection to centre which supports the performer in moments where they might get distracted, excited, and taken out of the moment of the chosen, task, event, dramatic choice and even character. Dynamic alignment is intimately connected to the notion of an *active aesthetic* as it happens in the *act* of *doing*. It is not something that is indicated, placed, or positioned. It is directional and active and one does not arrive there, but rather continues to activate within its dynamic.

Exercise #16
Psoas dynamic alignment in standing

Isolating the psoas while standing can be quite a challenge. It will start with the very same awareness initiating from the big toe that was learned in Ex. 14 *Hip thump*, and the path up and through the leg will be the same also. However, with gravity in action on the vertical axis new variables come into play.

This exercise introduces two new ideas: *directional energy*, which simply means in which direction you send your physicality and your awareness; and *opposing circles*, which will entail rotating one part of your body in one direction and the other in the opposite to create a dynamic balance between the two. This principle will be used later with the arms.

Standing for most is a place, a position, often one of a slow decay of the psoas' dynamic alignment, settling into "comfort" as the profound force of gravity takes its toll on the vertical axis.

We will learn this in a step-by-step fashion; however, the final action will be to work concurrently in opposing directions, counteracting the effects of gravity and harnessing the power of the psoas to lengthen and create readiness and ease of the breath-body. The challenge here is in not getting stuck or set. There is no position or placement. Every task or structure is a constant *doing* of directional energy. (Eventually there will be places of arrival and departure in the flow of choreography and blocking, but even stillness will remain dynamic in the act of doing.) Standing is active.

Step 1. From the standing position, do a little jump and land, releasing as much residual habitual tension as possible. (Recall "Etch-a-Sketch" in Ex. 9.) Allow the landing to align your body to what feels like your most balanced and poised standing position in this moment. Scan your body, witnessing any tension and releasing where possible. Let your arms simply hang and your tongue, jaw, and face relax. Let your knees remain soft and unlocked.

Step 2. Align your feet hip-width apart. Let your toes and knees face forward (not turned out). Working from *awareness*, press into the big toe side of the feet, lift and separate the four little toes, spreading them and stretching them before placing them back onto the floor, with the directional energy moving still through the big toe side of the foot into the ground as you lengthen up and out through the inside of the leg from the big toe.

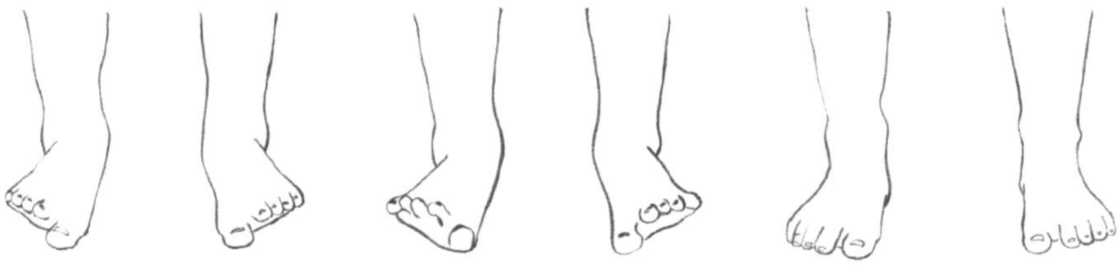

Etch-a-Sketch and repeat. Notice how when you get out of the way and let your body follow through with the effects of the inner toe action in standing, your buttocks are likely to jut out a little and the arch in your lower back will arch a little more than usual. This is normal.

Step 3. Pressing into the big toe side of the leg, lengthening up and out and plotting the path toward the psoas, rotate your thighs towards each other inwards and out the back.

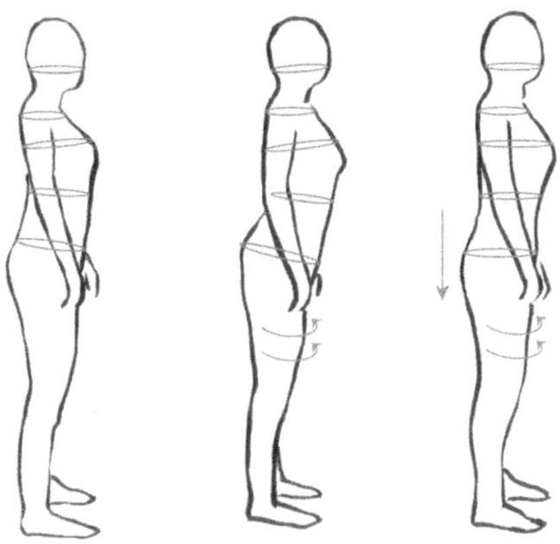

This will give the sensation of opening the buttocks like the opening of a book. This inward rotation of the thighs, accompanied with the action of the big toe, is not meant to feel comfortable. However, if you maintain this directional energy while you do the counter move, on the next step something interesting might occur.

Step 4. Draw the coccyx down ***without clenching the buttocks.*** The directional energy of the coccyx goes down as you open the creases in the thighs and lengthen your upper body up and out of the foundation established in the toes, up the inner leg, balanced on the equally actioned internal spirals of the legs, countered by the drawing down of the coccyx. Open the creases in the front of the legs and lift the torso equally, front back and sides, up and out of the pelvis.

Etch-a-Sketch.

Again: there is no stuck or degenerative position called standing. The big toe into the ground is *actioned* against the spread of the other four toes. The internal spiral of the leg is *actioned* against the drawing down of the coccyx. The lengthening of the torso out of the pelvis is *actioned* out of the stability created in the inside path from the big toe up through the legs and balanced by the coccyx descending. Standing is NOT a place or position when we are actively engaging the psoas in a balanced way. It is a doing, actioned anew with each and every breath. In this way it will also become both a place of poise and of readiness.

MOVING FROM FLOOR TO STANDING WITH DYNAMIC PSOAS ALIGNMENT

To move from the floor to standing while maintaining connection to the psoas and the perineal centre allows the transition to occur without any glitches to the sound when voicing. We learn it first by bending one leg under the standing foot. Plotting the path through the big toe of the standing foot, through the inside of the shin and the inside of the knee, up through the inside of the thigh and into the crease, we raise up on an exhale. The perineal contraction on the exhale, with its directional energy moving up the vertical axis of the body, activates the raising of the body.

To begin to do this, make it one extended movement as you come back up from the roll, on an exhale. So after your legs are over your head, on the exhale roll back to sitting with one leg under and the other "on the walk" (ready for the step, with foot on the floor) and let the exhale (with the perineal contraction) bring you to standing. And again, the perineal contraction on the exhale, with its directional energy moving up the vertical axis of the body, activates the raising of the body while at the same time maintaining the low centre. It is maintaining the low centre as we rise that can present a challenge. We often have the tendency to raise our points of centre as we reach for height, extend, or expand — when what is needed is the exact opposite.

In this move from floor to standing it is most important to learn to allow the contraction of the perineum (in balanced combination with the breath) in the directional vertical axis of the body, along with the plotting of the path from the big toe up the inside of the foot, leg and into the crease of the thigh, to be the action that raises you off the floor. What you DON'T want to do is to raise your point of centre into the chest and try to swing your body up from the floor, jutting out your upper chest and thus requiring the outside of the thigh to bring your legs to standing. It is a slow and smooth movement, with the breath moving you as the perineum leads the way, with centre staying nice and low as the path (again through the big toe, calf, inside of knee, inside of thigh, into the crease, and through to the back) brings you to standing.

Maintaining a connection to centre as you rise or extend, physically, vocally, and/or emotionally is always the challenge in this work. A beautiful thing is that in this practice, centring is constantly in action as it is aligned with the three-part breath and its continuous connection to the perineum. "Don't become the kite" is a little tool that can help you to remember to not leave centre.

Don't become the kite

To maintain an active connection to centre, especially in the height of the moment, can feel counterintuitive; however, it is vital to this practice. Imagine that you are flying a kite. There is you, holding the string, and there is the string, and there is the kite. In acting, singing, and dance there are many ways that we can lose the "you holding the string" and get seduced or excited and become the kite. We get caught up in the moment, the move or the sound and lose awareness of the task. Presence is lost, and, well, without the flyer, the kite is lost too. The problem with becoming the kite is that there is no grounding, no way to direct the movement, and no productive tension. It becomes a hysteria of sorts.

As actors, we can become the kite when we "ride an emotional state of being" and lose the moment-to-moment life of the character in service of sheer emotion. We may be producing tears or anger but there is a loss of complexity;

the moment becomes ungrounded, and very often the artist becomes disintegrated from breath-body and the ability to make dramatic choices.

As singers, when we rise up in the breath-body as we travel into the higher registers, we find that this is joined by a lifting of the chest and sternum, tightening the throat and creating facial tensions. We lose connection to the breath, harmonics are compromised, and catches occur.

As dancers, we can become the kite when we wind up in the torso during leaps and turns, disconnecting the upper body from the psoas and thus integrity of the feet, often manifesting in a sloppy or even damaging landing.

And, of course, the dancer can get caught up in the moment, the actor lose their connection to breath, and the singer their connection to the feet.

In moving from the roll to standing — in each of the above examples — *don't become the kite* will always start with a constant connection to the perineum on the intake and the exhale. In fact, each of the above examples of becoming the kite will be prevented by staying connected to the perineal centre through the breath. When you leave centre, use the outer leg muscles to stand and swing the torso up from the chest, you have become the kite, disintegrated, and, if you try it, unable to sound or breathe with continued connection and physical freedom in the transition from floor to standing.

ROLLING TO STANDING WITH AND WITHOUT VOICING

At this point we put it all together. All in one action: perineum, suspension, three-part breath, the roll, dynamic alignment in standing, psoas isolation through the plotting of the path through the big toe, remember "don't become the kite", return to centre. Three-part breath will take you from rolling to standing through the vertical axis in connection to the psoas. The voice, the moves, the shape, and the sound will eventually become a symptom, not the doing.

The task is to stay connected to the perineum throughout with the aid of the three-part breath. You will know that you have when you can complete the entire sequence without a glitch in the movement or the breath/voice and without the need to leave centre to return to dynamic alignment in standing.

You can choose to start by first standing, then on the exhale or while voicing move to sitting, rolling back, then forward to sitting and coming to standing all on one breath. Or you can break it down and start from standing, to sitting, to rolling back, while legs are over the head — suspend — then intake and, on the exhale/voicing, roll forward to sitting and up to standing.

You can also start sitting and, on the exhale/voicing, roll back, then forward and up to standing, then while standing — suspend — intake and then, on the next exhale/voicing, descend to the floor, back through the roll and forward to sitting.

This can be done with voiced scales, on a spoken phrase or on the slight pressure of ssss as per Ex. 10, *Three-part breath*. In the section dedicated to voicing, you will learn about a facial mirror centre in Ex. 31, *Accenting A*. If you are primarily working on the breath-body and want to fast-forward to smooth voicing while in movement, you may wish to skip to this section and then return to this point to learn about working with hands and arms for more options.

Regardless, *let the breath move you and let all movement and sound initiate from the perineum.*

Diagram of foot position as you come to standing:

Exercise #17
Sideways rolling in partners

This is an excellent way of developing rapport for duets or scene study and is an interesting ensemble-building activity. The main point, however, is to build up the ability to return to centre with each breath, moving through the breath-body, with an exacting use of the psoas, and with the added challenge of working with another.

Working in centre with a partner is very telling. When one person is not working from the perineum, or if they "become the kite", it sets the joint task of rolling astray — literally. One of the partners will actually start heading off in a direction other than the intended trajectory and this will unbalance the entire task. It's an unmistakable analogy for how partnerships work (and don't work). Meeting in the middle is key. Both parties need to come from awareness rather than focus. Staying centred in connection to the breath is essential. Witnessing one's own *stuff* and letting it go is key.

Again, the shape or choreography of the move is not the task; this will come as a symptom of the three-part breath in line with the perineal centre in connection to a collective breath-body. The doing of the doing is not the shape.

You will need a space of some length.

Step 1. You and your partner will face each other, just far enough apart to be able to hold hands with slightly bent elbows. Both of you will kneel on the ground with your knees in line with your hips. The same internal "plotting the path" up the inside of the legs that happens in the hip thump and dynamic alignment in standing as part of connection to psoas occurs here, even though it is the knees that make contact with the floor rather than the feet.

Step 2. You are both going to roll sideways while holding hands and maintaining eye contact. Decide which direction you are going to roll and then... Intake, releasing the perineum and pelvic floor downward (three-part breath), and on the exhale (sssss) the perineal contraction will engage up the vertical axis of the body and here we go! With a bend of the knee, collapse downwards in the intended direction. The side of your buttock and the outside of the thigh of the leg that is on the side of the direction you are moving in will first make contact with the floor. At the same time, you will drop the shoulder on the same side, reaching towards each other, making contact with the floor on your shoulder, rolling from the shoulder across the middle back towards the other shoulder, making contact with the knee on the other side, plotting the path through the inside of the thigh into the inside of the crease in the leg, bringing you back to kneeling, facing your partner with hands still held and eyes still in contact.

When your legs are in the air you can do one of two variations. You can extend them straight up, plotting the path through the big toe with the psoas connection intact, not becoming the kite (in this instance the kite would be your feet). You can also choose to bend the knees.

Notice if you lost eye contact. Notice if you left centre and, if so, at which moment in the sequence of the move. Notice if you landed further away from each other than when you started. Notice if you lost awareness and went to thoughts and feelings at any moment during the roll. How might this have affected centre or connection to the breath-body? Where in the task might you have gone to judging and diagnosing rather than the agreed task of letting the breath roll you while meeting in the middle with your partner, simply rolling sideways with eye contact?

Step 3. Repeat step 2 and roll back the other way.

Step 4. From here you can begin to roll together in a sequence of three to five rolls in a row, or across the entire space. (Return to the noticing self first and then the partnership if you find that things go astray.)

Variations: This exercise, once mastered, is excellent using the exhale during scales, a song that both know, or while reciting a script, pausing while in the kneeling position to intake after a phrase and continuing with the roll on the next exhale/singing/spoken phrase. It is helpful in that it aids in the intake (rather than inhale) as the body hits an exertion that requires an intake and exhausts the options for the controlling tensions that happen while inhaling. (See pages 106–109 for clarification on the difference between inhale and intake.)

For most this is fun. It's a wonderful way to end the day of a first workshop in this practice.

As mentioned previously, in this work we do not speak of posture, placement, or position, but rather of a dynamic alignment constantly aided by the perineal centre, actioned through breath and supported by an exacting use of the psoas. One of the challenges that can happen, especially during the flow of complex choreography that takes us from the floor to standing to leaping, or in moments of emotional catharsis, is that the parts of the torso that are needed to be kept independent in order to maintain three-part breath can collapse into each other. This can also happen by way of a returning to what is perceived as "comfortable" rather than the action of standing learned in *Dynamic alignment in standing*. Next we take the standing further, with a more precise way of understanding our own vertical alignment. Knowing how this works will allow you to land quietly after leaps, stop after a turn with stillness and in a position of readiness for the next move, and it will help to make clear how leaning too far forward or too far back on your feet can directly affect all the muscles of the body and, in doing so, directly affect your breath and therefore your sound.

Exercise #18
The sweet spot (exploring vertical alignment)

The sweet spot exercise is a way of exploring a vertical centre through your body that plots the path from the perineum and out the top of the head. It helps you to find a dynamic alignment in standing, walking, and leaping that sets you up to make optimum use of the psoas (see pages 123–125). In sports, a sweet spot is the place on a tennis racket, baseball, or cricket bat where you can hit the ball with the least amount of pressure and it will go the furthest. In audio engineering, it is the place between the speakers where the perfect combination of stereo sound can be heard. This exercise is called the sweet spot because it is about finding balance, poise, and maximum availability with the least amount of resistance. We will eventually apply this to standing, walking, and leaping while breathing, expressing, and sounding. This will have implications for dynamic alignment in future exercises, helping to maintain optimum vocal resonance in any position.

In this exercise, we lean back and forth, witnessing the shift in tension that is required to maintain the standing position in the act of leaning. Your task will be to allow yourself to maintain the standing position with the least amount of tension possible while noticing the transfer of necessary tensions as you pass through a vertical centre.

Preparing to work: Come ready to witness and work in awareness, with bare feet, a firm and clean floor, loose clothing, and a quiet mind.

Step 1. In the standing position, do a little jump and land, releasing any residual habitual tension. (Etch-a-Sketch, see page 108.) Allow the landing to align your body to what feels like your most balanced and poised standing position in this moment. Scan your body, witnessing any tension and releasing where possible. Let your arms simply hang and your tongue, jaw, and face relax. Let your knees remain soft and unlocked.

From the standing position, allow yourself to lean forward, bending from your ankles as far as you can to see how far you can lean before needing to step forward to catch your balance. Once you know where that is, do an Etch-a-Sketch and repeat the exercise, but this time while leaning back. After you know how far you can lean in both the forward and backward directions, we will for the rest of the exercise avoid needing to step off the standing position but instead aim to lean as far as we can without having to catch ourselves.

Step 2. Now that we know where the lean limits are, Etch-a-Sketch again, allowing the landing to align your body to what feels like your most balanced and poised standing position in this moment. Let your arms simply hang and your tongue, jaw, and face relax. Slowly lean forward and notice which muscles need to engage to help you maintain your standing position. Allow yourself to maintain the standing position with the least amount of tension possible, even while leaning. Allow yourself to move from centre to forward and back to centre a few times, really slowly, with awareness. Sense when the muscles engage as you move forward and when they release as you move back. Take your time and really explore. Once you have finished your exploration with leaning forward, Etch-a-Sketch and go from centre to back and to centre with the same exploration.

Tip: In order to be really sure that you are using the least number of muscles possible while leaning forward, see if you can release your jaw. Most people can. However, if you try and release your toes, you will fall forward. As you get more sensitive with your witnessing, you will notice that releasing your forehead completely while leaning forward will result in a fall forward (as will releasing your jaw when you are leaned back). This makes it clear which muscles are required to be engaged to maintain the standing position when leaning forward or back. Experiment with different muscles in both the lean forward and lean back directions. You may wish to shade in a copy of the following diagram, to illustrate the places that you sense muscle engagement, documenting your proprioceptive awareness of your vertical alignment.

Step 3. Shake it all out and Etch-a-Sketch. Now, with eyes closed, moving from centre to forward, through centre and all the way back, through centre to forward and again, witness the patterns of engagement. Release as you move through centre and notice what engages again as you lean in the other direction. Continue to lean back and forth, working to sense where you are doing the least amount of holding to maintain your standing position. It may be a slightly different centre than you expect or that you habitually stand in.

Tip: Some people find it helpful to consider the felt sense of the tension to be like sound getting louder in the shaded places on the diagram as you lean forward, getting quiet as you move through centre, and getting louder in other places as the muscle engagements shift to the necessary muscles for leaning back. What we are aiming for is that moment as you pass through centre where it is absolutely silent. It will be the place where your knees do not have to hook in at all, and where your jaw can release completely. This will be your sweet spot.

Step 4. You may be surprised where you are when you arrive at your place of least resistance. For some, the felt sense is further forward and for others it is further back than habitual. Once you arrive at the sweet spot, plot an imaginary line from the floor, through the perineum and out the top of your head. If you are more forward than usual, this line will be tilted forward; if you are more back than usual, the line will be on the diagonal backward. Allow yourself to walk through the space, maintaining the line at the diagonal that supports your sweet spot. Once you have explored walking, you can move to a light run. If you find that you revert to your habitual alignment, stop, Etch-a-Sketch and sway to find the sweet spot, create the imaginary line and move through the space again.

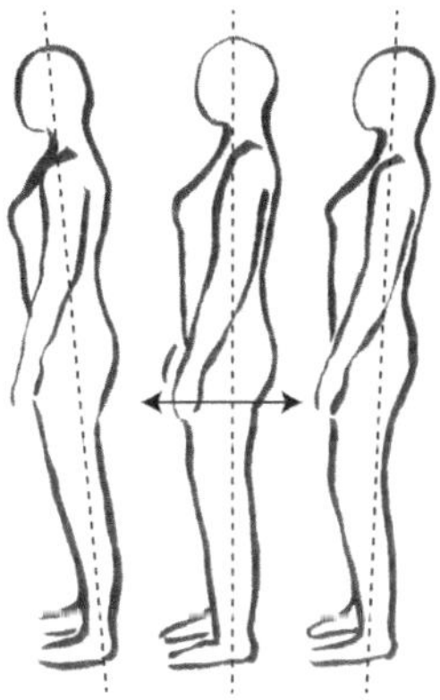

Variations

Hint: The sweet spot exercise works as a very effective exploration on the effect your alignment has on your vocal resonance. If you do steps 1 and 2 with a strong small mint in your mouth, breathing in and out and directing the vapour effect into the nasal passages and across the palate, you will discover that in different positions the mint travels to different areas and is shut out of others. This illustrates most effectively how the sweet spot is the best dynamic alignment for creating space in the facial resonating chambers. If working in partners, you can also put strong peppermint or eucalyptus oil on a hand and place it a few inches away from the person doing the exercise in steps 1 and 2.

Voicing: This exercise is also useful to do while voicing either a sustained text (the alphabet can work) or a sustained note. As you move through the sweet spot you can observe how the changing resonance (made clear with the mint variation) directly connects to harmonics and in some even pitch. For most people, leaning forward will result in a more strident quality to the tone and may even contribute to habitual sharpness. Leaning back can contribute to a dampening of tone and habitual flatness.

THE RINGS

Now that we have learned about dynamic alignment in standing, the next step is to learn a tool that will aid in dynamic alignment while rolling, bending, crunching, jumping, lifting, contracting, doing a headstand, cartwheeling, back bends, and pretty much anything else. One principle that helps in maintaining the integrity of the three-part breath in extended movement is that of The rings. *The rings* is not exactly an exercise, but, much like "Don't become the kite", it is a constant principle that we return to throughout the work.

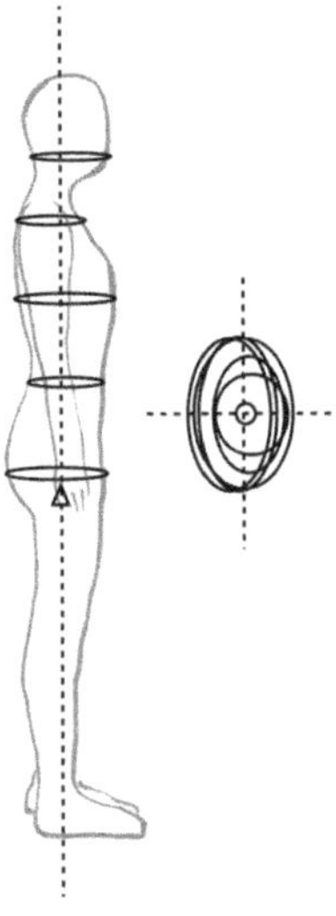

Imagine that you have rings making their circumference around the body in the following places.

- *Pelvic Girdle:* Around the area in line with the top of the pubic bone.
- *Diaphragm:* Around the area in line with the lower ribs/intercostals.
- *Sternum:* Around the circumference of the middle of the chest plate.
- *Clavicle:* Around the circumference of the collar bones.
- *Jaw:* Around the circumference in line with the jaw hinge.

The aim is to, in all movement, create space both during the intake and the exhale between all the rings, equally around their circumferences. This will happen as part of the three-part breath with the perineal contraction up the vertical axis.

This creates distance, back, front and centre equally, between the pelvic girdle, the diaphragm, shoulder girdle, and jaw. By working with the rings in this way, you can maintain the three-part breath and clear vocal production when folded over and in any physical position.

Once you have the concept of the rings as a tool, it is worth returning to the *Roll to standing* exercise and *Sideways roll in partners*, working now to expand the distance between the rings on both the exhale and the intake, and observing how this dynamic alignment in motion helps to stabilize the sound and breath and facilitate a less interrupted engagement with the perineum.

You might also note that in your sweet spot, the rings are at their most expanded naturally, with the back, front, and sides maintaining distance more equally than if you were leaning too far forward or too far back. Also, if you return to the *Dynamic alignment in standing* exercise, you will see how plotting the path through the feet with the rotation of the thighs working against the tilt of the pelvis creates a wonderful spring of directional energy that enables the greatest expansion between the rings on both the exhale and the intake. The rings are a tool for witnessing and remembering your dynamic alignment in motion. They will maintain the optimal spacing when you initiate each movement from the perineum, "Don't become the kite", and return to centre.

The rings is a concept that helps to proprioceptively draw awareness to the lengthening of the torso and helps us to remember not to collapse either front, back, or sides while in motion.

WORKING IN MOTION THROUGH DYNAMIC ALIGNMENT

At this juncture it should be clear how dynamic alignment works. It should also be clear that this is fuelled through the three-part breath and its continuous connection to the perineum, which supports a most exacting use of the psoas system.

Working in conscious practice with awareness while witnessing the doing of the doing will be key. Remember, each task is not the name, shape, sound, or emotional outcome of the exercise, but rather the doing of the exercise. We are continuing to work within the *active aesthetic* in the field of performing. Return to the previous chapters if any of these terms or concepts are unfamiliar at this point.

In Part IV we will apply the following work to character, text, and dramatic event. However, this work at this point is not just about movement and voice, even though it seems on the face of it to be conversing with physio-vocal propositions. It is very much about the actor as part of what is often called psychophysical work and, as such, is fundamental in harnessing presence and awareness in the act of doing a task, a crucial component in learning to access one's full potential through intent. This work also hones the conditioning of an integrative centre that offers optimal emotional availability. At every juncture, this work is about the integrative instrument and is holographic in structure (see pages 56–57).

WORKING WITH LEGS AND FEET, FROM SITTING TO STANDING, LEAPING AND TURNING

This next series of exercises gets us moving from centre while standing, plotting the path to the psoas while maintaining a constant connection to the perineum.

Many aspects of the preparation for this next sequence are the same as what we have been working with. In all these, the articulation of the toes, ankles, and arches will come into play. I recommend a warm-up that incorporates rotating the ankles, bending and stretching the toes back and then forward on the ground or in the air, in connection to breath, and massaging into the arches of the feet, pressing your fingers into the spaces between your toes. While standing or on the floor, rotate the ankles, the knees, the legs at the hip sockets. Find all the joints in your body and explore their range, with breath connected to the perineum. "Let the breath move you".

Find a clean floor, have bare feet and a mirror if possible. However, use the mirror wisely, to witness your body's releases and tensions rather than to judge the "look" of the move or of self.

It is crucial that you work in Conscious Practice, coming from awareness rather than focus, witnessing rather than judging and diagnosing, and that you work within the active aesthetic, attending to the chosen task or the doing of the doing rather than merely the exercise.

Exercise #19

Infinity from centre

Step 1. Find your best dynamic alignment in standing for today. This might entail working through the sweet spot and also a witnessing of the rings. Etch-a-Sketch and land where you feel in readiness, supported by the psoas, as unlocked as possible.

Step 2. As you continue to *Three-part breath* and make contact with the lowest part of the pelvic bowl (the perineum), lengthen up your vertical axis through the inside of the body, through the innermost centre of the rings, from the bottom chakra up out through the top of your head. Gently let the perineum sway in little alternating circles (the task is to isolate the perineum as much as possible), initiating from the perineum and eventually ribboning out through the arms and the legs as you extend the movement. Start with small movements, working to abstain from using the outside of the rings or hooking in any superfluous muscles. Isolate and initiate ALL movement from the perineum in connection to the breath.

> Witness: You will know if you have lost the vertical axis supported by an isolated engagement of the psoas when your legs hook in or your abdominals work to create the perineal movement. Notice your jaw and tongue. Your tongue should be able to rest gently in line with your lower teeth, as opposed to being stuck at the roof of the mouth. If you find that things are hooking in (for instance, if knees are locked, jaw tight, eyes focusing hard, shoulders up...), Etch-a-Sketch, reset, connect to the three-part breath, isolate the perineum, return to centre, and repeat.

Step 3. As you begin to find your vertical axis in motion you can now begin to extend the path of the perineum. Let the perineum move in the shape of a sideways eight — an infinity sign. Keep it small at first, maintaining the integrity of the dynamic alignment. (The arms and hands should remain as released as possible and are likely to move as a symptom, often as a gentle lift and fall in line with the ribboning out of perineal path.)

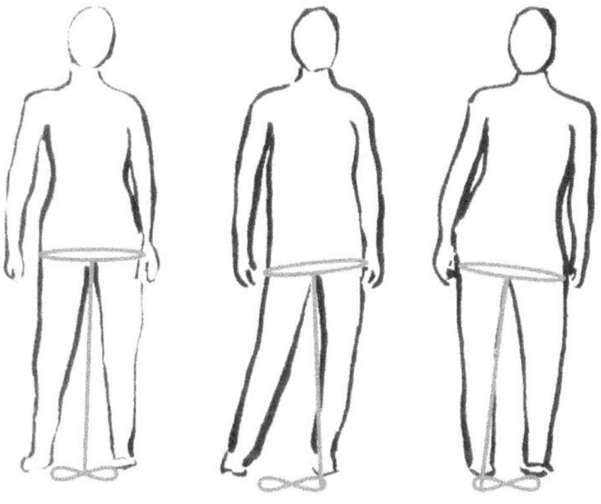

Helpful visualization: While thinking of a pencil or laser beam sitting at perineum, the bottom-most part of the bowl of your pelvis, directed at the floor, imagine that it writes a little ∞ (infinity sign) on the floor as it moves. Like all visualizations (which are subjective), only use this if it works for you.

Aside: When done correctly, this "looks" like a belly dance, specifically the type practised in the South Pacific. It has in common the fact that the movement initiates from below the belly button; however, this work initiates from *even* lower. IMPORTANT: students often when first "seeing the move" work to "do the look" and end up doing a sort of pop, jazz, or street-dance version of a hip thrust or pelvic undulation. The difference is that we are not relying on the abdominals here; rather, the abdominals are ribboned or *moved through,* supported by the three-part breath initiated from the perineum. The reason for this is that the abdominal engagement for the pelvic undulation and the belly dance will make it impossible to maintain the integrity of the three-part breath staying in connection with the perineal centre, making it also impossible to sound without glitches and jiggles, and will hook into the second chakra with its emotional states (which may not be an appropriate choice for a character).

Step 4. Once standing in place with the movement of the ∞ established, you can begin to start to extend the circle of the ∞ more on one side than the other so that, *as a symptom*, one leg will ribbon further out of the pelvic girdle, lifting the foot off the floor and allowing the option for travel sideways across the space. We are NOT moving the leg *and* circulating the pelvis. This is ONE action in line with the breath from the initiation of the perineum.

Step 5: After playing with travel across the space, you can then go back the other way. You can then go in diagonals, towards the front left, back right, and so on.

Notice which sides and diagonals within your body present the biggest challenges while maintaining the integrity of the psoas connection. Witness where you might have a tendency for the foot to land in such a position that you work from foot up rather than perineum down. Notice where and if your tongue changes position. "Isn't that interesting?" Notice which chakra might be congested as you work (there will be an equal relationship in the lower body — review mirror tensions on pages 117–119).

Hint: If one foot keeps on landing in such a way that you lose the psoas, you can return to the hip thump (remembering plotting the path). If you lose the integrity of the rings, you can return to the sweet spot. If you lose the perineum, you can pause in that position and find your three-part breath and notice all the above. Witness and be kind to yourself in the knowledge that each day is different. If you get all mucked up trying to "get it", return to the work of Part II. The task is not to "try and get it".

Next steps: Once you have become familiar with initiating movement from the perineum in constant connection with the three-part breath, you can start to create movement sequences that include sitting to rolling to standing, with and without voicing. Play with moving in any manner in the space with the perineum and the breath leading the way. When you lose connection to the perineum, start at the beginning and build from there.

Exercise #20
Silly walk(s)

The name of this exercise is playfully titled after a comedy sketch by Monty Python, presented on their show "Monty Python's Flying Circus", episode 14, titled "Face the Press". In it, John Cleese executes ridiculous manners of travelling through space with full extensions of his legs and with a wonderful sense of his own centre. Here the point is to work from centre, plotting the path through the big toe through the psoas, fuelled by the three-part breath.

Step 1. After doing *Infinity from centre,* come to dynamic standing, Etch-a-Sketch and find dynamic alignment in standing. Working from awareness, do a few three-part breaths. Facing sideways, feet in line with knees, knees in line with hips (no turnout in this instance), intake in preparation and...

Step 2. On the exhale, raise the leg up to a right-angle directly in front of you with a flexed foot. Even as the leg sits in midair, continue to plot the path through the big toes up through the psoas. This will invariably draw the little toe side of your feet towards your body as the big toe side of the foot lengthens through the inside of the leg away from your body. Continuing on the same exhale, bend the knee and bring the leg all the way back, extending past the back body, bringing your torso and leg forward in a parallel line with the floor. Continuing on the same exhale, bend the leg, straighten up and take a step, plotting the path through the big toe as it touches the floor.

Notice if you lose your balance raising the leg. What has happened to the foot on the floor? Did you lose the big toe? Did you move your weight toward the little toe? Remember that the big toe connection is the first action of stability, followed by plotting the path up through the inside of the calf, through the inside of the knee, into the inside of the thigh, through the crease of the pelvic girdle into the lower back (as in the *Hip thump*). Even as we lift the leg, the exact dynamics of the dynamic alignment in standing need to be held with integrity. This will be possible if we work through the vertical axis, through the inside of the rings, and NOT go to the outside muscles of the thigh or the abdominals. You will find that this is only possible with the aid of the three-part breath, allowing the perineal contraction to both instigate and follow through with the legs raising.

Next steps: After becoming familiar with the basic silly walk and becoming familiar with how and when your feet start to leave the psoas connection, you can begin to explore any manner of walking through the space. Working through existing blocking or choreography with these new principles can be telling.

Exercise #21
Leaping and jumping

Here we build on the skills above while learning the basic principles needed for any manner of leaping and jumping.

Preparation: Ex. 14 *Hip thump,* Ex. 19 *Infinity from centre,* Ex. 20 *Silly walk(s),* Ex. 18 *The sweet spot,* Ex. 10 *Three-part breath.* Make sure that you do the suggested warm-up that includes articulations of the toes, ankles, knees, and hip joints. Working from *awareness*...

Step 1. Find your sweet spot, Etch-a-Sketch. Start by walking, lifting each leg (initiating from the perineum), specifically drawing awareness to how your feet meet and leave the floor. Witness how in walking you lift through the leg, how the heel first makes contact with the floor, rolling into the arch and through the inside of the foot into the big toe side of the foot as you follow through, bending the toes, gently pushing off and continuing on the other side.

Step 2. In this step you will "plot the path" just as you did in Ex. 14 *Hip thump,* isolating the psoas (this time in motion), lengthening the rings as you maintain connection to centre/perineum through the three-part breath. As you walk through the space, plot the path through the big toe side of the feet and up through the inside of the leg into the crease and around to the lower back, releasing your coccyx gently down as your torso lifts up and out of the pelvic girdle equally on the back, front, and sides, extending the rings, lengthening through the inside vertical axis at the very centre of the rings, from the perineum out the top of the head. Plot the path, don't become the kite, remain in contact with the perineum on intake and exhale.

Step 3. In this step you move from walking to leaping. Continue as in step 2, walking with hands resting at the sides. Then, while maintaining perineal centre, step, step, step, leap: raise hands above your head while jumping off the ground. Release hands and continue, 1, 2, 3, *leap,* 1, 2, 3 *leap.* The lifting off the ground will happen on alternating feet. As your feet land, let the action of landing mirror that of the hip thump, through the toes (with the most action on the big toe side of the feet), plotting the path up the inside of the shin,

knee, thigh, and into the crease, letting these all bend and take the weight, springing back in readiness for the next step.

Step 4. Work through steps 1–3, but this time while sounding. You can use a script, a song, the alphabet, or a sustained "zzzzz". You will learn that it is only by maintaining the perineal centre with the psoas connection that an uncompromised flow of breath can occur, allowing for an uncompromised voice quality in movement. When you get to the leaping you will find that "don't become the kite" (page 134) is a most useful tool, assuring that you continue an even tone with no glitches even as you leap and land. Maintaining the integrity of the rings, lengthening back, front, and sides evenly as you leap and land will maintain the integrity of the three-part breath. (Singers may wish to jump forward to Exs. 31 and 33, *Accenting A & B,* and then return to this.)

Step 5. With the same basic principles, shift from leaping to spontaneous jumping in your own time. Landing through the big toe, plotting the path through the inside of the leg and into the crease to the back, absorbing the impact and bouncing gently back in readiness for the next action — remain in constant connection to the breath through the perineum. You will find that you can jiggle, leap, and jump without any glitches to the sound when practised correctly.

Next steps: Now that you have become familiar with the basic principles of leaping and jumping, try any manner of jazz-based or ballet-based leaps or jumps. Try fight blocking or just explore, and make adjustments to stick to the principles learned above. Remember: awareness first, breath/perineal centre, and plot the path — then the move!

Exercise #22
Turning

Here we build on the skills above while working with specific challenges in turning while maintaining the three-part breath, the rings, and the psoas connection. Start in dynamic standing (facing a mirror if you have one). You are going to make a full circle turn and land back in your dynamic standing position.

Preparation: Ex. 14 *Hip thump,* Ex. 19 *Infinity from centre,* Ex. 20 *Silly walk(s),* Ex. 18 *The sweet spot,* Ex. 10 *Three-part breath.* Make sure that you do the suggested warm-up that includes articulations of the toes, ankles, knees, and hip joints.

Step 1. Starting in dynamic standing, working from *awareness*, intake in preparation (releasing the perineum) as you raise one leg and turn it in with a big arch (as if you could hug a beach ball with your leg in front of you).

Step 2. The basic shape will be this: on the exhale (initiating the movement from the perineum), while maintaining the arch of the leg, take the leg around the back of your body, keeping the knee and arch as high as you can for as long as you can before you bring it down facing front again in dynamic standing. The task, however, will be to maintain connection to the perineum ("Don't become the kite"). You will also want to keep the dynamic alignment by maintaining connection to the psoas, plotting the path through the inside of the standing leg throughout the turn, and creating a path in the immediate placement of the turning leg back down to dynamic standing through the big toe and the inside of that leg. Keeping the rings equally expanded will help maintain the integrity of the three-part breath.

Helpful hint: Pick a spot in front of you to focus your gaze. Stay with that spot as long as you can and return to it as your head turns in the final moments of the spin.

Step 3. Follow steps 1 and 2 with sounding, as you did in the previous exercise. You will find yet again that an uncompromised tone and sustained breath is only possible with the constant connection to the perineum and the attending to the dynamic alignment through the isolation of the psoas and the lengthening through the vertical axis through the separation of the rings.

Next steps: As with the previous exercises, now that you have the basic principles, explore with all manner of turning. Remember: awareness first, breath/perineal centre and plot the path — then the move! — and return to centre. ("Don't become the kite.")

SHOULDER, NECK, ARMS, AND HANDS

In the previous exercises we learned how the perineal centre serves an exacting use of the psoas system through all manner of moving through space, leaping, jumping, and turning. This next section takes us to how we work with the hands and arms towards the use of arms going from the floor to standing, in lifts, catching back bends, and even in cartwheels, maintaining the integrity of an emotive, physical, and vocal integration.

Necks, shoulders, and arms are powerful absorbers of "stuff". There is a reason why there are sayings like we build our lives on the "shoulders of giants", or when someone carries around a grievance they have a "chip on their shoulder", or when we get snubbed we were given the "cold shoulder". When one is taking on a lot of stuff, they need "broad shoulders", and of course there was Atlas, that primordial Greek titan who "shouldered" the entire earth.

In this work a working independence of the hands, arms, clavicle, shoulder, neck, tongue, jaw, and sternum is key. When we do hold the world on our shoulders, these all tend to get locked together. It is important to find the ways that these operate independently and explore how the skeleton, and not the muscles, is perfectly placed to take the impact when pressing on the hands. If you take a detailed look at the anatomy of the shoulder girdle, you will see that the shoulder is not at all stuck or even one unit, but rather a concert of four joints. The shoulder joint, the *glenohumeral* joint, works as a ball and socket between the head of the humerus (or upper arm bone) and the glenoid cavity of the scapula (or shoulder blade). The *acromioclavicular* (AC) joint sits where the clavicle meets the acromion of the scapula. The *sternoclavicular* (SC) joint is situated where the clavicle meets the sternum (or chest bone) and the *scapulothoracic* joint is where the scapula meets with the ribs at the back of the chest. There is quite a bit more movement possible than we often experience.

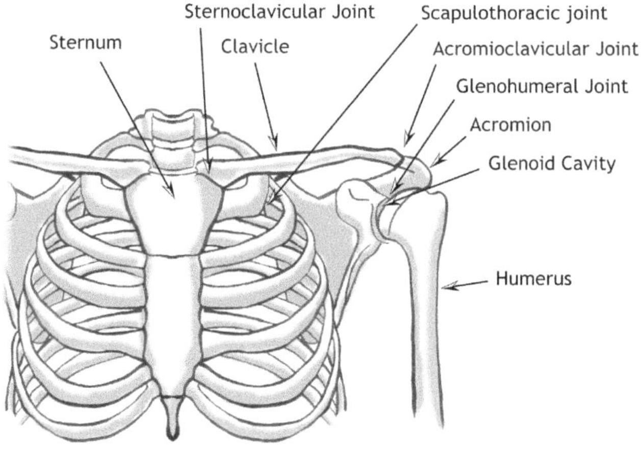

Movement of the hands, arms, clavicle, shoulder, neck, tongue, jaw, and sternum connect to the perineal centre through the three-part breath. Working with an exacting use of the psoas is as important as it was when we were working with the feet and legs. We will be working to release tensions so that more independent movement within the thoracic spine and the neck and shoulder area is possible.

For all of the below, I recommend a warm-up that includes moving the thoracic spine and the hands, arms, and shoulders, along with gentle work moving the neck. It is helpful to circle the wrists, elbows, and arms at the shoulder, along with stretches, including those with arms over your head and across the sides of the body. Use your favorites, discover new ones, and explore movement in these parts of the body. For some, ideas from the aforementioned texts by Olsen and Stapleton offer excellent ways to explore and condition the areas of the shoulders, neck, arms, and hands.

Exercise #23

Hand press (plotting the path)

In this exercise you will learn how to plot the path from the webbing between the thumb and index finger through the arm into the bottom of the scapula. Much as in the *Hip thump*, you will learn how many muscles that are not needed may hook in. We are aiming for an exacting use of the breath-body, plotting the path to isolate only the muscles needed and to witness superfluous tensions so that they may be released. In doing this, we will unlock and make independent the hands, arms, clavicle, shoulder, neck, tongue, jaw, and sternum.

Preparation: A clean floor, loose clothing, especially on the upper part of the body will be needed. (Avoid sports bras that pull or bind too tight at the shoulders.)

Step 1. Lie on your side with your legs gently bent in front of you for stability, with your head gently resting on your arm as it extends straight up past your head along the floor. Place the other hand on the floor in front of your chest in line with your breastbone.

Step 2. Begin by connecting to the three-part breath with its corresponding perineal contraction, taking directional energy up the internal central axis from the perineum out the top of the head on the exhale and with pelvic release on the intake. Working from *awareness*, on an exhale, gently press into the hand on the floor, plotting the path from the webbing between the thumb and the index finger up through the inside of the wrist joint, the middle of the wrist, and the upper arm *across the top back of the shoulder and down to the bottom of the scapula*. Notice any tendency for the neck, tongue, and jaw to hook in. If they do (and the path has gone up the neck, rather than down to the scapula) then start again.

Step 3. Once you are familiar with the path from the pressed hand down to the scapula, intake again, and on the exhale press into the hand, plot the path to the scapula and when the scapula engages, continue to press, bringing your body up to sitting. Let the neck, tongue, and jaw hang freely. You don't need them to sit up. Use only what you need: the press, the path, and the scapula.

Step 4: Switch sides and return to step 1.

Exercise #24
Partner wall press

This is a way to work with partners to understand and condition the role of the scapula in freeing the neck, tongue, and jaw while plotting the path through the hands.

Preparation: Ex. 10 *Three-part breath,* Ex. 18 *The sweet spot,* Ex. 16 *Psoas dynamic alignment in standing* and knowledge of *The rings* (page 142).

This is an exercise that is best done with a partner.

Step 1. Facing the wall, stand approximately two feet away. The first person will place their hands on the wall at shoulder height while the second gently places the flats of their hands on the scapulae of their partner, applying a gentle pressure but not pushing.

Step 2. The first person leans into the wall, plotting the path from the webbing between the thumbs and the index fingers up through the insides of the arms and down to the scapulae, bypassing any tension or holding in the neck, tongue, or jaw. When done correctly the scapulae will draw downward slightly. There will be no lifting of the shoulders. The second person is there to witness this action from behind and, with the touch, give a clear sense of the action of the scapula as it shifts down.

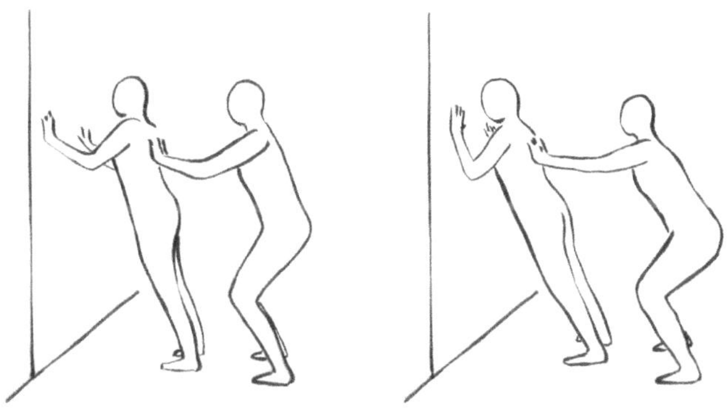

Note: Remember that when giving feedback or witnessing a partner's work, we do not tell them what they are doing, such as "you are pushing your shoulders up". We also do not draw conclusions, such as in "gosh, you're really tense". Rather, we express what we see in the present moment in full acknowledgement that this is our perspective. We do not diagnose, but rather notice what is happening in the moment. Be as specific as you can. Your feedback might go something like, "This time I noticed that as you moved toward the wall there was a slight tension in the left side of your neck, and as you moved further I felt the scapula move down and it seemed to resolve itself. I also see that the jaw on both sides seems to be holding. Is that your experience?"

Exercise #25
Arms of a clock

Here we explore and condition the independence of the arms, clavicle, shoulder, neck, tongue, jaw, and sternum while challenging the integrity of the dynamic alignment. The entire exercise takes place in dynamic standing perpendicular to a clear wall. Here you will connect to the three-part breath with particular awareness of the vertical alignment and the integrity of the rings. The aim is to keep the scapulae working in a downward direction as the arm rotates. At the same time you will maintain integrity of the rings, with particular attention to the ring that circles the shoulder girdle. We want to resist any hyperextension of the thoracic spine. This would result in the front of the ring raising up and the back pushing down, often causing a domino effect of the hip ring jutting out in compensation. The breathing will be key, as it supports the gentle lift of the body, front, back, and sides equally when connected to the perineum and up through the vertical axis. You can spend as long as you wish on any of these steps. The entire exercise can take up to thirty minutes if you wish.

Preparation: Ex. 10 *Three-part breath,* Ex. 18 *The sweet spot,* Ex. 16 *Psoas dynamic alignment in standing,* Ex. 23 *Hand press* and knowledge of *The rings* (page 142).

Step 1. In dynamic standing, stand perpendicular to the wall, approximately three inches away. Exhale, intake, exhale, connecting to the perineum in your three-part breath, and on the next intake raise the arm to 12 o'clock, with the hand flat on the wall, drawing the scapula down the back body. Let it sit there and take a few more breaths, working to release as much of the shoulder, tongue, jaw, and sternum as possible. A little bobble-head movement is useful here. Check to ensure that you are working from awareness. Notice

if the raising of the arms has extended the chest outward. If it has, on the next breath expand the rings, front, back, and sides equally, drawing awareness to the back body as it expands and levelling the rings. Remember the action through the big toes, connecting your standing position up and out by way of an isolated action of the psoas. (If this gets stuck, go back to your awareness, stop, drop the hands, Etch-a-Sketch, return to your sweet spot, find your dynamic standing, three-part breath and begin again.)

Step 2. As you become more confident that the rings are being supported by the breath moving through the vertical axis by way of the action of the perineum, you can then gently walk the hand to 1 o'clock. Check to see that your hip is staying perpendicular to the wall and that you are not turning toward the wall. You want to maintain the resistance. Repeat the bobble-head, the releasing of the scapula downward, the releasing of the tongue, jaw, neck, the realignment and separation of the rings through the action of the breath. Work into the floor through the action of dynamic standing in connection to the psoas.

Next steps: Continue in this way to 3 o'clock if you can. Do not over-stretch. Notice any sensations in your body and back off if necessary. The task is not to make it to 3 o'clock but to maintain the integrity of the dynamic standing as you move walk the fingers back in small increments between resting the hand on the wall. When you are done, release your arm, notice the difference between the arm that worked and the one that did not. Return to the beginning and work with the other side. Give yourself permission to let the other side be a very different experience.

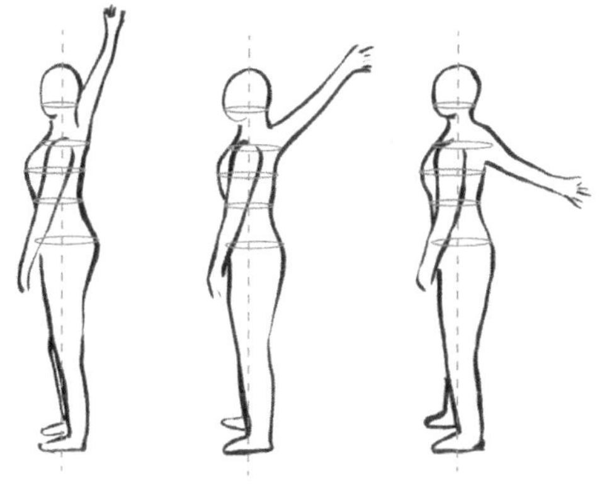

PREPARING TO TAKE WEIGHT IN HANDS AND ARMS

Now that we've worked to understand and begin to condition towards a greater independence of the hands, arms, clavicle, shoulder, neck, tongue, jaw, and sternum, we next work on strength and balance in the hands and arms towards more challenging movements that require the taking of weight into the arms.

Just as you worked with *opposing circles*, which entailed rotating one part of your body in one direction and the other in the opposite to create a dynamic balance between the two in *Psoas dynamic alignment in standing* (Ex. 16), we will use the same principle to create freedom and strength in the use of the arms. Here it will be through a combination of opposing circles in the arm with a plotting of the path through the webbing of the thumb and the index finger through to the scapula that will make cartwheels, back bends, and lifts all possible without compromise to the breath/voice and without raising the centre into areas or chakras that can unintentionally affect or impede emotional availability.

Exercise #26

Dynamic alignment in hands and arms while taking weight

Preparation: Ex. 10 *Three-part breath,* and a knowledge of the hands, arms, clavicle, shoulder, neck, tongue, jaw, and sternum independence (review pages 151–155). A yoga mat is helpful, as much of this work happens with the knees on the floor.

Step 1: Position yourself on the floor on hands and knees with your back flat and level; we'll call this *Table.* Let your hands be flat on the floor with your fingers directly facing in front of you (not turned out) and your thumbs facing in an easy diagonal toward each other. Your hands will be in line with your elbows and your elbows in line with your shoulders. Let your knees be in line with your hips.

Step 2. Working from *awareness,* press into the webbing between your thumb and index finger in a directional energy down through to the earth. Press firmly, with directional energy going through and down into the floor, not stopping at the floor. This will rotate your arms inward. The creases in your elbows will be facing towards each other. Imagine a circular motion at the middle of your wrist moving inward towards your legs. This is likely to bring your shoulders up toward your head. Ouch, can't voice THIS way! This is the first circle, to be countered in the next step.

Step 3. In the position of step 2, while maintaining the wrist circle supported by the continuous pressure into the webbing between the thumb and index finger, COUNTER this now with an opposite rotation of the upper arm in an outward direction. This action will draw the scapulae down towards your hip bones. A sensation of opening up your armpits to the space in front of you will likely happen.

Notice that when you rotate the upper arms out but do not apply the equal action by pressing into the webbing coupled with the internal rotation of the wrists, your arms can collapse and lose length and strength into the floor. We are working to keep a balanced pressure between the opposite circles to create a non-stuck and dynamic sense of being able to lift and move off the floor in an instant. Notice also if you get locked in the elbows or into rigid arms. This is not what we are aiming for. If this happens, take your arms off the floor, kneel, shake them out, and start again with step 1 until you find a dynamic balance between the action of the two opposing circles. A bobble-head movement can be helpful, as can voicing to see if independence of the hands, arms, clavicle, shoulder, neck, tongue, jaw, and sternum is being achieved.

Step 3. Once you find your best dynamic alignment of the arms through steps 1 and 2 (constant directional energy of the two opposing circles at the same time), then and only then tuck the toes under and straighten out the legs, plotting the path from the big toes as you raise into what, in yoga, is known as "downward dog" position. It is like an upside-down V. Do this while continuing the opposing circles and the pressure into the webbing between the thumb and index finger. Maintain the integrity of this dynamic alignment as you straighten the legs and your buttocks reach for the ceiling.

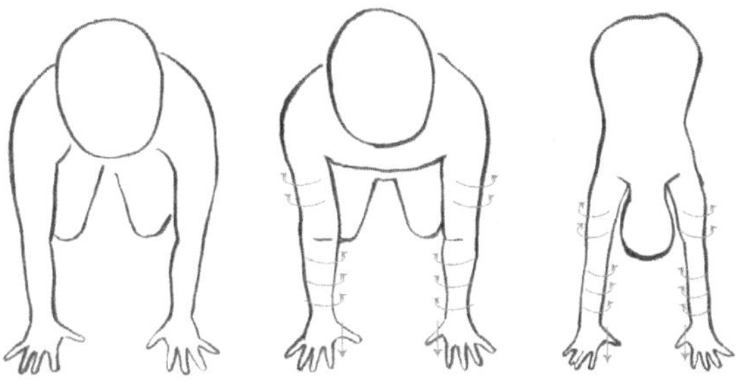

Notice if you tend to use "strength" rather than balance in the raising, meaning if your arms are doing the work, or your shoulders, tongue, neck, or jaw become involved. (We DO NOT want this, as this will create locks in the shoulder girdle.) When actioned correctly, nothing will be needed from your shoulder girdle. When executed correctly, with the constant and ever directional energy of opposite action of the circles, grounded into the earth through the pressure into the webbing of your thumb and index finger, this will create all the foundation needed. NO OTHER tensions will be necessary! This is dynamic alignment in the arms! If you engage anything other than the circles and the webbing, kneel, take your arms off the floor and go back to step 1.

Challenge: Return to the table and do steps 1 and 2. In table, from the three-part breath, initiating movement and breath from the perineal centre, voice a continuous note or execute a sustained zzzzz while bouncing your hands in little leaps off the floor. There will be NO glitch or interruption in the sound or breath as you raise and land if/when you maintain this dynamic alignment in the hands and arms. Magic! Think of the possibilities.

Exercise #27
Handstand and preparation

For lots of people a handstand can be very confronting. Going upside down can be disorienting, as can the idea of taking one's entire weight into their arms. For this reason we have here a very do-able way of entering into the proposition. But even if you have been doing handstands all your life, this is a new way of doing a handstand, as it is about the doing of the doing of dynamic alignment rather than just balancing your legs in the air.

Preparation: A clear flat wall and bare feet. Ex. 23 *Hand press*, Ex. 16 *Psoas dynamic alignment in standing*, Ex. 26 *Dynamic alignment in hands and arms while taking weight, Rings*, and Ex. 10 *Three-part breath.*

Step 1. Sit facing the wall with straight legs, with flexed feet against the wall, and a straight back (at a right-angle). Now take a note of where your sitz bones (ischial tuberosities), the bones under the flesh of your buttocks, make contact with the floor. It sometimes helps to literally pull the flesh away from your buttocks with your hands to find the pointy or bony feeling they make as they contact the floor. Take a few three-part breaths, working up the vertical axis, expanding the rings. Feel free to press gently into the floor with the tips of your fingers (connecting through the scapulae rather than going to the neck and shoulders) to aid this lengthening. Notice and release any holding in the neck, tongue, or jaw.

Step 2. The place where your sitz bones make contact with the floor is now the distance from the wall that you will put your hands. Turn and place your hands at this point on the floor. Your hands should be in line with your shoulders. Place your fingers facing directly in front of you (not turning out) and your thumbs pointing towards each other in a relaxed diagonal.

Step 3. From here you will return to your knowledge of *Dynamic alignment in hands and arms.* Working from awareness, create counter-rotation in the arms as described in Ex. 26.

Step 4. From here, after practising your three-part breath, initiating the next movement on an exhale connected to the perineum, take your feet up onto the wall at a right-angle and, on the exhale, press yourself to an upside-down right-angle.

Helpful hint (Partner work): This can feel in the proprioceptive experience like it is NOT a right-angle but taking you TOO forward, especially if this is a new experience. (Trust and know that you yourself measured it with the sitz bones.) Regardless, having a partner behind you with their hands placed at the creases of the hips with their body right up against your back body can be both a comfort and a help.

Step 5. Once your feet are there, this is the moment to work both the *Dynamic alignment of arms and hands* and the principle of *Dynamic alignment in standing* at the same time. Extend the rings at each intake and exhale. Note the freedom or constriction in the shoulder girdle. (If there is constriction, back off and reconnect to the *Dynamic alignment in hands and arms.*) Notice any constriction in the lower body. (If there is any, return to *Dynamic alignment in standing.*) Witness any feeling or thoughts. Return to awareness and do the doing of the task.

Next steps: Singing an entire aria, song, or acting a speech or monologue will be possible in this position when the full dynamic alignment (arms and legs) is working to free every pathway towards the perineal centre, making an exacting use of the psoas system. The three-part breath with the complete release of the pelvic girdle and outward movement of the intercostals and release of the sternum on the intake will also be possible. No tensions in the tongue, neck, shoulders, or jaw will be apparent, as will no holding in the thighs, feet, or pelvis.

Challenge: From here, if you have already got a personal practice of doing full handstands, you can work towards a full handstand incorporating the dynamic alignment principles. (It's good to start with a partner spotting the first time.) Even with the legs in the air, and not at the wall, remember the actioning of *Dynamic alignment in standing*. As you come down and your feet meet the earth, always plot the path through the big toe, through the inside of the leg into the psoas.

Exercise #28
Dynamic alignment in movement, two variations

Here we have two variations of movement that help the dynamic alignment in both hands and arms in relation to the perineal centre and the three-part breath.

Step 1. In both variations, start with your front body on the floor and arms resting along the floor in front of you with palms down. Do a few three-part breaths, drawing awareness to the three parts, particularly in the back body, as you plot the path from the perineal contraction up through the centre of the body out the top of the head. Exhale completely, intake in preparation and on the next exhale, initiating all movement from the perineum...

Step 2. ...press into the webbing between your thumb and index fingers and plot the path to the scapulae. Once it engages, press into the floor, peeling your thoracic spine off the floor as your shoulder blades trail down your back. Make sure your tongue, neck, and jaw are free of superfluous tensions. Stay connected to the perineum as you continue to exhale.

Step 3. ....on the continued exhale, initiating all movement from the perineum, draw the pelvis back to sit on your ankles as you bend your legs, landing in child's pose (see diagram).

Step 4. From here, intake again (releasing the pelvic girdle), and on the next exhale (with perineal contraction, initiating the movement from the perineum as always), tuck your toes into the floor (A) or wall (B), plotting the path through the big toe, up the inside of the leg and into the creases connecting to the psoas. Straighten the legs in dynamic alignment with the opposing circles, and maintain the opposing circles in the arms as the scapula trails toward the hip bones.

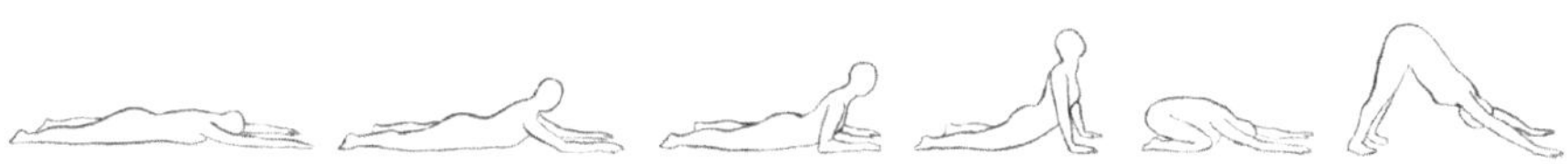

A.

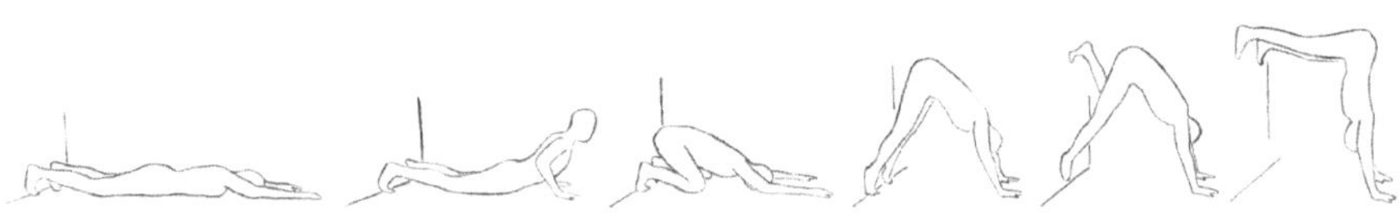

B.

Step 4 (continued). If you are doing variation B, then bring your feet to the wall as per the assisted handstand. Remember to maintain an active actioning of the opposing circles in both the arms and the hands, and remember to plot the path from both the big toe and the webbing in the hands. **All paths lead to centre, to the perineum, and to the breath-body.** We will return to this exercise after the section on voicing to incorporate sounding on the exhale.

Exercise #29
Dynamic alignment in back bends

Here we have a way to condition and learn dynamic alignment in preparation for all manner of back bends. You will need three people: the back bender, a partner, and a spotter.

Preparation: A good warm-up incorporating three-part breath is essential, as is an embodied understanding of dynamic alignment in both arms and legs. Plotting those paths from the big toe and webbing in the hands is important. As in all partner work, meeting in the middle is most important, as is both partners working from awareness throughout. A mat on the floor is helpful.

Step 1. One partner will kneel in Child's Pose (see diagram on page 162) with arms by their sides, palms up, and forehead resting on the floor. This person will need to be flexible enough for this to feel easy; they will be there for a little while. Once that partner is settled, the backbender will sit gently on the kneeling partner's buttocks, making contact at both their sacra. Breathe together and meet in the middle. The backbender will have their feet in line with their knees and their knees in line with their hips. Before exhaling completely, intake with the three-part breath and the backbender will roll back over the kneeling partner on the next exhale as their perineum contracts and they plot a path through the big toes up the inside of the legs into the creases.

Step 2. The backbender places their hands by the ears of the kneeling partner, who places their hand on the backbender's hands, applying gentle pressure in the side of the webbing between the thumb and the index fingers. This will create stability and help draw awareness to the webbing to aid in the plotting of the path through the arms to the scapulae. The back bender will work equally on the dynamic alignment of the arms and the legs and the connection to the big toes and the webbing in the hands.

Step 3. Here a spotter will assure that the feet remain in line with the knees and hips, and also check to see that the kneeling partner is breathing with ease and not feeling any discomfort from the weight. Once everything is settled, the spotter will go to the backbender's arms and assist in a very gentle stretch on the exhale by drawing the backbender's elbows closer together, moving them in line with the hands and shoulders. It can be helpful to stay in this position as the backbender explores how this strengthens the dynamic alignment in the arms and clears the path to the psoas and scapulae.

Step 4. (If either partner is fatigued, skip to step 5.) Once the backbender becomes familiar with the sensation of plotting the path in both the arms and the legs in this position, they simply apply equal pressure into the big toe sides of the feet and the webbing sides of the hands, connecting to the psoas and engaging the scapulae as they draw downward towards the hip bones. This will, in turn, raise the middle body into a full back bend. Backbender: do a few full three-part breaths. Make some sound. Release your buttocks to access the perineal centre more fully. (If you are working in dynamic alignment, and after you integrate the work of the next section on voice, you will find that you are able to sound and sing with no compromise to the voice while getting into and maintaining this position.)

Step 5. To come down, the backbender gently descends, making contact with the kneeling partner's back. Again, check that you are both meeting in the middle. Both breathe together, and, on an exhale, the kneeling partner will use their hands to draw up from Child's Pose to kneeling and the backbender will be gently assisted by the spotter into the counter-stretch of Child's Pose. If there is no spotter, gently press back to back, lifting the bender to sitting so that they can then release into Child's Pose. Take your time; breathe and witness any sensations.

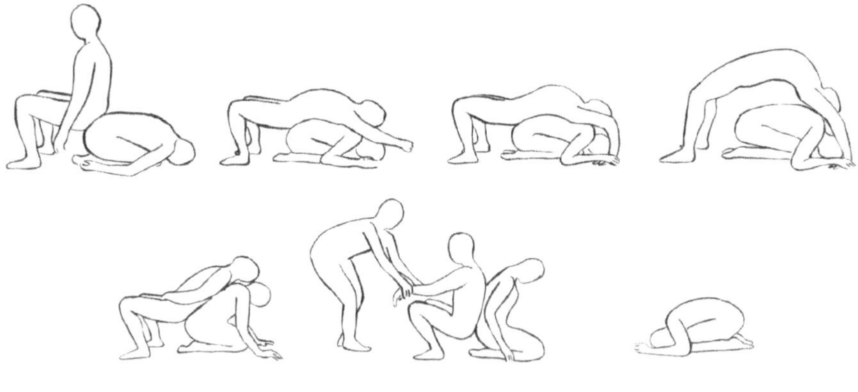

Return to this exercise after the section on voicing and integrate the possibilities of sounding on the exhale.

Exercise #30

Meeting in the middle, diagonal catches

This is an advanced version of meeting in the middle work and is excellent for establishing good working rapport in partners. It also incorporates all the dynamic alignment work.

Preparation: All awareness work, especially a detailed understanding of Ex. 7 *Meeting in the middle* and Ex. 11 *Rolling from centre,* along with all previous dynamic alignment work in arms and hands and all breath work, Exercises 23–29. For at least two people with a clear space to work.

Step 1. Partners face each other in dynamic alignment, standing about four feet apart. Meet in the middle, working from your three-part breathing connection to the perineal centre.

Step 2. Partners cross arms to clasp each other's wrists, with right arm contacting right arm. (Throughout any arm action for the rest of this work, at each clasp plot the path to the bottom of the scapulae, maintaining independence of the neck and shoulder.) Exhale completely, intake in preparation, and on the exhale both bend their legs towards a squat (as the perineum contracts upwards up the vertical axis), leaning back, relying on each other's weight to balance. Do a three-part breath, and on the next exhale, come to standing, maintaining equal tension in the leaning back and sustaining the meeting in the middle. Switch arms and do steps 1 and 2 again.

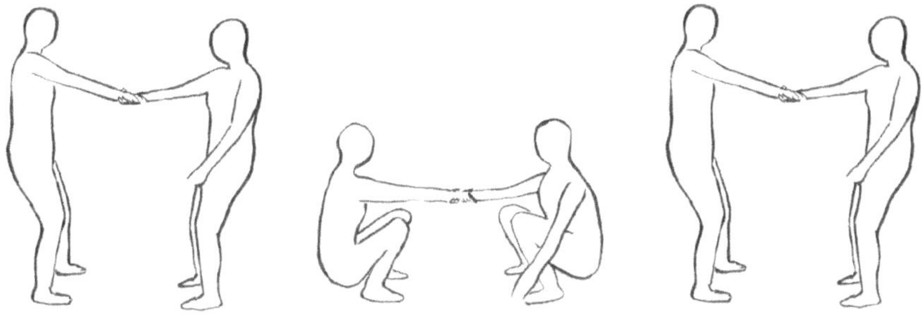

Witness: Are you both working from awareness rather than thoughts and feelings? Are you both meeting in the middle throughout the sequence? Have you both maintained a connection to the perineal centre throughout the move, in connection to breath? Are you plotting the path to the scapula? Are you working from the big toe side of the foot, plotting the path up the inside of the leg and into the crease connecting to psoas and ever extending the rings? Note what you can do to make this task clearer and start the task again.

Step 3. Stand again facing each other, meeting in the middle, and connecting to centre. This time, clasp right arm to right arm, then immediately release and switch to left arms. Allow this to become a sort of swinging motion in a mutual rhythm where when you clasp you both can lean back a little into the mutual support. Notice if this swinging action needs a reminder of the "don't become the kite" principle. Stay in connection with the perineal centre. Witness as above, and adjust as needed.

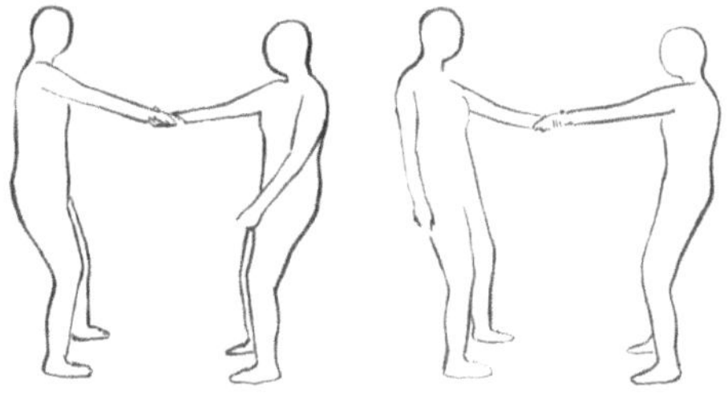

Step 4. Here it gets interesting. Once steps 1–3 are familiar, as you transition from right arms to left arms, one person squats and the other stands. Then the one that was squatting comes to standing as you switch arms, with the one that was standing now squatting. Work to do this in between the clasp as you transfer the hands. The task is to remain in centre and meet in the middle. Again, witness as above, and adjust as needed.

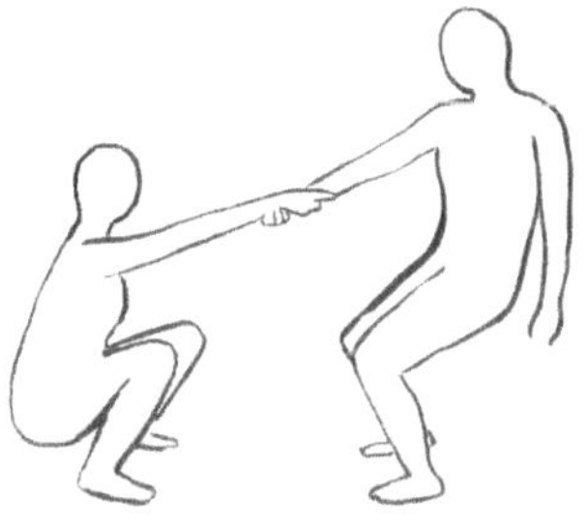

Step 5. To make this even more interesting, repeat step 4 but as you go to switch hands look behind you, away from your partner. Are you still meeting in the middle?

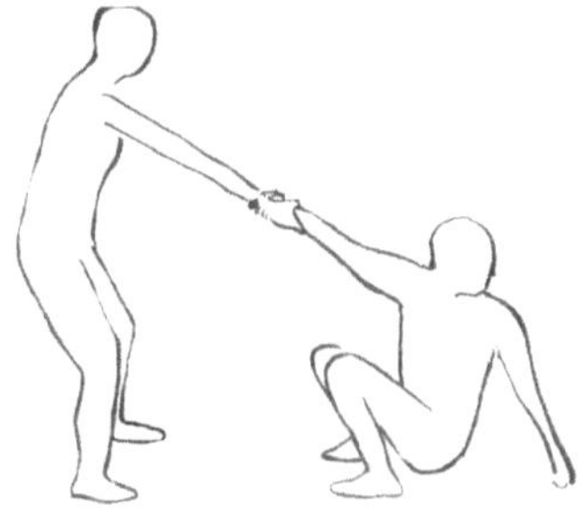

MOVING FORWARD WITH DYNAMIC ALIGNMENT INTO VOICING

As we have learned, dynamic alignment is directional, live, and active. One does not arrive at "it". There are some key actionings that make up dynamic alignment. These are a practice of returning to awareness and the continued connection to centre through the three-part breath with an expansion of the rings on both the exhale and intake. When making contact with the floor, the plotting of the path in the feet, up the inside of the legs, and into the crease to isolate the psoas system becomes part of the dynamic alignment, and when making contact with the floor with the hands we have the plotting of the path from the webbing of the inside of the thumb and index finger up the arms through the shoulders and down to the scapulae.

Return to centre is the motto. Centre as in being "centred" is practised as a constant return to awareness, so that every action comes from awareness in agreement with the task, rather than thoughts and feelings that take us out of the task. Centre is found in the perineal contraction and release, supported by the psoas isolation. The three-part breath supports and integrates the mind/body, emotive, physio/vocal centre. *In short, all movement, sound or emotive act initiates from centre, fuelled by breath. All actions happen in connection with centre from awareness.*

So — a cartwheel or back flip, for instance, happens from awareness first, where movement is initiated from the perineal centre as connected to the three-part breath. EVERY TIME a hand meets the floor, you plot the path. EVERY TIME a foot meets the floor, you plot the path. Maintaining a separation of the rings on the intake and exhale will allow all manner of movement, with a bent or crunched torso also possible without any glitches in sound, unintended jerks in movement or loss of connection to the perineal centre.

As we move forward you will learn that every type of movement is possible with unencumbered sound if you engage dynamic alignment and incorporate the following principles of working with voice.

NOTE

1 It was to my great horror that, while writing this book, the 2012 election in the States began to use "Etch-a-Sketch" as negative catch term denoting "forgetting". We had been using it in our way for years as a healthy clearing of tensions that may have accumulated in the body while working, concentrating, and "trying" too hard. For us, it is a clearing of the physical palate to allow for new possibilities of creation — in the spirit of the child's toy, invoking play and youthful naiveté, allowing and embracing the possibilities of the new without judgement or diagnosis.

Chapter 6

Voicing as a breath dance

IN THIS WORK WE DO NOT THINK OF SINGING, or voicing, in terms of sound. You will learn in the following pages how by the time any sound is produced it is really too late to "do" anything about it. It has already been made at the stage of awareness and through the path of the breath. The quality of sound, when produced by a living body, is rather the *symptom* of a sort of *breath dance*, initiated from a centre and released through a set of controlled counterpressures in the breath-body.

Unlike many approaches to voice, this work will not speak of "placement", "mask", or of "raising the palate" in the face, but rather, in keeping with an active aesthetic, and like activation of dynamic alignment in the previous section, will continue in the use of *directional energy* to set up the optimal conditions for integrative voicing. "Placement", "positioning", "posture", "alignment", "resonance", and the use of "mask" will all happen as *symptoms* of one coordinated action, as described in the next section.

You might also note the omission of any reference to "diaphragmatic breathing", especially when invoking any and all articulations of "breath-support". This is because any "doing" in the region of the diaphragm usually results in the tightening of the abdominals (among other things), which counterproductively impedes the diaphragm's movement downward. This will get in the way of an optimal pelvic release on the intake. For a detailed explanation of the workings of the diaphragm and the three-part breath, read the pages on centre and integrative breathing found earlier in Chapter Five (pages 106–112). In short, the three-part breath allows the diaphragm to do its work by getting us *out of the way*.

Another principle that may seem at odds with some trainings is that in this work, we do not "cover" or "colour" the sound after it is produced; rather, the quality (or character enhancement often ascribed to such) is considered at the beginning of the process, at awareness, before action. In short, we do not rely on band-aids or adjustments after the fact. Each sound, movement, intent, and action is born before the intake of breath.

Voice is the symptom of a breath dance that starts in awareness and initiates from the perineal centre, just like all movement and emotive choices in this work: one process that allows for acting, voicing, and movement both as a symptom and as one. If you have not done so already, please read Chapter Four, *Centre, Presence, and the Initiation of Task*, before engaging with the following exercises in voice.

If you have studied voice before, you may find a few of these exercises familiar in the initial shape or instruction; however, if you work through the practice you will learn that the *doing of the doing* of these is quite different. Returning to what is "comfortable", as in "Oh, I know this one" often patterns in old "stuff". (Recall Chapter Four, where we learned how one gets good at *exactly* what one practices.) As in the previous section, where we do not aim to get "it" or make the shape or execute a sound or movement of beauty, here we do not *aim* to have our belly move in any way, *feel* a vibration in a part of the face, nor do we aim to *make* a certain quality of sound, be it loud, resonant, on pitch, smooth of line, or any other possible product/aesthetic. Rather, we work in the doing of the doing, the practice of the practice: the active aesthetic. Any qualities, sounds, shapes, and feelings will emerge as symptoms of the integrative doing. The performer does not do the performance, be it the exercise, feeling, sound, movement, shape, or quality, but rather enters the field of performing where both performance and performer emerge.

This work draws from select work in *bel canto* singing, especially in taking the sounding off the throat and also in the way we execute the onset (the moment that sound is initiated); however, singing opera is not necessarily the goal and certainly not the only option. Belting, folk, rap, and spoken voice (or spoken word in the US), are all options included in this practice, which draws on key knowledge from speech therapists. Danish speech pathologist Sven Smith, in particular, is invoked, especially in the understanding of the importance of the complete exhale in order to make way for the inhale; however, as he referred to "abdominal breathing",[1] we depart from his work in a fundamental way for the many reasons expounded upon earlier in the section on integrative breathing.

In this work there are very important adjustments made to practices that you may feel familiar with. These adjustments are sometimes subtle, but they are essential. This is because not one of the practices drawn on was designed for the actor/singer/dancer as an integrative practice, making possible extended movement with full emotive potential, while at the same time voicing. So, as we give thanks and respect to the shape and form of other work, we move forward into an integrative and transdisciplinary solution of voicing for the interdisciplinary performer through the active aesthetic.

FACE AND HEAD AS MIRROR OF THE BODY

For a moment we will consider the head in isolation. Of course the head is part of the body entire. Recall the concepts of the holographic principle (see pages 56–57) and also how this was applied to an integral body organization of tensions in rolling with the idea of "mirror tensions" (pages 117–119). Interestingly, parts of your body map to the entire body/mind. For instance, the arch of the foot often corresponds to the arch on the ankle, often mirroring tensions in the lower back which affect the back of the neck. During the following work you might find that there is a connection between tongue and body, with the action of the back of the tongue relating to the perineal centre and the tip of the tongue relating to the top of the head. You may also observe that the jaw hinge and the hip sockets relate in both alignment and their corresponding sympathetic movement. When the rings are out of sync and the vertical alignment is influenced, we get both a holographic effect and a domino effect right up the entire body. We, as organisms, aim always to balance even in "imbalance". Where one thing goes off in one direction, another will compromise, creating a path that allows some version of standing, lifting, reaching, feeling, being, and yes, voicing.

Considering us as sounding "instruments" is sometimes a helpful place to start. We can be viewed as wind instruments. When breath goes out and hits the vocal chords, they vibrate, and a certain measurable outcome of sound is determined by the composition of the resonating chamber that is the body. Our alignment affects the resonating chamber and therefore the sound. You may recall some of the experiments in earlier exercises (using voice in Ex. 11 *Rolling from centre* and Ex. 18 *The sweet spot*) that highlighted this effect. In the next section, we will learn how to work more specifically with the tongue, jaw, and palate in coordination with the three-part breath to allow for any and all manner of movement and uncompromised sounding.

THE FACE AND THREE-PART BREATH AND TONGUE

If you will recall, in the three-part breath we exhale in preparation, letting all the air out, and then on the intake the (1) pelvic girdle releases downward followed by (2) the release sideways of the intercostals and then (3) the gentle raising of the sternum. Then there is a suspension (as opposed to holding or locking) and on the exhale (1) the perineum contracts up in the direction of the vertical axis and (2) the intercostals gently release followed by (3) the sternum responds. This basic principle will remain, but now, as we move into more advanced work, we will incorporate a few new things.

Intake: From now on, on every intake the tongue will release forward, initiating its movement from the very back of the tongue, with the tip of the tongue resting at the lower teeth.

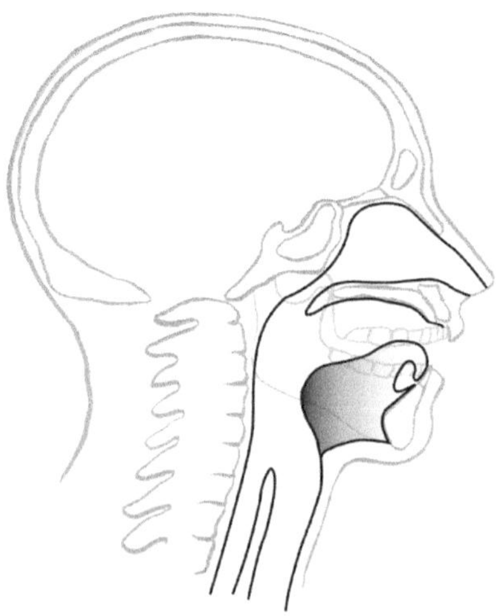

Tongue release during intake

Exhale: On the exhale (or while voicing), the tongue will then relax into a neutral position at the lower part of the mouth. Simply, the back of the tongue releases down and slightly back, without pulling the tip of the tongue away from the lower ridge under the bottom teeth.

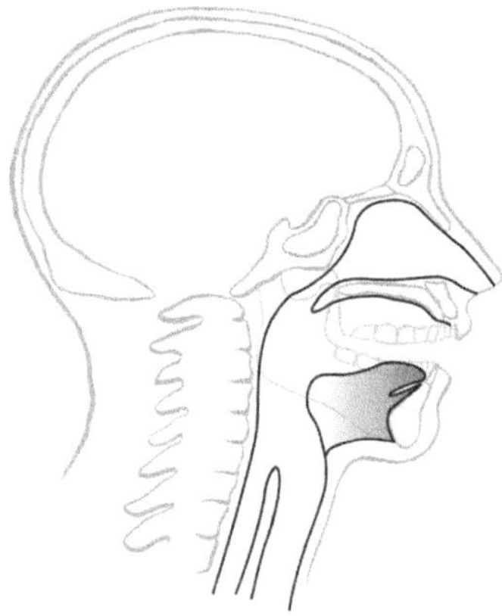

Tongue release during exhale

This action can *feel* counter-intuitive, as many of us tend to draw the tongue back on an "inhale" (rather than release it forward on an intake). When this happens it lowers the upper palate and blocks space in the mouth that allows for optimal resonance. It also tightens the neck muscles and compromises the dynamic alignment, as the back of the neck tends to shorten. Some people find that when they draw the tongue back on an inhale they also have a tendency to shift to the back of the heels, taking them out of the sweet spot and compromising optimum dynamic alignment in standing. When doing more extended movement, such as a backbend or handstand or even just lying in constructive rest, if you inhale and draw the tongue back it will be most difficult to sound. Try this, and then compare the difference with releasing the tongue forward on an intake in coordination with the three-part breath.

A most excellent gem of this work is in the fact that the lower your intake (meaning the more release in the perineal centre), the more upper harmonics will be sonically present when sounding. Also, the lower you allow your intake to be, the wider the range of pitch to which you'll have access.

Try this: in a standing position, inhale into your chest, and then sing a scale that goes as high as you feel comfortable doing. Note when the voice cuts out and how your body responds to the task.

Then, after practising the three-part breath, perhaps the hip thump and then a roll, try again. This time from awareness, exhale completely in preparation and then intake into the perineal centre with the tongue release and, on the exhale, sound up the scale. Most will attain a fuller sound and also a wider range.

Just to be sure:

- Move between various centres on the intake.
- Intake into the chest, then sound.

- Take a moment — Etch-a-Sketch.
- Intake into the solar plexus, then sound.
- Take a moment — Etch-a-Sketch.
- Intake into the belly, then sound.
- Take a moment — Etch-a-Sketch.
- And then intake into the perineum and then sound.

You will most likely experience a direct relationship between how low you allow yourself to intake and the availability of range and pitch.

You will also experience a direct connection to the tongue. The lower the release in the body, the easier it is to release the tongue. (If this is not working for you, review the work in Chapter Five.)

Moreover, if you witness your ability to stay in awareness, you may even note that when you breathe high, thoughts and feelings tend to take over and, in contrast, when you intake into centre, awareness remains throughout the task. (If the notions of witnessing and thoughts and feelings are not clear, return to the work in Part Two.)

Recall the tool "don't become the kite" on page 134. This works in all voicing, physical movement, and also acting (as explained in an upcoming section).

WORKING WITH THE EXHALE OR WHILE VOICING

Here we evoke some of the previous work. As expressed earlier, on the intake we get out of the way. This is why we call it an intake, rather than an inhale. It is on the exhale and while voicing that the work happens. It will take some energy, some engaging of new muscles and some releasing of patterned-in tensions that may have been conditioned into you from other less integrative practices. The good news is that if you have already worked through the *Three-part breath* and have a working understanding of the *Rings* and *Dynamic alignment* you will have an embodied experience of how this next stage operates as "productive tension", creating buoyancy, readiness, and the ability to move in any direction, physically, vocally, and emotively.

Exercise #31
Accenting A

This series of exercises is loosely based on the previously mentioned Accent Method by Danish speech pathologist Sven Smith. This incarnation, however, departs from his in key ways. Here, we work with the intake as part of the three-part breath and in keeping with the principles of dynamic alignment. (So in this work there is no mention of *inspiration* or *inhale;* neither is there mention of any manner of *abdominal* breathing, all terms that Smith used.) Further, in keeping with the premises of the active aesthetic, we (performers) do not do the exercise (performance), but rather we work with an exercise in conscious practice, entering in through the *way* of doing — starting in *awareness* — connected to the three-part breath and the perineal centre — supported by an exacting use of the psoas.

Preparation: This is best learned first in standing. Ex. 10 *Three-part breath* and all work up to *Dynamic alignment in standing* is essential (Exercises 8–16). Working with a group or with a partner is helpful at first; however, once you get the gist, doing it alone can be just as beneficial.

Step 1. For now, think through this rhythmic structure, done at a tempo of approximately 80 beats per minute.

Clap (as in two hands together) .....snap.....snap.....snap.....(clicking of fingers) *don't worry if you can't click, not a big deal...*

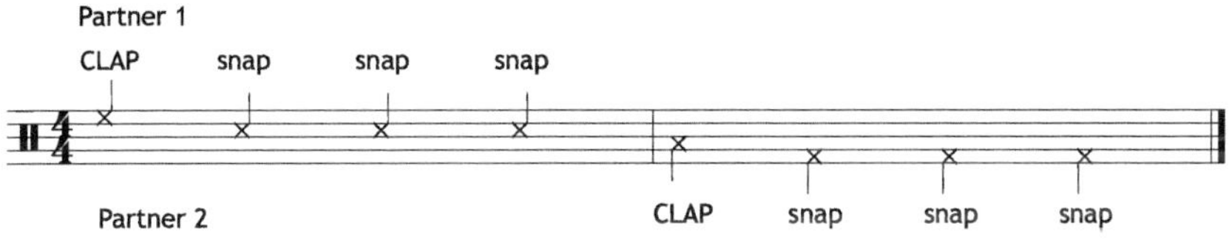

Partner (you silent) 4/4 Clap... ... ... Snap... ... ... Snap... ... ... Snap :|
You (partner silent) 4/4 Clap... ... ... Snap... ... ... Snap... ... ... Snap :|

Step 2: Once you have the hang of the rhythm and the clap, snap, snap, snap at 80 BPM, you will now, on your partner's clap, **intake** with the tongue release. Then, on the first snap and throughout the other two you will **exhale continuously**, letting all the air out. You will then **suspend with the air out** while your partner takes their turn: Clap/**intake** to snap snap snap/**exhale** and **suspend** throughout your turn.

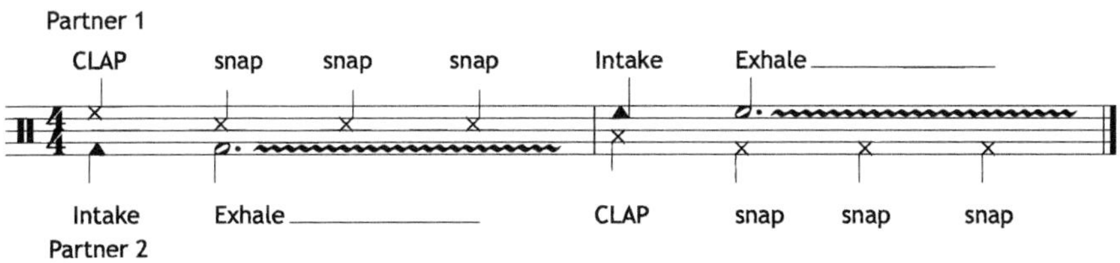

Key: This is the first time that we have done an intake this fast. In *Three-part breath*, we did it at a deliberate pace so as to become familiar with and isolate the three parts in action, those three parts being the release of the pelvic girdle, the outward movement of the intercostals, and the gentle raise of the sternum. Here, in the time of a CLAP, the tongue releases with the pelvic girdle, followed in quick succession by the intercostals and sternum release all in one beat. After a complete exhale and suspension, this will start to happen as a sort of rebound effect. It is important to remember not to go into the shoulders and chest. If this occurs, return to the previous exercises that worked on the tongue, jaw, neck, and shoulder independence. "Don't become the kite" is also a useful tool. Remember, the lower you allow the breath to go on the intake, the more release up the torso, access to the chakras, and integrity of the dynamic alignment up the vertical axis.

Step 3: You continue with the alternating pattern, but now play with what happens on the exhale. You can exhale on a zzzzz, or a vvvvv, on a flub of the lips bbbbb, a rolled rrrrr... play. Exhale all air, suspend, and then on the next clap/intake release tongue/perineum and intercostals and sternum. Don't become the kite.

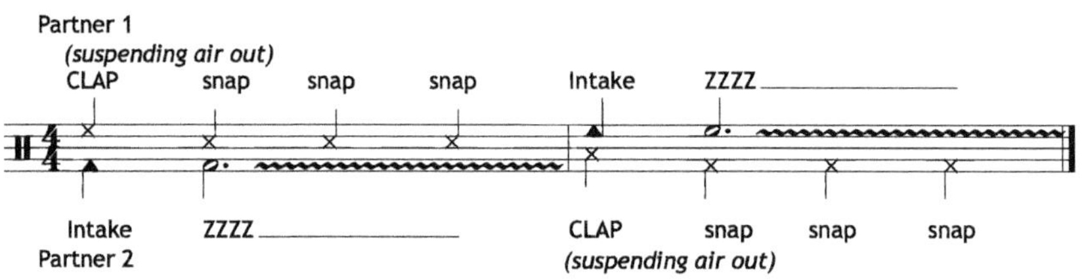

With practice, if you find that you are not emptying enough within the three beats, check that you are using enough energy on the exhale. Don't be stingy or too careful. This is a physical exercise. The more you let go, the more you'll have. Don't save it up, be generous. As you progress you can also extend the snaps a few more beats. Eventually you will able to zzzzz or vvvvv for the length of phrases of music or text as part of your practice.

Appoggio

Now that you have the basic idea of the intake in coordination with the tongue release and the three-part breath, we will build on this and more fully consider what happens on the exhale and thus while voicing.

On the intake, we release the tongue forward while the pelvic girdle descends in connection to the perineal centre. This is followed quickly by an outward action of the intercostals and a rise of the sternum, all of this in the time of a clap. Other than the action of the tongue, which does take some conscious muscular engagement, all that occurs on the intake should be a *getting out of the way*, a non-doing. The entire sequence happens as a counterspring-like action following a suspension of air out.

On the exhale, however, we will now learn a more precise way of working with the three-part breath that will both support an optimal use of voice while moving and sounding and help to remain connected to centre. This next step employs a level of *productive tension* reminiscent of and in keeping with the principles of dynamic alignment as already discussed.

The Italian verb *appoggiare* means "to lean", with the noun *appoggio* often translated in the context of voicing as "support". There are many articulations of appoggio technique that date back hundreds of years, stemming from the craft of *bel canto* singing. This variation draws from some, and leaves aside those that speak to notions of "alignment", "posture", "position", and "placement" as well as those that focus on creating movement or muscular happenings that will occur quite naturally as symptoms of conscious and doable actions. Here we build on the work already done and attend to the action of the intercostals and the sternum on the exhale.

Exercise #32
Exhale appoggio style

Preparation: This will take place in *Dynamic standing* position after finding your *Sweet spot*, Exercises 16 and 18. You will need to fully understand Ex. 10, *Three-part breath* and you will need knowledge of the *Rings* (page 142). A clear understanding and warm-up, including all of the hand, tongue, neck, and scapula work, is necessary, as is the ability to intake as per the previous exercise, *Accenting A*, in line with the three-part breath.

Step 1: Etch-a-Sketch and find dynamic standing and your sweet spot. Do a few cycles of three-part breaths.

Step 2: On the next exhale, raise one hand to gently rest on your sternum and the other to cup your intercostals on one side. Be mindful to plot the path of the arm so that the scapula releases downward as your hands move into position. Do a little movement of the neck (bobble head) to assure that you have maintained independence of the clavicle, tongue, jaw, neck, and scapulae.

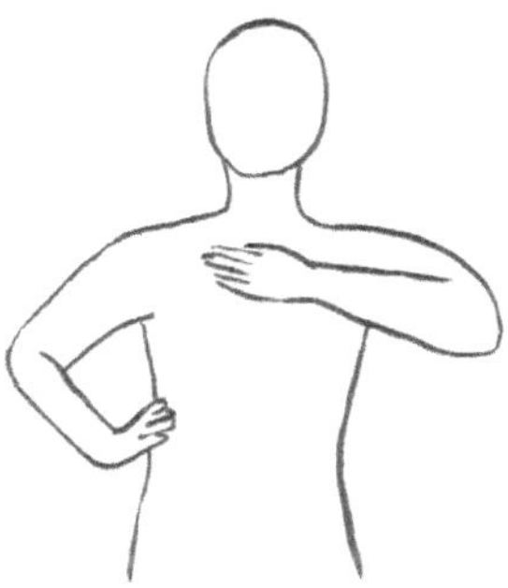

Step 3: With a clearly articulated three-part breath, exhale in preparation, suspend, intake (with tongue release) and let the next exhale continue as a smooth zzzzz for as long as it takes to completely empty. Witness what happens to your intercostals and your sternum as they empty. Suspend —

Step 4: Intake (with tongue release/perineum, intercostal and then sternum), suspend —

Step 5: At this point your pelvic girdle will be on the descent, the intercostals extended out sideways and the sternum gently raised as a result of the air that is in the lungs and the displacement of organs. This is where the work begins. On the exhale (do it on a ssssssssss), you will draw your awareness to the perineum as it begins to contract upwards in the direction of the vertical axis up the track of the chakras and out the top of the head. HOWEVER, THIS TIME when the intercostals begin to release inward you will suspend them out. You will resist the collapse. Your hand is there for your intercostals to *lean* against with constant directional energy out to the sides. Likewise, as your sternum begins to release downwards you will resist the collapse and the lowering of your hand. Exhale all air out, continuing to resist where your hands are, suspend, and intake.

Repeat.

Reflect: Working in this way with the appoggio, witness if there are any superfluous tensions arising in the tongue, neck, jaw, or shoulders. Witness the movement of the perineum. Remember that this is not a clenching, but rather a drawing upward as a symptom of the action of the exhale. Work to isolate just the muscles needed to work with the directional energy of the resistance against the collapse of the sternum and the intercostals on the exhale. There is no arrival, or position to get. *It is a constant actioning of resistance against the collapse, and it is initiated from and maintains constant contact to the perineal centre.* When done correctly, the resistance of collapse of the intercostals and the sternum provides a supportive foundation for a more relaxed, independent and articulatable tongue, neck, shoulders, and jaw.

Working with appoggio serves a few purposes. As you are not collapsed at the end of an exhale or long vocal phrase, there is no need for resetting on the intake. However, it is important to remember that non-collapse is in no way meant to be holding out or a locking, but rather a buoyant and dynamic resistance. The torso is already set up and poised for the springing in of the air with minimal adjusting. This will also make direct access to the perineal centre easier, since it supports a direct line down to the pelvic release on the intake. In movement, making sure that this is a constant actioning will be important. Awareness of a separation of the rings on both the intake and the exhale will support the action of the appoggio.

SOUNDING OFF THE THROAT

Sounding off the throat is important in this work, not for any aesthetic reason such as the quality of sound that it produces, but rather for its active aesthetic. When we sound on the throat while moving the neck, or jumping, or rolling, the sound gets interrupted, can sound muffled and can glitch. When you sound off the throat with the three-part breath and in connection to the perineal centre and working in dynamic alignment, it is possible to do all of those things without any interruption to the sound or loss of upper harmonics. But how do we sound off the throat, and what does this mean? It is really unhelpful to view vocalizing as the making of pleasing sounds. It is better to experience it as a breath dance that allows for the emergence of sound. By the time the sound has happened it is too late to do anything about it. Therefore, listening to your sound is really unhelpful.

To quickly summarize, up to this point we have established that on the intake the tongue releases in concert with the perineal release, followed in quick succession by the intercostals and sternum expanding. On the exhale or while voicing we will practise the appoggio as the perineal centre contracts upwards in the direction of the vertical axis up and out of the top of the head. (We won't become the kite, however.) As we voice or send sound out of our mouth we will do this not in the direction of between the lips, but rather over the upper palate and in the direction of above the upper lip, at the level of the philtrum (the little vertical indent at the top of your lip above the upper teeth). This can feel counter-intuitive, as we do tend to sense that sound comes from our mouth. Actually, the conditions for the production of vowels and consonants are made in the mouth, but the conditions for sound are produced by the entire body in direct connection to a centre.

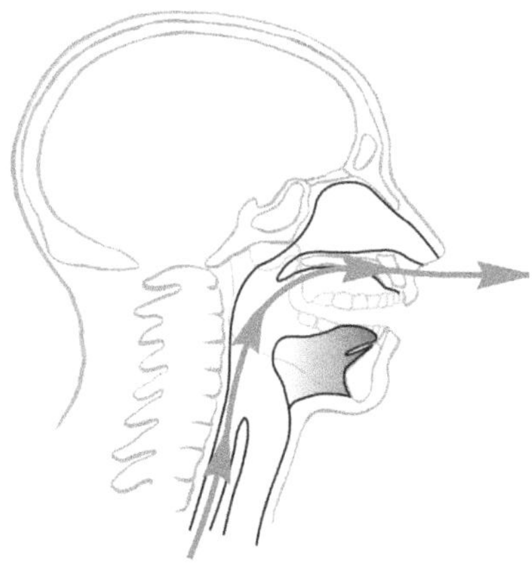

Interestingly, like the mirror tension in the roll (see page 117), there is a direct relationship between how low your breath releases into the perineal centre on the intake and how much you can direct the exhale off the throat over the upper palate and out the direction of the philtrum above the upper teeth.

Try this: if you breathe into the chest and then sound, you will find that your voice gets stuck in the lower throat. If you breathe into your solar plexus, your sound gets caught in the lower jaw. If you breathe into your belly button, your sound is likely to come out of the region of the lips, and if you breathe into the perineum with the three-part breath, you will begin to experience what it means to sound off the throat as a symptom of the breath moving in a directional energy out of the face at the level of the philtrum.

The centre of the face is at the level of the philtrum and has an active mirror effect in the centre of the body. Interestingly, this *breath dance* will also, as a symptom, open the nasal passages and raise the upper palate, allowing for optimum resonance.

Exercise #33

Accenting B

Here you will do everything in Steps 1, 2, and 3 for Ex. 31 *Accenting A*, adding the new elements. When you exhale or voice, you will direct the energy of the breath out over the upper palate and out through the facial centre (the level of the philtrum above the upper teeth). On the exhale you will now practise the appoggio.

This next stage of *Accenting* also introduces the option of new rhythms and pitch variations. When working with pitch, it is important to maintain the directional energy of the air out the centre of the face (the level of the philtrum) regardless of how high or low the sound is. Some have a tendency to raise the directional energy in the face as the note gets higher and also to lower into the throat as the notes get lower (remember, this often is mirrored in the torso with mirror tensions). This variation is not what we want. Maintaining the directional energy through the centre of the face, which means not becoming the kite on the high notes and not collapsing to the throat on the low notes, is crucial. Return to centre, both facial and perineal, is the motto.

Below you will find some possible variations:

Variation 1: (Working with rhythm and varying sounds)

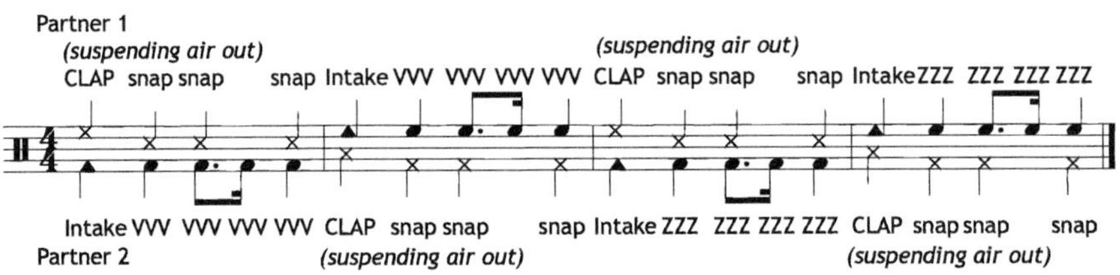

Variation 2: (Working up the chromatic scale with alternating sounds)

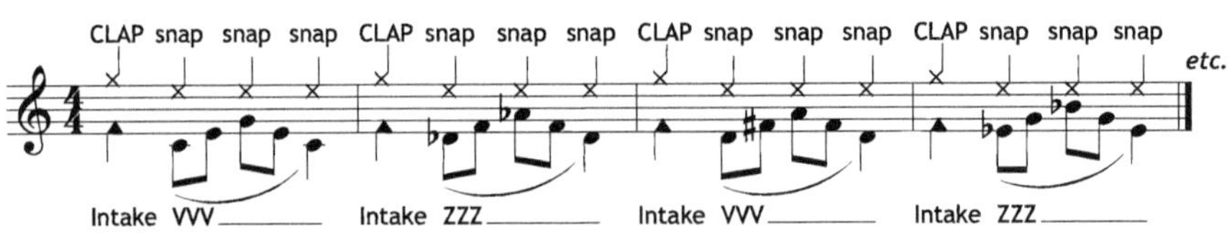

Incorporating new sounds as you progress: All of these can be done on a sustained vvvv, zzzz as written or with a roll of the tongue, a flub of the lips and eventually, after learning the next section on onset, with vowel sounds.

Working through all possible sounds and across the range is a wonderful way to warm up. Returning to the physical sequences and integrating the roll or the dynamic alignment in motion sequences creates a well-balanced conditioning.

EXPLORING RANGE

Much like the vertical alignment, up through the centre of the body (review Ex. 18), which is initiated by the perineal contraction and follows a directional energy up out the top of the head, there is mirror vertical alignment that follows a directional energy up the front of the face. This can be experienced as we sound up the range. It can be felt as vibration. In some interpretations of *bel canto* singing, this track, as it vibrates up the front of the face, coming to a point above the eye (interestingly, right where the sixth chakra and the third eye also sit), is the key to what is termed "squillo". Squillo refers to an optimum resonance that has a ringing quality produced by upper harmonics rather than physical pushing, often used by opera singers to help to carry the voice over a large orchestra without microphones. In exploring the squillo as part of a *breath dance*, we simply build on what has been thus far explained.

Exercise #34
Squillo sirening

Here we will explore the use of the squillo as part of a fairly common vocal exercise called sirening.

On the intake (which you will recall happens on an instantaneous recoil off the appoggio, in line with the perineal and tongue release followed by the intercostal and sternum release), you will direct the sense of the breath out through the level of the philtrum. So, to be clear, this will not be an "inhale", where you might draw the air back using lots of muscles, but rather while the tongue releases forward the directional energy of the intake will follow in line with the philtrum, releasing muscles in the face up into the direction of the sixth chakra or third eye.

Return to centre both in the face and the body, on the intake and on the exhale. We are never far from centre in this practice.

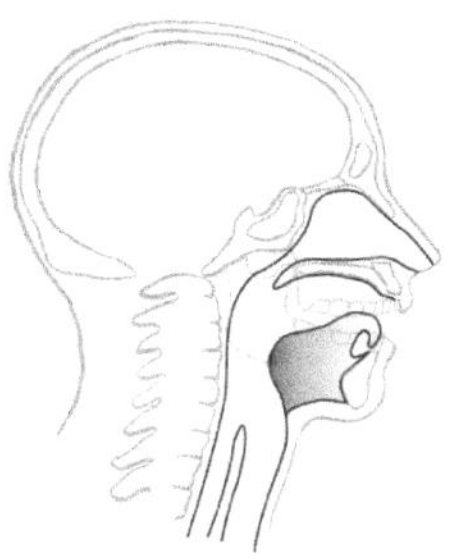

Intake

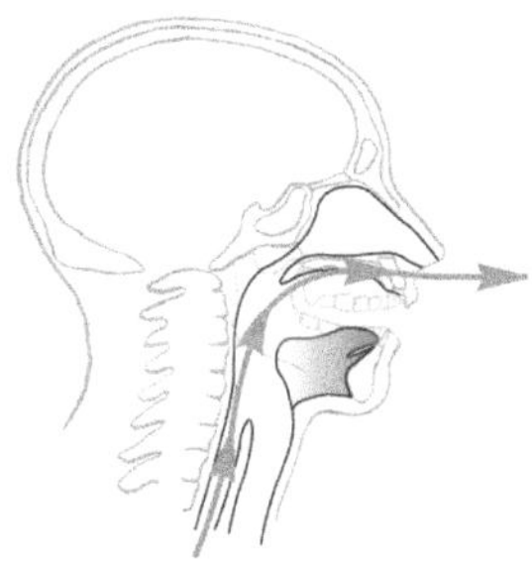

Exhale/voicing

This exercise works on a sustained sounded NG. NG just as in song. The siren will start low in pitch and travel up in pitch as one sustained note and then back down again.

Preparation: Ex. 10 *Three-part breath, Etch-a Sketch,* Ex. 18 *Sweet spot,* Ex. 16 *Psoas dynamic alignment in standing,* Exs. 31 and 33 *Accenting A and B,* and Ex. 32 *Appoggio.* Stand with knees soft so that you are poised to do a forward bend.

Step 1. Exhale in preparation and, on the next intake, with directional energy into the front of the face at the level of the philtrum, sound an NG, bending it up to the top of your range and back again. Note any experience of vibration.

Step 2. Do this again, but as you travel up the range release your head forward, taking your upper body into a forward bend, aiding in the release of the face.

> Note any new senses of vibration and any glitches of sound. Witness how the low point of centre in the body corresponds directly to the release of the face and the evenness of tone. (Do not aim to manufacture either of these; rather, let them be a symptom of the directional energy of the breath in line with the intake and exhale.) Note how the lower you breathe in the body, the further up the face the vibration tends to travel into the third eye.

Step 3. Repeat without the aid of the lean forward.

ONSET

Onset has to do with the moment the sound begins. Sound is produced by air hitting the vocal folds after they have joined together. We can sound a note that is airy to start (this happens when the vocal folds do not meet completely) and we can sound in a way that has a hard glottal explosion at the start. Both are fine as expressive options; however, as a starting point, what we are aiming for is something in between, a balanced onset.

A balanced onset is supported by all that we have spoken about thus far in the actions of the intake and exhale. It is especially important if we wish to move and sound, since a balanced onset makes the most economical use of the breath so longer phrases become possible. It is also important that we do not initiate the sound with explosive tension, because tension builds on other tensions, multiplies and creates a domino effect throughout the body. The key to a balanced onset is returning to the centre(s), face and body both, on the intake and the exhale/voicing.

Exercise #35
Onset with vowels

Here we take voicing a step further. Having progressed from *Accenting A and B* to further exploring our range on NG, we now introduce the concept of onset with vowels.

Preparation: Previous exercises in the voice section and Ex. 16 *Psoas dynamic alignment in standing.*

Step 1: You will intake EACH TIME (remember the tongue release) you see the symbol ^. As you work, you will sound on a vowel, with the directional energy out the centre of the face. Remember to practise your appoggio.

We will start on an *i* (as in sit)

i ^ i ^ i ^ i ^ then an arpeggio on *i* on do-mi-sol-mi –do : |and up the chromatic scale.

Step 2: Start again this time with a different vowel each time: ah, eh, ee, oh, and oo.

Step 3: Play with the basic sequence, mixing up your vowels and even alternating them.

> Note: Notice that there is a direct relationship between the release of the tongue on the intake and a balanced onset. Notice that the upper palate and the tongue will move into different positions as you produce different vowels; however, if you maintain centre(s), this will happen as a symptom with the least amount of superfluous tensions. Notice if you are coming from awareness and are witnessing. Work in conscious practice.

PUTTING IT TOGETHER: CRAFTING A PHYSIO-VOCAL PRACTICE

At this point you have all the tools available to work towards an integrative practice of voicing and moving. You may be a dancer who is wishing to speak, a singer who needs to dance, an actor working within physical theatre. You may be an opera singer who is being directed to move in ways that your previous training did not support in full. You may be a physical theatre practitioner negotiating new possibilities. You may be working as an interdisciplinary performer, participating in or inventing new modes of performance with new technologies that require interesting physio-vocal engagement.

Return to the previous exercises and their principles. You will find that they all connect to one integrated task: return to centre, supported by the three-part breath, in constant connection to centre. Every movement/sound is initiated at the perineum from awareness. Both sound and movement can be understood as a *breath dance*. An exacting isolation of the psoas is most important in any and all sequences of sounding and/or moving. This is supported through dynamic alignment while standing and in meeting the floor with hands and/or feet. (This includes unencumbered possibilities of backbends, cartwheels, and anything you can imagine.)

As an excellent way to condition and practise these, return to *Moving from floor to standing with dynamic psoas alignment* (page 133) and then *Rolling to standing* (page 135). The sequence offered in *Working in motion through dynamic alignment* is a wonderful challenge when incorporating work with voicing. You may wish to invent your own movement and sounding possibilities. Most importantly, apply the principles of Awareness, Three-Part Breath, Dynamic Alignment and the principles offered as part of Integrative Voicing, including the appoggio, onset and the *breath dance*, plotting the path in the face through the level of the philtrum on the intake and the exhale. *The more you release into the perineal centre, the more these actions become ONE doing. The further away from awareness, the further away from centre, the more these become a "negotiation". Here we aim for no negotiation but for one doing, from which all else "emerges" as a symptom of an integrative doing.*

In Part IV we will explore more exacting ways to integrate and work with any and all combinations of what have traditionally been taught as separate disciplines(s) of acting, singing/sounding, and dancing/movement. But first, let's look more closely at *acting*, the discipline that has a rich tradition of enquiry at the heart of what it means to *do* in a way that is "believable" or has "performative impact".

NOTE

1 For a good summary of Sven Smith's own work and details of his "Accent Method", which some of this work is in conversation with, see Thyme-Frøkjær, K. & Frøkjær-Jensen, B. 2001. *The Accent Method: A Rational Voice Therapy in Theory & Practice*. Milton Keynes: Speechmark.

Chapter 7

Acting is doing

BECAUSE OF THE WAY THE CHAPTERS in Part III of this book have been laid out so far, it might seem that we have worked through movement and voice and are only now arriving at a section on acting. This is not so. In truth, we have been learning how to hone our entire (physical-vocal-emotive-expressive) *instrument* — or better yet "integrative self" — toward acting as a discipline the entire time. As mentioned previously, the IPP is not a linear practice. Each exercise is in fact designed to be equally a vocal, acting, and movement exercise, or any combination thereof, to be used towards any aesthetic or disciplinary end. All the work thus far includes a deliberate practice of awareness in the doing of a doing, with breath and movement (even if that movement is practised as a stillness).

Acting, as will be discussed in detail in this chapter, is about *doing*. If you have, as recommended, worked with exercises 8–35 in Part III with the specific grounding offered in exercises 1–7 in Part II, then every physio-vocal exercise thus far in Part III has actually been done as an actor (even if you have not been aware of it). That's part of the beauty of an integrative practice.

If you recall, the main thrust of Part II, *Centre, Presence, and the Initiation of Task*, explored a fundamental core of what acting is as a discipline. Acting is essentially doing. Many actors will recognize that exercises 1–7, in addition to the Conscious Practice work, will seem much like what you might encounter in an acting class. Likewise, much of the movement and vocal work in Chapters Five and Six will resemble the type of approach you might encounter in an acting class. The more challenging exercises, however, might be required of an actor or performer training or wishing to work with physical theatre, or within various music theatre genres.

As mentioned at the top of Chapter One, the work in this book does not offer a technique but rather a practice. Acting as a discipline has a rich and highly articulated scope of techniques, systems, and methods. Acting as a discipline has a lot of rich discourse around it; it has been more historically articulated than other performance disciplines, possibly because there are so many conflicting and passionate treatises about what acting is and how to do it. In the following pages, we will discuss the implications of this for the actor aiming to work within more interdisciplinary modes of practice.

That acting has more discourse around it than dance/movement or sounding/singing may partly be because articulating how we sound and how we do movement is difficult. Sounding and moving can be perceived to be non-verbal or less "heady". You will have noted, however, that where there are articulations around what it means to breathe, what it means to be in centre and what it means to be present, and what and who is considered self in the practices of movement and voice, these aspects were explored within the previous chapters.

In this chapter, we discuss the practices of "acting". We do this to understand ourselves and our practice while acting, and to allow a more fluid understanding of what works and what does not as we practise across disciplines and, moreover, create a working tool kit of our own that we can draw on to integrate the disciplines.

Acting techniques can be boiled down, in various ways, to that of the practice of *doing*. As the IPP is about working across disciplines and with all aesthetic possibilities, you will find no new exercises in a discrete category called acting. You will, however, find possibly new propositions for you in the ways you may think and work around ideas of how you deal with the doing of the *doings*, particularly around expectations of emotion and character, and with these, movement and sounding. In Part IV you will learn how to make choices to support you as a practitioner in activating any combination of discipline(s) within the event. You will also see more details on how to work with acting as a discipline in Part IV, but first let's look at the discipline of acting as *doing*.

Acting is *doing*! But doing what? How? In which way? From where? For whom? Well, if acting is doing, what the doing is certainly changes depending upon which technique, system or combinations of practice(s) you use. Most actors today pull from a personal tool kit made of many systems and techniques and then negotiate (or even better, integrate) towards the purposes of the performance task, which may include movement and voice and sometimes dance and singing.

The nature of the *doing* that defines acting as a discipline has been described in many ways since Stanislavsky first transformed *text-based* acting from the gesture-ridden conventions of melodrama into a systemized psychophysical practice that could be used and developed in the service of a myriad of styles.[1]

As an actor, what you *do* changes depending upon whether you are acting from a script in a play or a musical score, or you are directed to work in a piece with no text, or a post-dramatic work where there may or may not be text but there is no narrative driving the action. As an actor, your doing(s) and the way you do will also change if you are working as part of an improvisation ensemble, a directed ensemble, and/or as part of a devising process.

For a useful inquiry into the many ways acting as a discipline in the West has been developed, negotiated, and practised since Stanislavsky, see Alison Hodge's book, *Actor Training* (Hodge 2010). I will not attempt to give a full account of the practices, or illuminate or justify the differences between techniques, but rather will survey the kernels of current acting practices through the lens of the active aesthetic, and then propose a way of working with acting through the IPP, integrating acting, voice/singing, and movement/dance towards the possibility of any chosen style and within a myriad of making processes.

REVOLTING AGAINST — DEFINING DOING

In Chapter One, we discussed how acting in many ways situates the *self* at the core of how it defines itself as a discipline. In addition to the defining placement of self, it is helpful to note that many practices were born out of a deliberate *revolt against*, or at least a marked discomfort with, aspects of the practices that came before them.

Stanislavsky revolted against the gesture-ridden pictorial conventions of the performance of his time, and worked to create truth on the stage, rendering acting as doing and the nature of that doing a respected craft. He imbued the act of acting with a sense of the sacred and gave us, actors, artistic integrity. Meyerhold rejected much of the "mysticism" surrounding this newly formed craft of the actor and worked to reinvigorate a sense of theatricality back onto a stage that had been overridden with naturalism, which he saw as often lacking atmosphere. Vakhtangov, in his "fantastic realism", came to the idea that a combination of Meyerhold and Stanislavsky was best. He aimed to retain the importance of truthful emotions while also allowing for theatricality. Michael Chekov, Anton Chekov's nephew, agreed with most of Stanislavsky's premises; he rejected, arguably, a central one, that of emotional memory, and leaned more on aspects of imagination. "Chekov argued that the emphasis should be on the character's feelings, not the actor's — not 'how would I feel?' but 'what does the character feel?' — and that this would enable the actor to transform into the character, rather than reducing the character to the personality of the actor" (Chamberlain 2010: 64).

By the time Stanislavsky's system made it to America and morphed into the Method, there were again different approaches, even within the Method camp. Krasner summarizes the main proponents like this: "For Strasberg, the essence of acting is psychological; resources abound in the actor's memory. For Adler, the essence of acting is sociological; actors draw from the given circumstances of the play." Meanwhile, "Acting for Meisner is in the doing; from this all other facets of the role emerge" (Krasner 2010: 155–157). And against this, at around the same time in America, Chaikin's Open Theatre revolted against the Method in workshops where "...from the onset [there] was a collective commitment towards exploring a new language for performance; one which was *not* based on naturalism or psychological motivation, but which was eclectic, inclusive, and innovative, based on questions rather than answers, on imagined possibilities rather than given formulae" (Hulton 2010: 166). Mamet, too, revolted against the psychological and character development elements in all derivations of the Stanislavsky "technique" and further returned to the text as the custodian of meaning, working against any fetishizing of an internally manifest truth and personal *belief* for the actor. He deemed all Method training and Stanislavsky-derived *techniques* "nonsense" and stated that "It is not a technique out of the practice of which one develops a skill — it is a cult" (Mamet 1998: 6). For him "The actor does not need to 'become' the character. The phrase, in fact, has no meaning. There *is* no character. There are only lines upon a page" (Mamet 1998: 9).

In Europe, Brecht's Epic theatre and his *Verfremdungseffekt* (not strictly a technique of acting, but certainly within the purview of the actor's doing) were a revolt against what he termed "culinary theatre", typified for him by a bourgeois sentimentality maintained by dramatic conventions he saw as casting a stupefying "witchcraft" over society, conventions that for him could be traced back to Aristotle, Wagner, and Stanislavsky. In what was in the 1960s and 70s termed "experimental theatre", both Brook and Grotowski made the training of their actors synonymous with the making of their work. Both required an integration of performance discipline(s) in the service of their company's aesthetic. (Implications of this are mentioned in Part I at various junctures.) For Brook, as summarized by Marshall and Williams, the actor "...moved beyond ego-driven virtuosity to a kind of psycho-somatic integration that he calls 'transparency'". Alive and present in every molecule of their being, they have "the capacity to listen through the body to codes and impulses that are hidden all the time at the root of cultural forms" (Marshall 2010: 189). Grotowski's Poor Theatre, by definition, situated the actor at the centre of the work. For him, the actor "was a holy figure, a type of 'secular saint' whose extraordinary discipline and ability allowed him or her to cast aside daily life masks in order to accomplish an act of self-penetration and disarmament" (Wolford 2010: 204). And, of course, there are many more mavericks of theatre not mentioned. The point here is that acting as a discipline is an ever-evolving one, where the actor as *self* is one constant part — but moreover that what we as actors *do*, and how we *do*, and towards which aesthetic, sits at the centre of that ongoing discussion.

The nature of *doing* for the actor seems to constantly return as a discussion, and in that return throws up a set of themes. It returns in different guises; however, a pattern is there, and it is a pattern of dualisms, such as internal/external, psychological/physical, personal/societal, higher/lower selves, sacred/secular, embodied/intellectual, and actor as custodian of meaning/text as custodian of meaning. In fact, different acting trainings are often defined by the different and often passionate rhetoric redefining the balance between these dialectical themes, creating a reorganization of self (actor) in action (doing) with either self and/or action in representation of a performance aesthetic and/or an ideology. It's a never-ending "same play with different props".

The Integrative Performance Practice does not have embedded within it one system, technique, or prescribed aesthetic for the actor doing the act of acting.

Further, it does not have within it a self-prescribed social or political dogma from which it requires the actor to operate. In fact, all of the aforementioned dramatic aesthetic outcomes brought forth through or by the many mavericks of acting as a discipline can be achieved with this practice. For you the actor, however, there may be adjustments and, in some cases, interventions in your *way* of doing the *doing* that is acting.

The Integrative Performance Practice maintains *no tension* between, around, or about the dualisms. In fact, if there is anything that might define this practice, it is in the very challenging that these are valuable dualisms at all! If there is any *revolt against*, it is here! In Chapter One we drew from phenomenology, performativity, and cognitive science to reconcile *self* and *doing*, as other than internal/external, psychological/physical, personal/societal, higher/lower, sacred/secular, or embodied/intellectual. We also introduced the term "event" to help us reconsider the dynamics of meaning making, repeatability and operations of performance. Drawing from current conceptual thinking in quantum theory and transdisciplinarity, operating within a holographic principle, we considered a possible *way*, or active aesthetic, that exceeds the linear, whereby the doing of the doing lives in and of ourselves and the world as an active field, a field of *performing*.

THE ACTOR DOING

From the beginning of this book we have been working through select ideas by way of this sentence:

A performer (A) does something called performing (B) towards performance (C).

In Part I we learned that from this middle field, performing (B), both the performer (A) and the performance (C) *emerge* as a *symptom* of the field of performing (B). We also discussed how it is in this field of performing (B) that the alchemy of the performer resides, in the doing of the doing or the way of doing. Two actors can work with the same set, costume, lights, with the same director and with the same script; however, without a doubt these will be very different events, very different performances. Why? Because the performer does not DO the performance. The actor does not DO the play or emotion, but rather enters the field of performing (B), and through their *way of doing*, a performance/play/emotion (C) emerges which also contributes to who they are as the actor/performer (A).

Much Western acting training works to strip us back to an *essential* self capable of enacting a certain nature of doing. Language around this self and this nature of doing tends to evolve around notions of truthfulness, authenticity, believability, creativity, naiveté, and presence. It is not always clear where this nature of doing resides or what it is in service to. As an actor, am I to be true to myself? To this moment? To my emotions? True to the script/score/blocking/choreography? True to my impulses? To the director's direction? To the character? To the given circumstances? To my own artistic integrity? To the "craft"? What exactly do I do, and for whom or what do I do it?

In this practice, *self* is not an essential place from which one acts. This means that there is no essential true and pure self to train or strip back to, but rather that self is recognized as a dynamic, moving, and ever-evolving entity, neither fixed nor static. It is not determined by personal narrative or by conditioning alone, but lives in the act of the act through all aspects of the inner/outer, psycho/physical, social/personal, conscious/subconscious, etc.

For the purposes of this practice, the *who* that is acting is supported, made present and connected at each and every *intake* and *exhale* through the three-part breath, with its isolation of the perineal centre. *Return to centre* is the motto. This supports emotional availability, gives greater access to physio-vocal possibilities, and helps to maintain awareness, rather than focus, allowing for an immediacy of the entire instrument in the execution of a wider range of creative choices. You may recall that in this practice the actor does not need to leave all their troubles at the door to enter the space cleansed. We recognize our *company*, and come from *awareness*, which differs from thoughts and feelings, to do chosen *task(s)*. We *witness* rather than judge and diagnose and *return to centre* again and again to *do the doing* of the *task* anew each time. If any of the italicized words in this paragraph seem undefined to you, and/or if their precise meaning within this particular practice is not clear, please review Part II before moving on.

In Part II we learned about a *way of doing* that supports integration and will take us through to the end of the book. At the beginning of this part, Part III, we explored some vocal and physical *what to do's*, allowing for greater integrative physio-vocal possibilities. In this chapter, we look at some of the *what to do's* present in the discipline of acting, examine some of the implications of these and offer some adjustments in approach that will help us work towards an integrative performance practice.

DOING ACTIONS

Since Stanislavsky, the doing of acting has ceased to be mere imitation and depiction. It has become, among other things, a practice that is both intimate and truthful about experience in the act of doing.

When Method acting teacher Sanford Meisner said the following, he encapsulated much of what Western acting training is about.

> The foundation of acting is the reality of doing... Are you listening to me? Are you listening to me? — You're not pretending that you're listening; you're listening. You're *really* listening. Would you say so? *That's* the reality of doing. Let there be no question about what I'm saying here. If you do something you really do it.
>
> (Meisner 1987: 16–17)

To really *do* listening — for instance, rather than indicate, pretend, or show listening — can be difficult. The difference between this type of *really* doing and that of *indicating* is considered key to many acting methods and was at the heart of Stanislavsky's early frustrations.

> In life all people can be normal people, while on the stage not everyone succeeds in being normal. In life everyone has organic lines, the actor on the stage alone has not got them. It is only on the stage that an actor can think of anything under the sun while singing a passionate love aria to the audience and at the same time clasping the leading lady to his heart without even bothering to look at her. When an actor makes a declaration of love on the stage he puts his hand on his heart, rolls up his eyes, sighs, and so on. If you ever tried to do the same in real life the girl you were in love with would certainly take offence and send you packing, but for some reason that sort of thing is considered quite normal on stage.
>
> (Magarshack 1986: 400)

While actor/singers may have evolved from such extreme melodramatic tendencies (we can hope), the fact remains that simply doing the doing of a task on the stage, while being watched, and further while working across performance disciplines, presents certain challenges. This is why the entirety of Part II is dedicated to learning to recognize elements of ourselves and our environments that create interference in the chosen doing of a task, and also why there are multiple exercises to help condition and train the actor/performer to operate in the field of performing (B), the field where the practice of disciplines intersect and, importantly, the doing of the doing happens. Meisner might call this "the reality of Doing".

I actually doubt that Meisner and I disagree here; however, language is important and creates patterns in practice(s). It is important to distinguish that *reality* is not an aim for the Integrative Performance Practice, but only one possible outcome. One might need to do actions that are fantastical, that incorporate the actions of a character while singing a cadenza, or the actions of a caricature while dancing a stylized medieval jig. For instance, in effective children's theatre the actor needs to switch between a truthful, intimate action and a large almost cartoon-like and even *indicated* action. With the IPP it is not only possible to move between different stylistic or discipline-related conventions, but it is easier, when you do the doing from awareness and in connection to centre. Here there is no reality, or truthful quality required of the doing, but rather simply the doing of the doing, the entering of an active aesthetic whereby truth and reality are only emergent options. Indicating and melodramatic gesture are also options. The choice is yours, but, as you may recall from previous chapters, so is the responsibility. In the IPP the *integrity of the doing* is maintained by doing the doing, from awareness, in connection with centre.

In system-derived trainings, *doings*, often called "actions", are bound in a linear logic or "through line of action", which comes directly from the text as plotted in the narrative through the realization of a character in the "given circumstances" of the play/score. These doings are fuelled by the character's desires, wants, intentions, or objectives (all words used for the same thing, depending upon which version of the System/Method you are working with). In each scene a character will have an intention, and all the scenes' intentions will plot a path through the play to the "super-objective".

For Stanislavsky, actions executed in this way adhered to what he called "a logic of physical actions". Physical because "It is easier to lay hold of physical than psychological action; it is more accessible than elusive inner feelings. Also physical action is easier to fix; it is material, visible" (Stanislavsky 1959: 46). However, for him this "physical action", when connected to intention or character's want, was intrinsically bound with the psyche and the spirit; it became a "psychophysical" action. With the methods of physical action the mind/body connection was made: "Thoughts are embodied in acts"... "and a man's actions in turn affect his mind. His mind affects his body and again his body, or its condition, has its reflex action on his mind and produces this or that condition" (Stanislavski 1975: 4).

There has been much fetishizing around supposed dualisms of external/internal, psychological/physical, and conscious/subconscious approaches to action within the development of Western acting training. In the IPP we do not even consider *doings* from the perspective of these dualisms. In this work *the integrity of doing*, as it comes from awareness in connection to centre, solves this problem before it starts. Further, in the IPP we depart from the requirement of a *character's intention* to render an action truthfully. Integrity of action happens in attendance to the doing of the doing, entering the field of performing within the *event*. (This use of event will be discussed in detail in Part IV; the theory of event was introduced in Chapter Two, What is integrative performance.)

In this work there is no reliance on a "logic of physical actions" and the attendant firm belief that there is a *linear through line* dictated through the text to a "super-objective". One could *choose* to work in this way, especially when dealing with realistic interpretations of texts where the logic of human behaviour is what is to be evoked. However, in instances such as post-dramatic work where narrative is not the driving force, or in modern dance that uses the spoken word, or in intermedial work where there might be an exchange between technology and human behaviour, or in less naturalistic interpretations of plays/scores, the use of a character's intention and the through line of action will either disrupt the actions' integrity or impose an unintended aesthetic on the work.

BEING/DOING CHARACTER

The way an actor approaches character sits at the heart of many acting practices. For Stanislavsky, "Only after an actor has thought through, analyzed and felt himself to be a living person inside his whole part there opens up to him the long, beautiful, beckoning perspective...Against this depth of background he can play out whole actions, speak whole thoughts, rather than be held to limited objectives, separate phrases and words" (Stanislavsky 1996: 177).

There are actors from certain branches of the American Method who connect the above idea of feeling oneself "to be a living person inside his whole part" with the aforementioned "reality of doing". They take this to an extreme and choose to immerse themselves in the character, living, breathing, and eating like that person might have lived. This approach can help one to condition the physique, to explore the experience of being the character and help one pattern in quirks and choose qualities of action, but it also leaves little distance between the actor's sense of self and a temporary illusion of being the character.

For an Integrative Practice this is not recommended, since the body, mind, and skill set of a character, as true to life as it may be, is most likely not capable of performing seven performances a week. Moreover, it may not be able to live its story through song or dance. In the IPP we need to be able to respond to all the elements within the performance event with our complete instrument. Interestingly, Stanislavsky's actual stance was closer to the work of the IPP than such examples of the American Method. His fictitious student in *Building a Character*, speaking about a successful characterization, says, "while I was acting I felt exceptionally pleased as I followed my own transformation. Actually I was my own observer at the same time that another part of me was being [the character]...Yet can I really say that that creature is not a part of me? I derived him from my own nature. I divided myself, as it were, into two personalities. One continued as an actor, the other was an observer. Strangely enough this duality not only did not impede, it actually promoted my creative work. It encouraged and lent impetus to it" (Stanislavsky 1996: 21).

In this work the practices of *coming from awareness* rather than focus and *witnessing* rather than judging and diagnosing (as described in detail in Chapter Four) dissolve this dualism and also allow for observation while working in the flow of presence in the field of performing (B).

In this work, *becoming* the character to the extent of losing centre, the three-part breath and your ability to witness is likened to a sort of hysteria, described earlier in the section *Don't become the kite*. This is not to say, of course, that your character has the same centre, tensions, voice, or emotional life as you the actor. However, in this practice you activate the qualities of your character through the perineal centre and your character's voice through the level of the philtrum fuelled by the three-part breath; your character's tensions are embodied as you are still able to plot the path of the dynamic alignment. If you need to leave any of these for a creative choice of emphasis, then you simply return on the next breath and as the next physio-vocal emotive task may require. This is possible if you come from awareness rather than focus and if you witness as you work within the field of performing, working in a *conscious practice* with its continued return to centre. All of the exercises in this chapter have aimed to set this up for you. One way to be sure that you are working from an integrative practice as you embody your character is to do *Rolling to standing with and without voicing* (page 135), and Ex. 28 *Dynamic alignment in movement* as your character. When working with others, meet in the middle as practitioners, but do Ex. 30 *Meeting in the middle, diagonal catches* as your characters.

Next, you will learn how to integrate text, be it music or word, choreography, blocking, or direction, and support yourself to create choices that will allow the emotional life of the character to emerge as a symptom of various doings and happenings within the event, while making it possible to sound/sing and move/dance without compromise to disciplinary aesthetics.

In the next chapter we will learn how to make choices so that our character lives physically and emotionally within a performative matrix, made possible through an active framework, which includes actions, obstacles, and the happenings within the chosen performance event. We will also learn to make choices that help to support characterization *through* the integrative instrument. Your character might just happen to sing rather than speak, or your character may carry a deep wound as part of their history; your character may be more like a stock caricature with fleeting and sudden physical and emotional gestures and no deep history; your character may not speak at all, but rather communicate through elaborate choreography. We will learn how all this is possible through an active aesthetic.

NOTE

1 Stanislavsky's system is often misconstrued as serving only naturalism and realism, mostly because of his profound collaborative relationship with playwright Anton Chekov. What is not so commonly known is that his work in opera and his love for music influenced his system from the beginning. His observation that musicians had a language and actors had none was very apt. Further, his directing of opera in his later years served as an exploration of various styles. For Massenet's *Werther* he focused on characterization and the relationship between characters. In Tchaikovsky's *Eugene Onegin* he chose a minimal approach and had the actor/singers perform in their street clothes with no makeup, so that the acting, music, movement, and poetry were their only recourse to making theatre. In Puccini's *La Boheme*, he explored that elusive place that lies between the words and the music. Pavel Rumyanstev, a singer and student, documented much of this work, which can be found in the book *Stanislavski on Opera*. His last opera, and therefore arguably the ultimate expression of his system, was Rimsky-Korsakov's *A May Night*. It was chosen for its theatricality and accessibility to a younger audience. He produced an un-naturalistic, physical, and fantastical production that still adhered to his basic philosophies of truth on the stage.

PART IV

Integrative performance analysis

Chapter 8

Working in the field of performing through text

IN THIS CHAPTER we get to put it all together and learn to fashion all manner of integrative possibilities. We will learn how to analyze and organize creative and practical choices around what we do as performers. The choices will be, at the same time, both creative and technical (in support of possible cross-disciplinary challenges). They will cover any required integration of acting, movement, and vocalizing and will work in correlation with text. You will learn that the best choices are those that are not complicated; however, there is a certain level of complexity involved in the planning. You will know when you have made the right choice because it will allow you to do *one* doable action, from which any combination of disciplinary expressions can emerge.

TEXT IN INTEGRATIVE PERFORMANCE ANALYSIS

As mentioned previously, *text* in this work includes all types of material that are *prescribed* (pre-scribed, written beforehand). This includes words, choreography, blocking, music, and also the structures of exercises, such as the ones offered in Parts II and III. As introduced in Part I, text is not an object that *holds* some inherent meaning which you, the performer, are obliged to depict or allow to passively come through you (unless of course this is a deliberate and chosen creative choice). Since text(s) set themselves free in the act of performing and therefore hold no essential meaning, we will work with text as just another active partner in the process of making and doing in the field of performing (B). Text in this work is viewed as a collaborator in the doing of performing. Text is also seen as just one of the components woven into the performance event as we map our trajectory through the work. *Event* is what *happens* in performance (C).

Let's again review our working terms:

We are people called *performers*, who do something called *performing*, towards an outcome called *performance*.

A	B	C
Performer	**Performing**	**Performance**
Who is doing.	Way of doing.	What is done.

In Part I we introduced the notion of event, and in this chapter we learn to work with the concept of event as a chosen lens through which we make creative and practical choices. Event, however, contains more than just our actions; it also contains little events that we will call *happenings*. We will learn soon how these happenings emerge as the result of different kinds of *actions* against *obstacles*.

Since the Ancient Greeks, through Wagner and in our current climate, with its myriad of contemporary hybrid, intermedial, and interdisciplinary forms emerging, theatre-makers have been looking for an integrative methodology. This practice offers a possible solution. In Integrative Performance Analysis (IPA), we recognize that it is the *event* that *happens* on the stage (or in the space) through the *act* of performance. As discussed in detail in Part I, this happens actively, in a middle field we have termed performing (B). You may recall, as discussed in Chapter Two, if the desired effect is to have all the *operations* of the various disciplines working together in a network to allow for an event, then we need to attend to these *operations*, which contribute to the happenings within that event.

In this chapter we learn how it is possible to integrate the disciplines as part of an active aesthetic as we work in the field of performing (B). Here the text, the design elements, the technical theatre aspects, the spectator/audience dynamic, and of course the performance disciplines will be *activated* as part of a chosen event. Let's first break down the components of these operations and then apply them to practical examples.

ACTIONS IN INTEGRATIVE PERFORMANCE ANALYSIS

Actions are doings. Most actors know of actions as things that their character does to get what they want, to achieve their intention or objective. There is often a sense of internal motivation in this type of action. The action, when discussed in this way as part of acting technique, adheres to a logic of human behaviour derived from Stanislavsky's work (discussed in greater detail in Chapter Seven).

In the IPA actions can indeed be like the above, but they also include other doings. Actions can lie outside those of a character's motivation, which are often hung on a linear narrative and adhere to a logic of human behaviour. If we were to try and overlay actions as spoken about in the discipline of acting on a Cunningham modern dance work, or most art songs, or a postdramatic theatre work where the event is neither gleaned from the character's journey nor the central thrust of the drama, we might diminish other possible happenings that were envisioned into the events of these forms.

In Integrative Performance Analysis, actions are doings. However, here doings also include the throw of a light, the cough of an audience member, the extension of a leg, the swell of the orchestra, the projection of an image, or the reach of one character to another in the effort to convince. Actions can also include performance practice *tasks* as described in Parts II and III, such as *working from awareness*, *engaging dynamic alignment in the hands and arms*, *returning to centre*, or *releasing the tongue on the intake*. Actions can be many types of doings. What makes them actions within the chosen event, however, is how they are incorporated into what happens within an event. For that, we need to introduce obstacles. (If the idea of *task* is not clear, please review Chapter Four.)

ACTION AGAINST OBSTACLES

For those who have studied theatre, the saying "conflict is drama" is not a new idea. If Romeo and Juliet met, fell in love, got to hang out together, got married and then lived happily ever after without any obstacles in their way, well, there would not be a play.

For actors this works on a practice-based level. Actors know that they cannot "do" emotions. The actor does not do crying. To try to cry often causes tension and often takes the activity outside of what is believable. Such an action would also then become *to try to* cry, which differs from crying. When an actor is working toward a desired outcome of an emotion within a naturalistic form, they are taught to do actions towards a want of the character, as in "I need to find my keys because I can't leave the house if I don't and I am late for the audition of a lifetime". The obstacle is that "no matter where I look, how hard I try to remember where I put them, how many times I ask my housemates, the keys are nowhere to be found". The actor stays with the urgency of the need to find the keys as they do actions as the character within the given circumstances of the play, against the obstacle of not finding them, and that tension allows for the emergence of a *real* and present emotion or state of being. This is much like our working sentence: the performer (A) does not do performance (C), but rather does something called performing (B) from which performance emerges. Here the "performance" would be the emotion associated with frustration that one couldn't find their keys.

When actors learn technique in this way there is a large distinction between playing an obstacle and playing *against* an obstacle. If our same sorry character did eventually find their keys, scrabbled to the audition late, found everyone had left and then went into the nearest bar, got blindingly drunk, stumbled home and was trying to put the keys into the door... the obstacle (against the action of trying to get in the door) would be the state of being drunk. Here actors learn that they don't *play* drunk. They try to get into the door, *against* the obstacle of being drunk. Perhaps every time the key meets the doorknob there appear to be three blurry keyholes; the character works against this obstacle in their action: to get the key into the keyhole. They do not squint their eyes and wave the key around, since squinting one's eyes and waving keys around are not actions towards opening a door. Playing against helps to strengthen an action and the obstacle and, as a result, makes the moment, which includes the state of drunkenness, the need to get in the door, and the entire characterization, more believable — for both the actor and the audience. This *against-ness* is about *engaging* at a very basic level.

Even as we work in disciplines other than acting and in work that is not dependent on character, this dynamic of working *against* an obstacle is going to be important as we move further into the IPA. When you *do* or *play* an obstacle it ceases to be an obstacle; it becomes an action, and thus changes the event.

The action-against-obstacle dynamic serves as a fulcrum, where the integration of singing, acting, and dancing can occur. For instance, action against obstacle is at the heart of producing sound. When air moves through our windpipe and then hits up against the obstacle of our joined vocal folds, vibration happens and sound emerges. We learned in Parts II and III that we do not perform or "do" a note, but rather a bunch of other doings, from which the note emerges. We also learned that we do not "do" a leap. Movement can be seen as tension against release, or extension against contraction, or the initiation of force against the pull of gravity. The leap emerges. All of our doings come from awareness, fuelled by the three-part breath. (Return to Part III if this is not clear.)

At the centre of all the disciplines of acting, singing, and dancing is the basic dynamic of *action against obstacle creates happening.*

In the IPP the idea of action against obstacle is embedded at every level. In Part II we spoke about what it means to work in awareness and with a "crispy presence" (as opposed to in a trancelike state). We also introduced the concept of "staying in the discomfort" rather than "getting it". We learned about witnessing self rather than focusing as you attend to the task; this, too, was about ways of working in a productive tension — action against obstacle. When we began to work physio-vocally in Part III, with the opposing circles in the dynamic alignments of the arms and legs, working against each other always and never resting in a position or posture, this was also action against obstacle. The productive tension produced by an outward direction in the intercostals on the exhale and/or voicing during the *appoggio* is also a prime example. This *against-ness* is central to the field of performing (B). This is why it is very important to enter this dynamic from awareness, connected to the perineal centre, fuelled by the three-part breath. It is the best way not to slip into *doing the obstacle*, especially when working across performance disciplines.

EVENTS AND HAPPENINGS IN INTEGRATIVE PERFORMANCE ANALYSIS (IPA)

Happenings are little events. Multiple happenings make up an event. Happenings emerge from the dynamic of action against obstacle. The event is what happens. An event can be the entire work, play, exercise, or an incremental moment, scene, or section. The funny thing about an event is that if you want to be aware of the operations within it, you cannot take it for granted, because even if you are not aware of it, there will always be an event: something will happen. You can't *do* an event, or a happening for that matter.

Events are highly subjective, meaning there are lots of ways to see them, determine action in them and have them actioned within. Consider the situation of a violent fight between two lovers. This fight could be activated as an Internet-generated work, a scene in a play, a ballet, an opera, a musical theatre work, a physical theatre piece; this situation, that of the fight, could be one of many Events. A violent fight between two lovers, regardless of the intentions, the language, the movement, the musical notes, or the technology, could be activated as any of the events below (and also others).

- A relationship ends
- A relationship is reborn
- Two make love
- Murder attempt
- Just another night in the Smith house

Each of these chosen events will cast a different lens on the fight scene, through which the integrative performer will view and do the actions against different obstacles, creating different happenings to make up that event. The event in the IPA is a way of bracketing the actions, obstacles, and happenings that are part of the dynamic that make up that event. We will soon learn how to use this as an *active framework*.

Let's take this explanation to a larger canvas in *Romeo and Juliet*, Shakespeare's play of the "star-crossed lovers". It's a malleable story; Berlioz turned it into a *symphonie dramatique*, Prokofiev a ballet, Tchaikovsky an overture-fantasia. Bellini and Gounod's operas are performed regularly, as is the Bernstein/Sondheim/Laurents musical theatre adaptation *West Side Story*. A quick search on the Internet will show you an array of physical theatre adaptations. It has made its way to film, has influenced pop and jazz music, and was even recently made into an interactive performance work in tweets in "Suchtweetsorrow" in cooperation between the Royal Shakespeare Company and The Mudlark Production Company. The "star-crossed lovers" component is rich with conflict and hangs on the *theme* of love. Often *theme* is considered the unifying or constant factor across disciplines and genres.

In the IPA, in much the same way that it is argued that one does not *do* emotions or *do* performance, we do not *do* a theme without that doing being one of depicting and indicating. The design, the performers' actions, movements and sounds, and the mise-en-scène can at best *adhere* to or *depict* a theme. Themes, however, are *activated* in a field of performing within the dynamic operations of the dramatic event.

Even with the *love* theme, the *event* of *Romeo and Juliet* is still very variable. What *happens* on the stage/performance space/environment is the *event* in the *act* of performance.

Events within the love theme of *Romeo and Juliet* could be:

A. family feud comes to a bitter end
B. manipulation of church official results in youths' demise
C. society drives teenage lovers to suicide
D. love prevails over prejudice

Here we see that the event is not something that is *written* into the prescribed, text, or design, or even technology, but rather is a choice of how one activates this text in the act of performance. Context may influence it, but it does not determine it. Events help us to determine what happens between the texts, performance, design, technology, concept, and disciplines of performing. The event in this instance helps bracket the crossings, collisions, and intertwinings of the dynamic operations within it. As a first step, event is used as an *active framework* for the purpose of making choices. (We will speak of how the interdisciplinary performer activates these choices shortly.)

The first step when exploring the implications of a chosen event is to ask, "What happens when such an event occurs?" Every event is made up of lots of happenings. These are not necessarily in any order. The best way to explore this is to step back from the text, step back from any linear understanding of how the story unfolds, step back from any attachment to any character's logic of behaviour, step back from any limitations of old technology or fetishizing of new technology, step back from any conventions around the performance discipline(s), and take a larger view, a view of the event, and then enjoy the brainstorming process.

So, for the purposes of brevity, let's pick the first event mentioned above. (You can brainstorm on the remaining.) What happens in feuds, and moreover when "feud comes to a bitter end"? Happenings within this might include: Anger, Augmented Stories Of Blame, Demonizing Of Other Side, Loss, Sadness, Alliances Made, Testing Of Loyalties, Bully's Rise To The Top Of The Clan, Pressure To Take Sides, Accidents, Retribution, Lines Drawn, Both Sides Become Defined By The Battle With The Other, Loss Of Awareness Of Rest Of The World, Violence Resulting In Death And Loss, Mediators Emerge, Mediators Get Caught In The Firing Line Or Become Impotent, Vying For Alliances With Those Outside The Feud, Pledges To Never Forgive, Curses Wished On The Other Side, Clan-Like Markings Emerge, Incest And The Genetic Problems That Come With This, Betrayal, Retardation Of Both Families' Growth, Tensions Boil Over…

And the list can go on and on. It will be as detailed and interesting as your imagination will allow. It also does not have to be expressed as "situational" or in language; any combination of movement, sounds, or visuals might express a felt sense of what happens as this event. However, at this stage of analysis, they will be considered as *happenings*. Not as actions or obstacles, but things that emerge out of actions against obstacles.

When "Tensions Boil Over" is a happening, we then look to a possible action against obstacle that might result in tensions boiling over. The action might be to stay calm against the obstacle of someone insulting your loved one; if the obstacle is strong enough, and you play against it with urgency, then you may lose your temper in any number of ways: tensions will boil over. One can also choose a non-narrative example such as a performer shaking from centre, working from the smallest of movements to the largest as it extends out to the extremities, slowly, against the constraints of another performer holding them around the middle of the torso. It could be vocal, made with light, props, puppets… it can be anything that is actioned against an obstacle, resulting in the happening "tensions boil over".

Once a larger event is broken down into happenings, you might find that a happening is big enough to be the event of a scene or moment within the larger event. Happenings are, in effect, little events. If the happening is to become an event of its own moment, then you drill down again to more specific happenings. So if the happening "tensions boil over" becomes an event within the overall event of "feud comes to bitter end", then "tensions boil over" becomes a scene or moment in its own right, and it is broken down to further happenings. These might be: Suspicious Glances, Alienation, Opportunists Taking Advantage Of The Chaos, Demonization, Instigating Violence, Pressure, Tension, Escalations Of Distrust, Rage, Teasing, Testing, Name Calling, Sides Taken, Fake-Outs, Revenge, Appeals For Calm, Violence… all are possible happenings within the event "tensions boil over".

These happenings, now that they are drilled down to suit the moment or scene, can then be broken down to actions against obstacles.

If we look closely, we will see that this list of happenings for "tensions boil over" can make up the "fight scene" in Act 3 Scene 1 of Shakespeare's play, Act 1 Scene 6 in Prokofiev's ballet, or the duel in Act 3 of Gounod's opera, and also the Rumble in *West Side Story*. All of the happenings listed can be elements when the fight scene is activated as "tensions boil over" as part of "feud comes to bitter end".

With a different overall event for *Romeo and Juliet*, such as any of the previously mentioned options — manipulation of church official results in youths' demise, society drives teenage lovers to suicide, or love prevails over prejudice — the happenings that you drill down to will obviously be different. They will also be activated differently.

ACTIVATING THE EVENT

As this book is about how we as performers operate in the field of performing, the idea of activation is key. We will eventually learn how we *do* one thing at any one time as part of the weave that makes up the event. This one thing will allow for any combination of disciplinary outcomes. But first, let's look at how we locate the *doings* of our discipline(s) within the weave of actions, obstacle, and happenings.

When we look more closely at the fight scene as we have thus far drilled down, this is where the Integrative Performance Analysis gets interesting and deviates from linear, disciplinary, or strictly narrative approaches. The dynamic of the performing elements does not adhere to a simple cause and effect trajectory; it is more in keeping with the holographic, and is transdisciplinary, as discussed in Chapter Three (please review pages 58–60). The happening of one moment can at the same time be an obstacle of another and the action of yet another. What is aimed for in this practice is that they all connect under the umbrella of the chosen event as part of an active framework. The way we execute them is possible because we are working within an active aesthetic. (If this term is still not clear, please review pages 60–1 in Chapter Three.)

How does this work? How can an action also be at the same time an obstacle? What are the implications and the possibilities for us as performers making choices within our practice? It is actually much like how we operate in life. Let's return to our working example to make sense of it. If, for instance, Romeo does the action *to make peace* against the obstacle of *rage*, this can result in *Violence*. However, Romeo's same action *to make peace* can serve as an obstacle against Tybalt's need *to Blow off steam*, creating the happening of *Instigating violence*. The happening of *Violence* then can also become an obstacle for Mercutio as he does the action to *Survive while in shock*; this can result in the happening *A curse placed on both their houses*. All of these are, of course, chosen to serve within the choice of the event "tensions boil over" as part of "feud comes to bitter end".

What is so important here and slightly different is that in this *active* architecture, NOTHING depicts or shows, but rather everything DOES (unless the event calls for depiction and showing). It is the focus on the *way of doing* within the active framework of the event that makes this particular play of activity able to be actioned as active aesthetic. It is in the doing of the doings within this bracketed moment/scene or section where the performance and performer is activated through the field of performing, whether the doings are a surprising flash of thunder, the move of an arm, the utterance of a particular line of text, or an exhale; all are woven into the event as either an action, obstacle, or happening (and sometimes more than one of these) within the chosen event. As soon as something is engaged with outside of the event, the event can change. This can happen, of course, but it is the constant returning to the dynamics of the event that is the practice of the practice unless a new choice is made. We will return to this discussion within this conversation about activating text, but first let's look at this dynamic as it pertains to our practice, the practice offered in Parts II and III.

How might practice work within this idea of an active architecture? If we look at Ex. 11, *Rolling from Centre* and how we initialize our practice of *Rolling from Centre*, we begin to see how working with this particular type of analysis can aid the integration of our doings. In doing the Roll, the event might be *Warming up* or *Connecting the breath-body in preparation for a specific song* or *Finding centre*. Let's look closely at the first one for the sake of analysis, *Warming up*. Happenings within this event,

Warming up, might be *witnessing, adjusting, feelings of resistance and release, constant returning to centre, letting it go, repeating the task, three-part breath, releasing shoulders*... However, if we find that we do an action of *judging* against the obstacle of *annoyance that we are not getting it right*, the happening of *frustration* might emerge, which in turn can then present as an obstacle against the action of *releasing perineum in the three-part breath*, resulting in the happening of *tension in the shoulders* (Becoming the kite; see page 134). When we engage an action, or push against an obstacle that is not within the chosen or agreed event, we then change the event. In this example, we have left the event of *Warming up* and entered something more akin to *Punishing* (which of course is not a difficult thing to do). Conscious Practice is about witnessing the doing of the doing so that you remain within and/or return to the agreed event. (Review pages 90–94 for details on Conscious Practice.) No exercise, like no text or design, holds the event, but rather they live within it. When you keep the actions and the obstacles within the event, your doings are integrated; when you leave, you literally and figuratively, physically and intellectually become disintegrated. As you will recall, the perineal centre, three-part breath, and working from awareness are tools embedded within this practice that help to make leaving the event of the task a little more difficult than in other practices.

PUTTING IT TOGETHER

One of the main ways that this work differs from some others is that technique does not serve the text(s). We do not think of technique as a pictorial tool there to bring the text or director's/choreographer's/designer's vision alive, but rather the text(s), concept, technologies, and the technique(s) are integrated, under the umbrella of the event, within the field we call performing (B). Everything becomes activated in a mutually interdependent dynamic. You may recall that this is one of the key aspects of working within an active aesthetic.

With this approach the word *practice*, rather than *technique*, is very deliberately used. This is because when there is a technical challenge or an aesthetic obligation, we weave all the actions, obstacles, and happenings into an integrative practice. A challenge that might require technical attention, with "techniques" such as three-part breathing, dynamic alignment, the isolation of the psoas muscle system, intake, or meeting in the middle, is practised as either an action, obstacle, or happening within the chosen event.

Example #1: an acting/singing/blocking challenge

Let's take, for example, a moment in *West Side Story* where both singing and acting present a possible challenge. Actors may recognize the action-against-obstacle dynamic, but keep in mind that here we are not primarily justifying actions in service of a narrative and the character, or working necessarily within a logic of human behaviour. In this work, such organization of action against obstacle is just one choice as part of the integrative dynamic. If you are an actor familiar with this choice, by the end of this example you will see how shifting out of the pure narrative can help allow for integration.

In the Bernstein/Robbins adaptation, the feuding factions are not two families but two gangs made up of different nationalities in the 1950s. The Montagues become an Anglo gang called the Jets. Riff (Mercutio), who is Tony's (Romeo's) best friend, leads them. The Capulets become a Puerto Rican gang called the Sharks, led by Bernardo (Tybalt). Tony and Maria (Juliet) have fallen desperately in love in the first act. At the moment that we will explore, the Jets and the Sharks have had their fight and Tony has just killed Bernardo, who is Anita's love and Maria's brother. Tony has come to Maria asking her to run away with him; Anita, who is mourning for her love Bernardo, walks in as Tony leaves and goes on a tirade, trying to drive home to Maria the dangers of loving a boy who is not of her own kind. Her song is *A Boy Like That*.

The Event for this could be *A Warning*. As this is a dramatic work, in the structure of a narrative and with the throughline of a character's journey, we might see this in acting terms, where Anita has an intention or objective within which she carries out her actions against the obstacle of *Maria's blind and undying love for Tony*.

Anita's actions within the event could then be *to convince Maria of the danger, to make her see her point of view, to scare her, to bully her, to override her love for Tony with the loss of her brother, to appeal to her sense of sisterhood, to wake her up, to hold her to a loyalty to her family*... Maria, of course, would counter this at every turn with her own actions against and obstacles inherent in the event of *a warning*, perhaps with her counter-intention, which might be *to make love win over violence for the sake of all*. This is clearly a charged acting moment. As it is charged, the performer playing Anita in this song would design an active framework supporting her integrative instrument with knowledge of the aesthetic requirements of the scene. There are many repeats, and, as Stanislavsky taught us, never repeat anything for the same reason. The first two repeats escalate the intensity. "A boy like that/who'd kill your brother"... "A boy like that/will give you sorrow".... There is a new moment and a new reason at each moment.

Here we have an acting challenge, not to *ride the state of being* or to *play* a general emotional state as part of the tirade. This could, if approached from the performer (A) doing performance (C), lead to a hysteria of sorts, and all manner of *becoming the kite* (see page 134). If the actor decided that the doing of the doing was to act out the intensity by *showing* how angry she is, then she would leave the event of the drama and enter her own event as a the performer. She would most likely also leave centre and create the type of tensions that would affect her vocal body. Anita, after all, is not showing or acting, she is convincing and imploring for sanity against the obstacle of Maria's blind love.

Here we will do the actions against obstacles of the character. It is through the character's doings that we can integrate select movement and voicing tasks as they present technical challenges. Technique is not *applied* as an accompanying layer or a third line of the score, to serve aesthetic requirements of the drama; rather, we enter into the field of performing, where we do the doings of the character through chosen tasks within the integrative practice as we witness. We do one doing at a time, whereby Anita's voice and body emerge as part of the dramatic event of the scene.

This, however, is not only an acting moment, it is written as musical theatre and requires physio-vocal considerations. The music for this song is effective, with a sense of turmoil and urgency activated through its chromatic harmonies and alternating triple and quadruple meters. In this work we do not treat music (or any text) as accompaniment, but rather as an active partner in the event. The performer might choose to have the shifting meters be the happenings of her heartbeat, as a result of her action *to get her point across to Maria* against the obstacle of *the sense of shock of just seeing Tony and Maria together*. As another choice, the shifting meters could also be an obstacle as an *unsettling inner rhythm*, against an action *to get herself steady*, where the happening might be *increased urgency*. Both of these are choices within the event *A warning*. This is where choices come in, and making them to support your integrative instrument, especially when there are technical or disciplinary challenges, is where this practice and analysis comes into play.

Let's drill down to one moment in this song, *A Boy Like That*. In the third verse we get a challenge. Anita has been imploring Maria to see sense; she has pressed that Maria should stick to her own kind, not a boy that could kill her brother; she points out that Maria could find another and, just as the musical climax arrives, she drives home the complete insanity of the situation: "and he's the boy that gets your love and gets your heart" (Bernstein 1956: 182).[1] Here the performer is asked to sing up a chromatic sequence through a possible break in the female voice without a glitch or loss of tonality while acting a heightened emotional scene of marked intensity. The performer also has to deal with the challenge of singing from the "r" in *your* to plotting the breath through the "h" onto the vowel in *heart*.

For a trained mezzo-soprano this might not be where the biggest challenge lies; however, this role, when cast in the genre of musical theatre, is invariably cast as a dancer with a big voice (because the other requirements of this character include excellent dancing), but, interestingly, as a result this dramatic moment is often treated as an "acting" moment rather than a vocal one. (By now, however, you will understand that with the IPP there is no such thing as an acting, dance, or vocal moment: they are all one and the same.) We will proceed with this example in this context for the purposes of explaining how you can use the IPP and IPA to integrate the disciplines in action.

Let's add that, at this moment, the director has asked the actress playing Anita to grasp Maria by her upper arms and shake her as if to wake her out of her insanity. Even without the acting, such a vocal climb in this part of the voice can present a challenge. Even without the singing, this dramatic climax for the actor can also present a challenge. Shaking in the arms can also engage the shoulders, tongue, and jaw, which could present challenges for the required sustained tone throughout the phrase. Focusing on two or three difficult things at once will take us out of the dramatic event and into a technical negotiation of the performer (A) doing the performance (C). So what do we do? We make this moment one action, against one obstacle, with an emergent happening that supports the musical/dramatic aesthetics and the disciplinary challenges within the chosen event, which in this case we have chosen to be *a warning*. Here's how...

Because this moment is quite rapid, with fast intakes of breath, it is clear that the three-part breath, on the intake, with the tongue release and perineal release rather than an inhale, is going to be essential if we wish to maintain the integrity of the dynamic alignment in the arms while doing the shaking. The intake will also help us to get a clean onset rather than a glottal attack. The use of appoggio as discussed in Chapter Six will also help keep the tone even, especially when directing the energy of the breath out over the upper palate and out through the facial centre (the level of the philtrum above the upper teeth). This will help the vowel adjustment from the words "your" to "heart". All of these become one action as part of the three-part breath and as discussed in former chapters. (Review Chapter Four and Exercises: 7 *Meeting in the middle*, 23 *Hand press (plotting the path)*, 25 *Arms of a clock*, 31 *Accenting A*, 32 *Exhale appoggio style*, 33 *Accenting B*, 35 *Onset with vowels*.)

The required dance of the breath/body as described above can all happen in a moment before the phrase in question. All the elements of an integrative intake can be actioned as *to make her see the seriousness of this situation* against the obstacle that *you are losing her*; the happening is likely to manifest in the breath-body and emerge as a clear onset with sustained directional energy through the level of the philtrum.

Another choice could be to intake with awareness to the perineum with the action *to prepare for a fight from Maria* against the obstacle *Maria is looking more determined to get her own way* with a happening of *conflict escalates*.

Plotting the breath path through the level of the philtrum connected to the dynamic alignment in the arms becomes the action *to drive the point home* against an obstacle of *chaos*. Either way, it's all one action, against one obstacle at any one moment, from awareness, fuelled by the three-part breath, initiated from the perineum. The language you use for yourself and what you put where is about choice. Each choice is designed to integrate the practice of performing within the chosen event, here *a warning*.

These are but examples of some of the choices by which you can use Integrative Performance Analysis within Integrative Performance Practice to be responsible for and able to respond to the aesthetic and technical requirements of an interdisciplinary performer.

Let's now play with a different challenge within a different genre.

Example #2: singing/acting/movement

In this example we look at Gounod's *Roméo et Juliette*, an opera in five acts. The *Ballade of Queen Mab* is sung by Mercutio, a baritone. It correlates with Shakespeare's famous Queen Mab Speech. In Act I, Romeo, Benvolio, Mercutio, and the lads have crashed the Capulets' party. There is a sense of adolescent cavorting. Mercutio is a witty, energetic juvenile, and he interrupts Romeo, who is about to speak about a dark and prophetic dream, perhaps too seriously for such a fun evening. Before Romeo can even start, Mercutio takes the stage, literally and figuratively, and weaves this dreaming into an elaborate fantasy, "La reine Mab t'a visité" (*Queen Mab has visited you*).

In Shakespeare's version, Mab is no bigger than an agate stone; she climbs over men's noses when they are asleep, her chariot is an empty hazelnut, and she gallops at night through lovers' brains. She plagues kissers with blisters (which some scholars attribute to herpes). Sometimes she drives over soldiers' necks and they dream of cutting foreign throats. She is the hag that, when maids lie on their backs, presses them and teaches them first to bear (which some interpret as young women learning to pleasure themselves).

It's a fantastical series of images born of adolescent hormone-filled mind/body playing with danger, the grotesque, sexual boundaries, naiveté, and violence. The text of the aria is shorter, as is common in opera, largely because the music is time-consuming and repeats were part of the formal structure of a Ballade, but the energy of the moment is similar. The musical language offers some of this energy; it is very physical, with running scales and a melody that is fast and erratic. It can be challenging to articulate at such speed, maintaining a through line from vowel to vowel, allowing for evenness of tone with no loss of harmonics throughout the range. However, for a trained baritone, this is very possible, especially when standing in place.

There is a part in the Ballade, as in Shakespeare's text, where Queen Mab's chariot is described. *Son char, que l'atome rapide Entraine dans l'éther limpide, Fut fait d'une noisette vide Par ver de terre le charron!...* (Her chariot, which the rapid particle draws through the limpid ether, Made out of an empty nutshell by an earthworm, the cartwright.) At this moment it is not unusual for a director to stage some manner of galloping, with a physical illusion of a chariot made as the boys (often filled out by chorus members or dancers) become the different elements of the image as they join Mercutio's excitement. What is often a little odd is that the baritone playing Mercutio is often left out of the full physicality of the moment. If we choose to activate Mercutio as an energetic youth who (for one reason or another, depending upon the chosen event, its actions and obstacles) is painting a detailed and elaborate picture of this Queen Mab, rather than a baritone standing and singing an aria in an opera house, then some integrative performance practices might be helpful.

As we learned in Part III, skipping, leaping, and even galloping are more than possible without any compromise to tone, pitch, or harmonics if one does them as part of an integrated action, initiated from centre and fuelled by the three-part breath in line with the principles of dynamic alignment. This exacting use of the psoas muscle will maintain the integrity of breath in all manner of leaping or jumping without a glitch in tone. (Review Exercises: 9 *From inhale to intake*, 10 *Three-part breath*, 14 *Hip thump — Plotting the path towards psoas*, 16 *Psoas dynamic alignment in standing*, 18 *The sweet spot (exploring vertical alignment)*, 20 *Silly walk(s)* and 21 *Leaping and jumping*.)

In addition to the above, any manner of arm gestures, small, grand, and erratic ones, are also possible without compromise to the vocal line or the diction when dynamic alignment in arms and hands is adhered to as one action made in concert with the three-part breath initiated from centre. (Review: "The rings", "Don't become the kite" and Exercises 18 *The sweet spot (exploring vertical alignment)*, 23 *Hand press (plotting the path)*, and 25 *Arms of a clock*.)

This ballade, as in the other examples, can be activated as one of many events. An obvious one could be a "boys will be boys moment"; the event here might be *boys cavorting*. In a more subtle take, one that is arguably better supported by Shakespeare's text rather than Gounod's adaptation, Mercutio could be seen to be in love with Romeo himself and sensing that he is losing Romeo to his increasing admiration of girls. Mercutio speaks fast and comes up with fantastic ideas, and takes everyone out of a sensitive moment; this could be a way of avoiding his deeper emotions and Romeo's alike. The event in this instance could be *avoidance of painful emotions*. Another take could draw from the sort of gang mentality that *West Side Story* tapped into. The event could be *camaraderie cemented*.

For our purposes, we will choose the first event, *boys cavorting*. Happenings within the event could be *testing, play fighting, competition, dares, grossing each other out, joking, ribbing, dirty tricks, bullying, making fun of girls, embarrassment, mocking elders, egging each other on, escalating danger, play acting, bonding...*

In the following musical example you will find a moment within this ballade where Mercutio sings about how Queen Mab visits the couch of the Virgin and makes her dream of kisses. The moment in question happens after the music has already shifted from the fast-paced *allegro*, which takes us through the first two verses to an almost schmaltzy *poco ritardando*. This shift in tempo can be activated as *to mock most seriously* against an obstacle of *breaking up with laughter* within the event of *boys cavorting*. Where you see Tempo 1° in the musical example following, the orchestra returns to its running scales; we return to the fast-paced chorus verse and with a snap "Mab...", the spritely activity continues to the end.

The text says, "after a sigh startles, when you lie on your couch. O virgin! She lightly brushes your mouth And makes you dream of kisses! Mab, queen of falsehoods, etc." Here we will explore a physically engaging staging of this moment.

If, on the first phrase starting at A, Benvolio and the other boys are in full flight within Mercutio's fantasy and aiming to *push it further*, their actions might be *to up the game, to egg him on, to partner up with Mercutio in the control of this game, to test how far he'll go*... against the obstacle *the fun could end*. The boys might at the top of phrase B *make alliances*, which would have the happenings of *knowing glances, planning of the next move, coordinated actions*... These could manifest as the happening of three boys going to the ground on hands and knees in a row to create the couch on which Benvolio might, while in front of Mercutio, give him a playful little brush down the cheek on the mouth. The action of this brush could be *to provoke* against the obstacle *trying not to laugh*; Mercutio might then *rise to the bait* and, with a happening of *hamming it up in a most suggestive way*, swoon onto the boys, who have created a platform with their backs across the floor, making contact on the words "effluere ta bouche". On the next phrase, C, he could then, as he sings the words "Et te fait rêver de..." in a most effeminate way, lean back, and as he gets to the *fermata* lean his head back, as if *to drink the nectar of the most delicious kiss* as his head bends off the boys' backs towards the audience in a suggestive way... "de baisers!" As the music at that exact point snaps back to Tempo 1°, with the support of his hand on the floor and the assistance of the boys backs as they rise, he could do a half backbend, let his legs go over and land poised and ready for the last verse starting on the note E — "Mab!"

When the acting and the choreography are not integrated as one action with the singing, staging like this could be quite a negotiation and could adversely affect the voice; however, most importantly, it could take the event out of *boys cavorting* and into an event of *a technical negotiation of a baritone* with its own distinct and not-so-interesting actions against obstacles. So what do we do?

If we integrate the breath-body so that the singing and moving both equally emerge as symptoms of the action as the character, this is possible. This happens, again, as learned in the earlier chapters, from awareness, initiated from centre and fuelled by the three-part breath with an isolation of the iliopsoas system. The swaying into the sitting on the couch can happen without a glitch in the voice if on the sway you "don't become the kite" and the integrity of the rings is maintained as part of the dynamic alignment in standing. These tasks could be integrated into Mercutio's action *buying time to think of the next funny thing to do*. This is, of course, all connected to the three-part breath and the perineal contraction isolating the psoas. If the lean back onto the couch is executed from the perineum with the contraction up the internal axis of the body, lengthening the rings, here Mercutio could be *sidling up to his comrades pushing boundaries*. Then, on the intake before the words "de baisers", the tongue releases forward (this could be to *prepare for the punch line*) so that the A# (on the fermata) and following F# and B can plot the path out through the level of the philtrum without any glitch or compromise to tone. In the bar and a half where Mercutio comes to standing, the hand makes contact with the floor, plotting the path through the webbing between the thumb and pointer finger, working in dynamic alignment to allow for tongue, jaw, and throat independence (this could be *to gear up for the next level*) and after the flip, as the feet make contact with the floor, he plots the path on an intake, connecting to the perineum, isolating the psoas, and in one action landing poised and ready for that E on "Mab". And here Mercutio *rallies the troops up again*. (Review the aforementioned exercises, plus Ex. 26 *Dynamic alignment in hands and legs while taking weight*, and Ex. 28 *Dynamic alignment in movement, two variations*.)

None of the above goes against any of the dramatic actions discussed above in the event *boys cavorting*, or against any of the possible obstacles. In fact, they are more in keeping with a spritely, show-offy adolescent than the actions of an opera singer in his prime. Either is fine, but it is a choice. There is no such thing as not doing in the field of performing (B), and an event will always be happening. It is also helpful to choose dramatic, vocal, and/or movement actions and obstacles that help integrate the disciplines in practice rather than leave you in a position to do the action of negotiating them.

Example #3: a dancing/voicing/acting challenge

In this next example we will explore an increasingly common interdisciplinary performance challenge. Trained dancers are being asked more and more to vocalize text while they move and act. Here we will look at a few moments of the famous balcony scene in the widely performed ballet written by Prokofiev and in this example work with the choreography of Kenneth MacMillan. We will add select text from Shakespeare for the purposes of exploring dance with integrated voiced text.

This scene takes place after the ball. It starts with Juliet on her balcony, dreaming of Romeo. He enters below and she runs to join him. The moment in this example is part of the ecstatic *pas de deux* (duet) where they express their love for each other.

This happens in Prokofiev's score in Act 1 scene 2, beginning eight measures before rehearsal number 142, and approximately 4:15 minutes into MacMillan's choreography from the start of the balcony scene.

This choreography starts with Juliet's run to Romeo, followed by supported multiple pirouettes (Juliet turns a few times with Romeo's arms around her waist). This is directly followed by a grand ronde de jambe en l'air, ending in an arabesque en pointe (meaning that on the last turn her leg extends in front of her, then moves above the level of her hips through to the side towards the audience and then directly behind her, all on the tip of her left toe).

There is then a lift with a battement front followed by a grand ronde de jambe en l'air, this time while being lifted, and she is lowered then into a panchè arabesque (meaning that following the arabesque she kicks her leg forward; as she is lifted in the air, the leg travels from the front across the side and to the back, where she is then placed back on her left toes as her right leg goes directly toward the ceiling in a split).

After coming out of the panchè arabesque, she turns and faces him, and then he supports her in two falls, one to the left and the other to the right, with her torso bending back across his arms as he does a single port de bras (an arm gesture, in this instance toward the ceiling).

As she recovers, he kneels with another port de bras; she moves from facing him to turning and leaning back onto him with an interlocked arm gesture followed by a travelling lift.

During this lift he moves through the space as she is in the air; at the same time, Juliet moves from an extended leg lift or front développé extension to a battement derrière as he swings her down. (Another way to say this is that when she is in the air as he is travelling, and while she is balanced across the back of his shoulder, she swings her left leg up towards the ceiling and then, as he lowers her, down across the apex of his body in the direction of her back, with a slight backbend.)

This pattern can happen two or three times, depending upon the artists (we will choose three, with the first in silence). Romeo then sets her down and they face each other in an embrace before continuing.

In the following chart we have lines of Shakespeare's text from the balcony scene lined up with the MacMillan choreography. If we go with an event choice of *a union is made*, then the actions against obstacles in the second column present possible choices.

Romeo: O, wilt thou leave me so unsatisfied?	*(During Juliet's supported pirouettes after she has run to him)* R's action: *to try and still her for his own*, against *her flirtatious spins*. J's *spinning* is the happening of her feelings, which are the result of her action *to come down off the balcony* against *her apprehension*.
Juliet: What satisfaction canst thou have to-night?	*(Grand ronde de jambe en l'air, ending in an arabesque en pointe)* J's action *to extend herself* against *never having challenged her nurse/world*. R works *to support her in her rhythm of coming to terms with their love* against the obstacle *the rhythm of his own lust*.
Romeo: Th'exchange of thy love's faithful vow for mine.	*(After the lift with the battement front, grand ronde de jambe en l'air with the panchè arabesque)* J's happening is that she is *extending beyond anything she has ever known*. That becomes R's obstacle in knowing that this is new for her, and his action is *to test if she will have him* against *their families' history*.
Juliet: I gave thee mine before thou didst request it; And yet I would it were to give again.	*(She turns and faces him and then he supports her in two falls, one to the left)* R's action is *to hold the faith that she will be his against fear*. J's action is *to test his loyalty to their union* against *her own fear*.

Romeo: Wouldst thou withdraw it? For what purpose, love?	*(Supported fall to the right)* R's action is to *give her assurance* against the obstacle that *she will not believe it.* J's action is to *surrender* to him against *loyalty to her family*. Her happening is *a decision…to give herself.*
Juliet: But to be frank and give it thee again.	*(Standing as he kneels)* J's action is to *promise herself in full awareness* against *the world as she knows it.* R's action is to *promise* against the obstacle of *surrender* — including his idea of *manhood as he understands it.*
Juliet (Continued): And yet I wish but for the thing I have.	*(After she turns for the supported fall, saying "I have" on the lift, they travel in silence as her leg lifts the first time into a front développé extension, from there to a suspended battement derrière, and back toward an extension)* J's action is to *give to him* against the obstacle that *he might not hold her.* R's action is to *take her* against the obstacle of *fear.*
Juliet (Continued): My bounty is as boundless as the sea,	*(As her leg lifts the second time)* J's action is to *test her love for him* against the obstacle *of the possibility of his not being able to hold that love.* R's action is to *prove that he is the man for her* against *his fear of his childish understandings of manhood.*
Juliet (Continued): My love as deep; the more I give to thee,	*(At the second battement derrière in lift)* J's action is to *surrender* against the obstacle of *fear.* R's action is to *hold her world* against the obstacle *of his old world view.* The happening is that *they commune.*
Juliet (Continued): The more I have, for both are infinite.	*(As her leg lifts the third time)* J's action is to *trust and make love* against the obstacle that *this moment will end.* R's action is to *make love* against the obstacle of *not being able to get closer yet.*
Juliet (Continued): I hear some noise within. Dear love, adieu.	*(After the third battement derrière, and then she stands facing him)* J's action is to *begin to say a sweet goodbye for now* against the obstacle of *the physical pain that comes with that.* R's action is to *bring her down gently so as not to compromise her integrity* against the obstacle of *having to wait for a later time to make love properly as husband and wife.*

It is true that it would be more likely for a modern dance or physical theatre piece to integrate text and choreography in this way. It is also true that a reduced ensemble of musicians rather than a full orchestra would most likely be employed to accompany spoken voice; however, this particular choreographic example has been chosen for its complexity and also its interesting place, living in between an established balletic choreographic aesthetic and an aesthetic climate that is increasingly incorporating interdisciplinary performance.

As previously discussed, one of the most challenging things that get in the way of integrating the performance disciplines are disjunct techniques of breathing. In this work the three-part breath, with the intake rather than inhale, along with the appoggio on the exhale, is going to be key throughout for the dancer/voicer. (Review Exercises: 9 *From inhale to intake* and 10 *Three-part breath*.) When done correctly, with the perineal contraction and its inherent vertical alignment, all movement becomes part of a breath dance, initiated from the perineum and supporting an exacting isolation of the psoas. This isolation of the psoas is at the heart of much ballet technique anyway. Voice here becomes a breath dance as dance becomes fuelled by the breath, which has an emergent property of vocal sound. As also discussed, the lower your point of centre, which corresponds to the pelvic floor release, the less throat engagement there will be with the voice. This will result in a sounding off the throat and make it possible to bend the neck and upper body in any way without compromise to tone.

(Review "Don't become the kite" and "Rings" along with Exercises: 14 *Hip thump*, 15 *Bridge to leg lift conditioning*, 16 *Psoas dynamic alignment in standing*, 18 *The sweet spot (exploring vertical alignment)*, 19 *Infinity from centre*, 25 *Arms of a clock*, 26 *Dynamic alignment in hands and arms while taking weight*, 29 *Dynamic alignment in backbends*, 30 *Meeting in the middle diagonal catches*, and all of Chapter Six, *Voicing as a breath dance*.)

When working with IPP within forms of dance that use a turnout as a consistent part of the movement vocabulary, a certain adjustment needs to be made in order to keep the integrity of the three-part breath and also a balance of the rings. In IPP we learn dynamic alignment in standing by plotting the path through the big toe up through the inside of the leg to isolate the psoas, with a marked lack of turnout. You may recall that feet are to be in line with knees, and knees in line with hips. This is the optimal position for learning to isolate the psoas in connection to pelvic release on the intake and its connection to the perineal centre. This psoas isolation is, however, still possible with a turnout, if that turnout is made with as little use of the quadriceps as possible and initiated from the perineum, working through the hip flexors and maintaining the integrity of the rings with no extraneous thoracic hyperextension (pushing out of the chest). If, en pointe or in a turnout, the same directional energy present in the opposing circles in dynamic alignment in standing is employed, this will further aid in maintaining the psoas connection throughout grand battements and also while running and leaping. This use of dynamic alignment will make it possible to sound without glitches or compromise to tone or resonance when the breath-body is connected as one in integrative action.

Let's drill down further and look at the moment in this example where Juliet says:

> My bounty is as boundless as the sea,
> My love as deep; the more I give to thee,...

In this moment Juliet is in the throes of a travelling lift sequence. She has just moved her leg down behind her as she is draped across Romeo's shoulders (the first battement derrière in the lift), and she is about to be lifted again as she extends her leg to the skies.

Juliet (Continued): My bounty is as boundless as the sea,	*(As her leg lifts the second time)* J's action is *to test her love for him* against the obstacle of *the possibility of his not being able to hold that love.* R's action is *to prove that he is the man for her* against his fear of his *childish understandings of manhood.*
Juliet (Continued): My love as deep; the more I give to thee,	*(At the second battement derrière in lift)* J's action is *to surrender* against the obstacle of *fear.* R's action is *to hold her world* against the obstacle of *his old world view.* The happening is that *they commune.*

As her leg raises she will say, "My bounty is as boundless as the sea". The appoggio (a slight resistance to the collapse of the intercostals — review Ex. 32) will need to have been initiated in preparation on the exhale/voicing in the moment before. This task will make sense, as it is very much a part of the happening of *suspended excitement*, in line with the event, and it will also keep the trunk in readiness for the intake as she drapes across Romeo's body. From here, the artist will have in place the contraction of the perineum upward (which, as mentioned earlier, aids in lifts anyway), and be poised for the intake as part of the three-part breath on the lift while in the battement derrière. She will intake as part of her preparation for the action *to test*. Juliet will work, in connection to the psoas as initiated through breath and in isolation with the psoas, to really *test her love for him against her fear* (this fear could present as gravity, or any struggle to isolate the psoas, depending upon the artist). This movement will be fuelled by an exhale that plots the path through the level of the philtrum and is voiced as "My bounty is as endless as the sea". All *to test her love for him* against the obstacle that *he may not be big enough for her love* within the event *a union is made.*

While Juliet is literally and figuratively suspended here, there is a new intake with tongue release and appoggio (in preparation for the intercostals being bent in the repeat choreography to come) in line with three-part breath as part of the happening *she realizes that he passed her test, he is her destiny.* Her next action is *to surrender.* This is activated with the descent down to the second battement derrière, on a voiced exhale, with the text "My love as deep; the more I give to thee…" and it continues.

When beginning to work with dance and voicing, it is helpful to first work with Ex. 33, *Accenting B*, regarding the actions as part of physio-vocal choreography within the event.

The three examples in this section are not offered as models of performance, but rather as part of an ongoing discussion about ways of working with the Integrative Performance Practice and Analysis across disciplines and genres. What is important is that we never simply do dance or do acting or do singing. We enter a field of performing, the doing of the doing of dance, acting, and singing. It is in this field that integration is possible, that a unified practice of breath from one centre is developed, honing the body in the most economical and balanced way with an isolation of the psoas. We work from awareness, not focus, and witness rather than judge and diagnose, so as not to get stuck on performance aesthetics that, through practice, can have the practitioner negotiate and disintegrate the practitioner. Rather, we remain in, or at least constantly return to, the active field of performing, a live field. This field is where we can be responsible for and respond within the chosen event. That event can be an exercise, a performance moment, or anything really.

EVENT IN IPA: A SHIFTING TEMPLATE HOLDING MULTIPLE DISCIPLINES WITHIN MYRIAD GENRES

Event serves as an arch or umbrella that contains and brackets a chosen scene/moment/space or place in time within which doings and happenings occur. It provides an *active framework*. It is non-linear, changeable, and unstable. For this reason we use it as a *shifting template* within which we work in the field of performing. As you can see from the examples in this chapter, you can drill down to a tiny moment or expand to an entire work using the IPA as a tool to examine, intervene in and/or make choices about how you might activate the event and its happenings toward integrating various combinations of doings within performance disciplines.

The non-linear and holographic aspect of viewing event in this way helps to activate and integrate by design. All of the above examples were working within the basic dramatic structure of Shakespeare's Romeo and Juliet, for which we chose an über-event, *feud comes to a bitter end*. In the first example, Anita shakes Maria and sounds through a possible break in the voice as part of *a warning*. In the second, Mercutio invokes Queen Mab, a mercurial, dangerous sexual figure, while living at the edges of danger as part of *boys cavorting*. In the last example, Juliet tests her own feelings (against the stability of her promise and Romeo's ability to hold it) in the extension of a leg as part of *a union is made*. These were organized as happenings within the event *feud comes to a bitter end*.

Such a shake, an invocation, or an extension of the leg can represent, depict, and even show an aesthetic moment within a disciplinary category. However, when these are activated as actions against obstacles, creating happenings within the event *feud comes to a bitter end*, something different occurs. Their *way* of doing, their active aesthetic within the field of performing (B), is brought to the fore, harnessing the performers' alchemy, that which adheres to the idea that meaning *happens* in the *act* of performance. Performers (A), in the IPP, are not merely there to depict the aesthetics of a discipline or of a performance (C). With the use of the IPP in the structure of the IPA, the performer enters a field of performing (B) by design. When an interdisciplinary performer's *doings* are activated as part of this shifting template, then Anita's shake, Mercutio's invocation, and Juliet's lift will have in them activations of the event *feuds comes to a bitter end*. Every action, obstacle, and happening will be woven into an interlocking web of dynamic activity within an active framework by way of its *way* of doing, as opposed to the *what* it does. Much like the structure of the holograph described in Chapter Three, the bit, the part, and the local will be in the whole, the entire, and the global. Each moment, gesture, breath, utterance, or emotive expression will foreshadow, backspeak, and also contain within itself an over-arching integration of the event — through its *way*.

Events, however, are unstable. They can absorb and/or get shifted by the unexpected. For instance, when we do a doing such as to *try and sing/move/act that note/shape/emotion correctly*, we most likely leave or alter that dramatic event, since our own technical challenges are not usually a part of the chosen dramatic event. It is also true that accidents do happen, such as a cell phone in the audience going off, or a set piece, costume, or technical malfunction. This is where we return and integrate what has occurred into an action, obstacle, or happening within the chosen event. For instance, a phone going off in the audience can be feathered into and integrated as part of the event by becoming an action, obstacle, or happening. Within the examples given, that phone going off could become the happening of *a siren* in the event *a warning*; or the action of one of the boys *farting for effect* in *boys cavorting*; or an obstacle of *a sign of the nurse coming* in the event *a union is made*. When working from awareness within this event, it becomes simply a part of the moment. It is not a break in the moment; everything that occurs is an active part of the event and, in doing so, constitutes that event by design within the *active framework*. When these accidents happen, we witness and return to the event rather than focus and justify.

It is possible, as stated before, to take the event out of that of narrative. It is also possible to work with action against obstacle in less recognized performance disciplines and structures. The implication for the holographic structure within event as a shifting template is not to be underestimated. It means that building from the field of performing does not need to come at the beginning, middle, or end of the creative process. One gesture, note or emotive experience can give birth to an entire work. You can start in the middle, at the beginning, or at the end. You may not even know as you go. You will witness and then have some level of choice, however, as to how the actions, obstacles, and happenings are performing (B) within a chosen event. These actions, obstacles, and happenings can include aspects of performance practice, technique, choreography, musical score, spoken text, images, technical aspects, design aspects, space, place, and also audience, participators, and those experiencing and engaging with the work.

In this process, because we analyze and activate performance through a field of performing, we get an equalizing of sorts in the area of what or who holds the meaning of a work, piece, or structure. There is no recognized inherent hierarchical order; no one component, be it the play, the score, the design, the choreography, or the director's concept, that has singular status as the custodian of meaning. Each component and each operation becomes a meaning maker as it is activated in the act of performing. It is because of this that the Integrative Performance Practice used with the Integrative Performance Analysis is a useful tool not only in narrative-based performance work but also in intermedial work, performance art, postdramatic theatre, installation art, immersive theatre, and as a part of devising processes.

NOTE

1 Found on the third system of page 182 of *West Side Story* score, ©1956, 1957, 1959 by The Estate of Leonard Bernstein and Stephen Sondheim. Leonard Bernstein Music Publishing Company LLC, Publisher. Boosey & Hawkes, Inc. Sole Agent.

Chapter 9

Conclusion

I TOOK IT TO HEART WHEN I LEARNED that Stanislavsky said, "Create your own method, don't depend slavishly on mine. Make up something that will work for you! But keep breaking traditions, I beg you." I invite you to take this to heart too and play with, apply, and explore whatever this book has had to offer you as you develop your work and as you craft your very own integrative performance practice.

By now you will have gathered that this book joins a long tradition of viewing practice as a process; however, it takes it a little further in that here we concentrate specifically on the process of the process, referred to as the *active aesthetic* or the *way of doing*. In Part II this was introduced and explored through exercises and back references to the theory section that came before it. In the theory section, Part I, we explored the theoretical basis of an active aesthetic by looking at what a *performer* does in *performance*, and we established a field of *performing* to help explore some of the subtleties in the idea. We started from the perspective of what it means to learn, experience, know, and embody a practice as an artist/self. We then looked at how the expectations and understandings of what performance is within today's climate have led us in many ways further away from a process of working across disciplines as a performer, even while the aesthetics of performance have become more interdisciplinary. At the end of Part I we shifted to key concepts within quantum physics, holography, and transdisciplinarity to help establish a working field of *performing* whereby an active aesthetic could provide a different way of valuing meaning within our work, allowing for the possibility of an integrative practice and performance analysis that recognizes the act of doing as the generator of meaning.

Part III, the bulk of the book, took us through the IPP with detailed practical exercises, accompanied by a few pauses for critical accounts of other key techniques and methods of working, especially where these presented contradictory articulations of how to approach aspects like breath, centre, alignment, presence, and awareness, and the act of doing. Here we learned exacting and integrative understandings of awareness, the perineal centre, presence, three-part breath, and dynamic alignment. Each of the exercises presented were equally acting, singing, and movement exercises.

Breathing is not only the domain of the singer; neither is an exacting use of centre and the iliopsoas muscle to allow readiness, balance, and poise only that of the dancer. Doing from awareness is not just an actor's process, but also the dancer/ mover's and singer/voicer's.

After completing the work in Part III, I hope that you now understand the above terms and understand that it is possible to sound, move, and act — even in the most emotional roles, with complex choreography and with virtuosic singing — without compromise of either expression or technical exactitude. It is likely that you have discovered that any movement, sound, or emotive act can be more integrated when initiated from centre, fuelled by breath, and when coming from awareness. Further, the more you release into the perineal centre and initiate from the perineal centre, the more these actions can become ONE doing. The IPP is designed not as a negotiation of the performing disciplines, but rather as one practice through which any combinations of discipline(s) can emerge as a symptom of an integrative doing.

In Part IV we looked at Integrative Performance Analysis and learned a way of organizing creative and practical choices around what we do as performers. Through three examples, we saw how the choices we make are often both creative and technical (in support of possible cross-disciplinary challenges). As you take this work forward into your own working propositions, you will learn that the best choices are those that are not complicated. There may be a certain level of complexity involved in the planning, but you will always know when you have made the right choice because it will allow you to do *one* doable action, from which any combination of disciplinary expression can emerge.

There is nothing in this book that was invented from scratch. The iliopsoas, awareness, breath, and centre were certainly not invented during the development of the IPP. Neither was it the first time that the idea that "meaning happens in the act of doing" was posited. What the IPP does do is reconfigure many of the ways we consider these aspects and offer, perhaps for the first time, an exacting approach whereby these elements work as effective integrators, empowering the performer in the act of performance as they practise across the disciplines within any genre, style, or aesthetic.

I will end here with something my first performance teacher, my grandfather Alec Rubin, used to say to me:

"You always know when you are learning the right thing, because somewhere deep inside you knew it already."

Bibliography

Adair, G. 1991. In: R. Andrews (ed.) *The New Penguin Dictionary of Modern Quotations*. London: Penguin Books.

Anwar, Y. 2011, February 23. Meditation Beats Dance for Harmonizing Body and Mind. *UC Berkerley News Center* [Online]. Available: http://newscenter.berkeley.edu/2011/02/23/meditation-dance/ [Accessed July 27, 2011].

Association for Psychological Science 2011, May 25. Thoughts that Win. *Science Daily* [Online]. Available: http://www.sciencedaily.com/releases/2011/05/110525164120.htm [Accessed August 26, 2011].

Association for Psychological Science 2011, June 3. Want to Solve a Problem? Don't Just Use Your Brain, But Your Body, Too. *Science Daily* [Online]. Available: http://www.sciencedaily.com/releases/2011/06/110602111448.htm [Accessed September 10, 2011].

Auslander, P. 1995. "Just Be Your Self": Logocentrism and Difference in Performance Theory. *Acting (Re) Considered: Theories and Practices*, ed. P. Zarrilli. London and New York: Routledge, 59–67.

Barba, E. & Savarese, N. 2006. *A Dictionary of Theatre Anthropology: The Secret Art of the Performer*. London: Routledge.

Barthes, R. 1977. *Image, Music, Text*. London: Fontana Press.

Bay-Cheng, S., Kattenbelt, C. & Lavender, A. 2010. *Mapping Intermediality in Performance*. Amsterdam: Amsterdam University Press.

Bedau, M. A. & Humphreys, P. E. 2008. *Emergence: Contemporary Readings in Philosophy and Science*. Cambridge, MA: MIT Press.

Benedetti, R. 1997. *The Actor at Work*. Boston, MA: Allyn and Bacon.

Bernstein, L. & Sondheim, S. 1956. *West Side Story*. London: Boosey & Hawkes.

Bogue, R. 2004. *Deleuze's Wake: Tributes And Tributaries*. Albany, NY: State University Of New York Press.

Bohm, D. 1994. *Wholeness and the Implicate Order*. London: Ark Paperbacks.

Broadhurst, S. 1999. *Liminal Acts: A Critical Overview of Contemporary Performance and Theory*. London: Cassell.

Brockes, E. 2011. Simon: Simon Says. *The Guardian*, September 23, 2011.

Bryon, E. R. 1998. *The Integrative Performance Theory: an Anti-Hermeneutic Approach for Opera*. PhD. Melbourne: Monash University.

Bryon, E. R. 2009. Interdisciplinarity and Embodied Knowledge: Towards an Active Aesthetic using Integrative Performance Practice. *Tanz im Musiktheater – Tanz als Musiktheater. Beziehungen von Tanz und Musik im Theater. Bericht über ein internationales Symposion, Hannover 2006.* Würzberg: Königshausen & Neumann.

Buddhananda, S. 2000. *Moola Bandha, The Master Key.* New Delhi: Yoga Publications Trust, Thomson Press.

Burns, D. D. 1980. *Feeling Good, The New Mood Therapy.* New York: Avon Books.

Butler, J. 1988. Gender and Performance, Selections from Gender Trouble. *In:* D. Welton (ed.) *Body and Flesh: A Philosophical Reader.* Oxford: Blackwell Publishers.

Butler, J. 2011. *What Does It Mean that Gender is Performative?* [Online]. Available: http://bigthink.com/ideas/30766 [Accessed February 2, 2012].

Calais-Germain, B. 1993. *Anatomy of Movement.* Seattle, WA: Eastland Press.

Campbell, J. 1991. *A Joseph Campbell Companion: Reflections on the Art of Living.* New York: Harper Collins.

Capra, F. 2003. *The Hidden Connections.* London: Flamingo.

Carlson, M. 2004. *Performance: a Critical Introduction.* London: Routledge.

Cerbone, D. R. 2006. *Understanding Phenomenology.* Durham: Acumen.

Chaikin, J. 1980. *The Presence of the Actor.* New York: Atheneum.

Chamberlain, F. 2010. Michael Chekhov on the Technique of Acting: "Was Don Quixote True to Life?". *In:* A. Hodge (ed.) *Actor Training.* 2nd ed. Oxon: Routledge.

Colebrook, C. 2002. *Understanding Deleuze.* Crows Nest, NSW: Allen & Unwin; London: Orion [distributor].

Conquergood, D. 2002. Interventions and Radical Research. *The Drama Review* 46, Vol. 2, 145–368.

Dale, C. 2009. *The Subtle Body, An Encyclopedia of Your Energetic Anatomy.* Boulder, CO: Sounds True.

Damasio, A. 2006. *Descartes' Error.* London: Vintage.

Damasio, A. 2010. *Self Comes to Mind, Constructing the Conscious Brain.* London: William Heinemann.

Derrida, J. 1988. *Limited Inc.* Evanston, IL: Northwestern University Press.

Doidge, N. 2007. *The Brain That Changes Itself, Stories of Personal Triumph from the Frontiers of Brain Science.* London: Penguin Books.

Erkert, J. 2003. *Harnessing the Wind: the Art of Teaching Modern Dance.* Windsor: Human Kinetics Publishers.

Fisher-Lichte, E. & Jain, S. 2008. *The Transformative Power of Performance.* New York: Routledge.

Foucault, M. & Bouchard, D. F. (eds.) 1980. *Language, Counter-Memory, Practice: Selected Essays and Interviews,* Ithica, NY: Cornell University Press.

Franklin, E. 2002. *Pelvic Power, Mind/body Exercises for Strength, Flexibility, Posture, and Balance.* Hightstown, NJ: Princeton Book Company.

Franklin, E. 2003. *Pelvic Power for Men and Women.* Hightstown, NJ: Princeton Book Company.

Franko, M. 1996. History/Theory — Criticism/Practice. *In:* S. L. Foster (ed.) *Corporealities: Dancing Knowledge, Culture and Power.* London: Routledge.

Garber, D. 2005. Descartes, René (1596–1650). *In:* E. Craig (ed.) *The Shorter Routledge Encyclopedia of Philosophy.* Oxon: Routledge.

Goffman, E. 1959. *The Presentation of Self in Everyday Life.* Garden City, NJ: Doubleday.

Goldsmith, K. 2004. *I'll Be Your Mirror: The Selected Andy Warhol Interviews. Thirty-seven Conversations with the Pop Master.* New York: Carroll and Graf

Gopnik, A. 2009. *The Philosophical Baby: What Children's Minds Tell Us About Truth, Love & the Meaning of Life.* London: The Bodley Head.

Gordon, M. 1987. *The Stanislavsky Technique: Russia: A Workbook for Actors.* New York: Applause Theatre Book Publishers.

Graham, M. 1991. *Blood Memory.* New York: Doubleday.

Graham, W. 2005. Heraclitus (fl. c.500 BCE). *Internet Encyclopedia of Philosophy* [Online]. Available: http://www.iep.utm.edu/ [Accessed December 3, 2013].

Greene, B. 2004. *The Fabric of the Cosmos.* London: Penguin Group.

Grof, S. (ed.) 1984. *Ancient Wisdom and Modern Science.* Albany, NY: State University Of New York Press.

Hackney, P. 2000. *Making Connections: Total Body Integration Through Bartenieff Fundamentals.* London: Routledge.

Hampden-Turner, C. 1981. *Maps of the Mind.* London: Mitchell Beazley Publishers Ltd.

Hanh, T. N. 1990. *Breathe! You are Alive: Sutra on the Full Awareness of Breathing*. Berkeley, CA: Parallax Press.

Hodge, A. 2010. *Actor Training*. Oxon: Routledge.

Howarth, J. 2005. Epistemic Issues in Phenomenology. In: E. Craig (ed.) *The Shorter Routledge Encyclopedia of Philosophy*. Oxon: Routledge.

Hulton, D. 2010. Joseph Chaikin and Aspects of Actor Training: Possibilities Rendered Present. In: A. Hodge (ed.) *Actor Training*. Oxon: Routledge.

Jackson, S. 2004. *Professing Performance: Theatre in the Academy from Philology to Performativity*. Cambridge: Cambridge University Press.

Kayes, G. 2004. *Singing and the Actor*. London: Black Publishers Limited.

Knowles, R. P. 1996. Shakespeare, Voice and Ideology: Interrogating the Natural Voice. In: J. C. Bulman (ed.) *Shakespeare, Theory and Performance*. London: Routledge.

Koch, L. 1997. *The Psoas Book*. Felton, CA: Guinea Pig Publications.

Krasner, D. 2010. Strasberg, Adler and Meisner: Method Acting. In: A. Hodge (ed.) *Actor Training*. Oxon: Routledge.

Lugering, M. 2007. *The Expressive Actor, Integrated Voice Movement, and Acting Training*. Portsmouth, NH: Heinemann.

Madison, D. S. & Hamera, J. 2006. *The Sage Handbook of Performance Studies*. University of North Carolina, NC: Sage Publications.

Magarshack, D. 1986. *Stanislavsky: A Life*. London: Faber and Faber.

Mamet, D. 1998. *True and False: Heresy and Common Sense for the Actor*. London: Faber and Faber.

Marshall, L. & Williams, D. 2010. Peter Brook: Transparency and the Invisible Network. In: A. Hodge (ed.) *Actor Training*. 2nd ed. Oxon: Routledge.

Maturana, H. R. & Varela, F. J. 1992. *The Tree of Knowledge, The Biological Roots of Human Understanding*. Boston, MA: Shambhala Publications, Inc.

McGregor, S. L. T. 2004. *The Nature of Transdisciplinary Research and Practice*. Kappa Omicron Nu Human Sciences Working Paper Series [Online]. Available: http://www.kon.org/hswp/archive/transdiscipl.pdf

McKenzie, J. 2002. *Perform or Else: From Discipline to Performance*. London: Routledge.

Meisner, S. & Longwell, D. 1987. *Sanford Meisner on Acting*. New York: Vintage Books.

Merleau-Ponty, M. 2002. *Phenomenology of Perception*. Oxon: Routledge.

Moore, S. 1984. *The Stanislavski System*. New York: Penguin Books.

Morris, E. & Hotchkis, J. 1979. *No Acting Please "Beyond The Method", A Revolutionary Approach to Acting and Living*. Los Angeles, CA: Spelling Publications.

Nelson, R. 2013. *Practice as Research in the Arts: Principles, Protocols, Pedagogies, Resistances*. Basingstoke: Palgrave Macmillan.

Nicolescu, B. 1997. The Transdisciplinary Evolution of the University Condition for Sustainable Development. *International Congress, Universities' Responsibilities to Society*. Bangkok: Chulalongkorn University.

Nicolescu, B. 2005. Transdisciplinarity — Past, Present and Future. *Second World Congress of Transdisciplinarity: What Education for Sustainable Development? Attitude — Research — Action*. Vitoria/Vila Velha: Brazil.

Olsen, A. & McHose, C. 1991. *Body Stories: A Guide to Experiential Anatomy*. Barrytown, NY: Station Hill Press.

Pavis, P. 2001. Theatre Studies and Interdisciplinarity. *Theatre Research International*, 26, 153–163.

Pert, C. B. 1997. *Molecules of Emotion: Why You Feel the Way You Feel*. London: Simon & Schuster.

Phelan, P. & Lane, J. 1998. *The Ends of Performance*. New York: New York University Press.

Power, C. 2008. *Presence in Play, a Critique of Theories of Presence in the Theatre*. Amsterdam, NY: Rodopi.

Rancière, J. 2007. The Emancipated Spectator. *Artforum*, 45, 270–281.

Schechner, R. 2002. *Performance Studies, An Introduction*. New York: Routledge.

Searle, J. R. 1997. *The Mystery of Consciousness*. London: Granta Publications.

Shewell, C. 2008. *Voice Work: Art and Science in Changing Voices*. Chichester: Wiley-Blackwell.

Siler, B. 2000. *The Pilates Body*. New York: Broadway Books.

Smith, D. W. 2011. Phenomenology. In: E. N. Zalta (ed.) *The Stanford Encyclopedia of Philosophy*. Fall 2011 ed. Stanford, CA: Stanford University.

Stanislavski, C. 1996. *Building a Character.* London: Methuen.

Stanislavski, C. & Rumyantsev, P. 1975. *Stanislavski on Opera.* New York: Theatre Arts Books.

Stern, C. 2007. Erick Hawkins. *Dance Teacher Magazine* [Online], 29. Available: http://www.dance-teacher.com/2007/09/erick-hawkins [Accessed December 3, 2013].

Stevenson, R. L. 1911. El Dorado. *Virginibus Puerisque.* Swanston (ed.) London: Chatto and Windus.

Talbot, M. 1992. *The Holographic Universe.* New York: Harper Perennial.

Thyme-Frøkjær, K. & Frøkjær-Jensen, B. 2001. *The Accent Method: A Rational Voice Therapy in Theory & Practice.* Milton Keynes: Speechmark.

Turner, V. 1969. *The Ritual Process: Structure and Anti-Structure.* Chicago, IL: Aldine Publishing Company.

University of California — Santa Barbara 2010, December 5. Brain Maps Created for How Humans Reach. *Science Daily* [Online]. Available: http://www.sciencedaily.com/releases/2010/12/101203091459.htm [Accessed July 27, 2011].

Van Gennep, A. 1960. *The Rites of Passage.* Chicago, IL: University of Chicago Press.

Whitaker, R. D. 1997. *Exploring and Employing Autopoietic Theory: Issues and Tips.* Paper presented at Biology, Language, Cognition and Society: International Symposium on Autopoiesis. 18–21 November, Belo Horizonte.

Wolford, L. 2010. Grotowski's Vision of the Actor: The Search for Contact. *In:* A. Hodge (ed.) *Actor Training.* 2nd ed. Oxon: Routledge.

Yusuo, Y. 1993. *The Body Self-Cultivation and Ki-Energy.* Albany, NY: State University Of New York Press.

Zarilli, P. 2000. *Kathakali Dance-Drama: Where Gods and Demons Come to Play.* London: Routledge.

Zarilli, P. 2009. *Psychophysical Acting, An Intercultural Approach After Stanislavsky.* London: Routledge.

Index

Bold page numbers indicate illustrations